Additional Praise for
Top Hedge Fund Investors

"In *Top Hedge Fund Investors*, Rittereiser and Kochard have put to rest any lingering doubts that hedge funds have become an essential component of successful investment programs. When a collection of extraordinarily talented individuals, like those profiled in this book, dedicate their lives to a common discipline, we can be sure that these strategies have reached a permanent level of prominence in the investment world. *Top Hedge Fund Investors* profiles men and women with passion, courage, intellect, tenacity, inquisitiveness and resiliency, who have helped establish a standard of excellence in hedge fund investing that all those who read this book will benefit from emulating. We are all richer for the authors' efforts to bring together this outstanding volume of Stories, Strategy and Advice from some of the best hedge fund investors in the business."

> —Mark W. Yusko
> CEO & Chief Investment Officer
> Morgan Creek Capital Management

"*Top Hedge Fund Investors* offers a refreshing perspective and unique insight into the shrouded world of hedge funds. We get a glimpse beyond the numbers and gain an insider's view of this complex industry. As one who has been with this business for nearly thirty years, I can attest that this book rings true."

> —Lawrence P. Chiarello, Partner
> SkyView Investment Advisors LLC

"Great subject, terrific insights from top allocators to hedge funds. Eldon, Meyer and Hodge show how to avoid making unforced errors when investing. They and the other Investors make this the best book I have seen on selecting money managers."

> —Douglas Sperry Makepeace, President
> Sperry Fund Management LLC
> New York City

"An insightful tour of the Hedge Fund World, with some of the most experienced guides that demystify a lot of the wrong ideas people have of this industry and its players."

> —Michel Amsellem
> Member of the Advisory board Banque Heritage

"Given the importance that 'hedge funds' have gained in financial markets it behooves all investors, not just professionals, to understand the underlying principles used by prominent hedge fund investors. *Top Hedge Fund Investors* provides an interesting description of the investment philosophy of some of the leading practitioners of this relatively unknown segment of the financial markets, and how they have organized their firms."
—Charles Falcon
Retired Corporate Finance Executive

Top Hedge
Fund Investors

Founded in 1807, John Wiley & Sons is the oldest independent publishing company in the United States. With offices in North America, Europe, Australia, and Asia, Wiley is globally committed to developing and marketing print and electronic products and services for our customers' professional and personal knowledge and understanding.

The Wiley Finance series contains books written specifically for finance and investment professionals as well as sophisticated individual investors and their financial advisors. Book topics range from portfolio management to e-commerce, risk management, financial engineering, valuation, and financial instrument analysis, as well as much more.

For a list of available titles, visit our Web site at www.WileyFinance.com.

Top Hedge Fund Investors

Stories, Strategies, and Advice

CATHLEEN M. RITTEREISER
LAWRENCE E. KOCHARD,
PHD, CFA

WILEY

John Wiley & Sons, Inc.

Published by John Wiley & Sons, Inc., Hoboken, New Jersey.
Published simultaneously in Canada.

For general information on our other products and services or for technical support, please contact our Customer Care Department within the United States at (800) 762-2974, outside the United States at (317) 572-3993, or fax (317) 572-4002.

Wiley also publishes its books in a variety of electronic formats. Some content that appears in print may not be available in electronic books. For more information about Wiley products, visit our Web site at www.wiley.com.

Library of Congress Cataloging-in-Publication Data:

Rittereiser, Cathleen M., 1960–
Top hedge fund investors : stories, strategies, and advice / Cathleen M. Rittereiser Lawrence E. Kochard.
    p. cm. – (Wiley finance series)
Includes bibliographical references and index.
ISBN 978-0-470-50129-0 (cloth)
1. Hedge funds. 2. Mutual funds. 3. Investment advisors. 4. Portfolio management.
5. Investments. I. Kochard, Lawrence E., 1956- II. Title.
HG4530.R58 2010
332.64'524–dc22

2009054065

Printed in the United States of America

10 9 8 7 6 5 4 3 2 1

For

My father, Walter Kochard, for always listening when I talked. Family dinner conversations when he was a broker at E.F. Hutton in the 1970s inspired me to work in this exciting business!
L.E.K.

My father, Bob Rittereiser, and uncle, Freddie Rittereiser, the two top Wall Street leaders in my book
C.M.R.

Contents

Preface

Foundation and Endowment Investing: Philosophies and Strategies of Top Investors and Institutions, the first book Larry Kochard and I wrote together, profiles 12 well-regarded chief investment officers at leading university endowments and foundations. Inspired by Larry's fruitless search for such a book when he became CIO of Georgetown University, *Foundation and Endowment Investing* chronicles the investment philosophies, strategies, and challenges of leading CIOs and shares their ideas and advice with investors.

Modeled on books like *Market Wizards* by Jack Schwager (Marketplace Books, 2008) and *Investment Gurus* by Peter Tanous (Prentice Hall Press, 1999), and published by John Wiley & Sons in January 2008, *Foundation and Endowment Investing* was reviewed in the July/August 2008 issue of the *Financial Analysts Journal*:

> The investment success of other educational institutions' endowments and of some foundations has made the workings of endowments/foundations of growing interest. Kochard and Rittereiser have produced a well-written, enlightening book on the subject.

The stories of such accomplished investors—most known only within a segment of the institutional investment community—provided readers with valuable information and ideas. Descriptions of their long-term investment process taught investors useful lessons about asset allocation, manager selection, and alpha generation. Their opinions and advice left readers with a better understanding of the top investor mind-set.

Larry Kochard best describes the value of writing and reading about successful investors in this excerpt from the conclusion of *Foundation and Endowment Investing*:

> Successful people in any field don't stick their head in the sand—they are always hoping to learn new ideas from other innovators and leaders in any field. As investors we all want to do a better job establishing a disciplined and successful investment process and

generating better returns on our portfolio, whether it benefits an institution or our families.

Now that we know how much we can learn from interviewing different types of investors, we look forward to hearing their insights.

I too found the experience of interviewing and writing about such accomplished investors to be engaging, enlightening and, quite honestly, entertaining. Moreover, Larry and I agreed that our complementary skills and perspectives, and our format—overview, interview, review, and preview—would work well in books about other interesting and important investment industry insiders.

Having met and become colleagues and friends through our work in the hedge fund industry—Larry on the investor side and I on the marketing side—we already knew a group of investors who fit the profile.

Like foundation and endowment CIOs, the investors we endeavored to profile had expertise in a powerful, exclusive, and misconstrued industry segment. No other book told their stories, described their strategies, and shared their advice for becoming top performers, until Larry Kochard and I wrote the book you now hold in your hand or read on a screen: *Top Hedge Fund Investors: Stories, Strategies, and Advice.*

Most hedge fund profile books, like *Hedge Hunters* by Katherine Burton (Bloomberg Press, 2007) or *Inside the House of Money* by Steve Drobny (John Wiley & Sons, 2009), describe hedge fund managers, the men and women in the markets running money. In *Top Hedge Fund Investors*, we profile nine top-performing, well-regarded investors, each with a long history of investing in those hedge fund managers.

Once the province of wealthy individual investors, hedge funds have become more important market participants, more prevalent in investment portfolios, and more available to institutional and individual investors. Investing in hedge funds requires sophisticated knowledge, access, and experience. We believe an increasing number of investors will need to learn how to choose a hedge fund investment and would benefit from reading the different perspectives from a number of successful hedge fund investors.

Top Hedge Fund Investors chronicles the challenges and rewards these investors face in selecting hedge fund managers, managing risks, and constructing portfolios. By telling their stories, they describe their strategies and offer their advice for succeeding at investing in hedge funds.

The following chapters provide:

- Overviews of the evolution of hedge funds as an investment and an industry, showing how and why this group has become a bigger and more influential investment force

- Interviews of top hedge fund investors—the pioneers and next-generation, high-net-worth individuals, funds of hedge funds, and institutions—resulting in nine revealing profiles
- Viewpoints, lessons, insights, and advice beneficial to all hedge fund investors regarding particular challenges in the areas of due diligence and manager selection, growth and change of the asset class, proliferation of funds, headline risk, and balancing qualitative and quantitative factors when making an investment decision
- Reviews of the financial crisis of 2008, problematic hedge fund strategies, the Bernard Madoff fraud, and previews of how these recent events will influence hedge fund investors in the future

Top Hedge Fund Investors will prove valuable to anyone involved in investing in hedge funds as well as to hedge funds seeking a better understanding of their clients.

Larry Kochard and I feel privileged to have worked with and learned from these leading hedge fund investors. We cannot express enough gratitude for their participation. Our goal was to capture their thought processes, so that we, and our readers, would understand their philosophies and gain investment insight. We believe we have achieved our goal.

Acknowledgments

Writing *Foundation and Endowment Investing: Philosophies and Strategies of Top Investors and Institutions* as first-time authors, we did not know what to expect. I felt privileged to work with a publisher like Wiley, learned a tremendous amount from our subjects, made new friends, and had new experiences. I found the process challenging, frightening, and gratifying.

Two years later, writing *Top Hedge Fund Investors: Stories, Strategies, and Advice*, I again learned a lot, met and worked with wonderful people, and experienced frustrating and satisfying moments. Yet enough had changed—namely, economic conditions—and enough had stayed the same—books take the same amount of time to write every time—that I had a completely different, humbling experience. But in the end, we have proudly produced another book about interesting investors that other investors and readers should find valuable.

Neither of us could have accomplished this project on our own, and we could not have done it without the people we recognize and thank here.

First, the extraordinary hedge fund researcher and author Alexander Ineichen deserves our praise. We relied on his work extensively. He delivers knowledge and historical perspective with edgy humor and authority.

A number of individuals helped us identify top hedge fund investors to serve as profile subjects, made crucial introductions, or provided the means for us to make important connections and promote the project. They include the following:

Susanne Gealy, Teacher Retirement System of Texas and Preston Tsao, founder, Metropolitan Circle of Private Investment Offices in New York, introduced us to subjects and helped us network in the family office community.

Frank D'Ambrosio, a senior hedge fund marketing executive then at SkyBridge Capital, proved instrumental by introducing me to his colleagues. Anthony Scaramucci, managing partner of SkyBridge Capital, asked the firm's advisory board member, Frank Meyer, to participate, and along with partner Victor M. Oviedo, invited me to interview Meyer live, onstage at their SkyBridge Alternatives (SALT) conference. I am forever grateful.

Others who offered suggestions, support, and substantiation include:

Roger Ehrenberg, IA Capital Partners; Ken Grant, Risk Resources; Dr. Nicola Meaden-Grenham, Dumas Capital Limited; Rick Sopher and Brad Amiee, LCF Edmond de Rothschild Asset Management Limited; Thomas Munster, CapitalRock Advisors; John Watras, Concept Capital; Louise Wasso-Jonikas, Angelo, Gordon & Co.; Maarten Nederlof, PAAMCO; Charlotte Luer, LJH Financial Marketing Strategies; Virginia Macias, Lim Advisors; Brian Moss, Optima Funds; Tanya Ghaleb-Harter, Bank of America; Tracie Gunion and Barbara Tollis.

Several media outlets, conference organizers, and industry associations offered their support to this project and to *Foundation and Endowment Investing*:

David Stewart, Global ARC; Amanda Rodrigues, GAIM USA; Lisa McErlane Yao, Institutional Investor Conferences; Lisa Vioni, Hedge Connection Inc.; Elana Margulies, HFMWeek; Connie Adamson, NACUBO; and the entire team at O'Reilly Media.

Particular thanks go to Mohan Virdee and David Griffiths, at Markets Media for having me chair their inaugural *Eye on Endowments and Focus on Foundations* symposium in October 2009 and edit the follow-up *Review and Outlook* magazine for endowment and foundation investors. The investors, colleagues, and industry experts—too numerous to mention— who participated in and supported the projects also deserve thanks.

The Georgetown University Investment Office provided valuable assistance throughout the process. Larry also thanks the members of the Georgetown Investment committee for their support and his students, past and present, for their inspiration.

Rose Fiorilli, executive coach and founder of Rubicon Advisory Group, provided me with clarity, focus, and inspiration. Friends Kimberly Blue, Rebecca Randall, and Carey Earle helped me through one of the most challenging years ever, and Barbara Selbach and Jeff Skelton set the wheels in motion over holiday dinner in December 2001. Thanks also to my best little buddies: Tyler and Andie Stolting, Ellie, Tim, and Will Anderson, John Rittereiser, and Charlie Rittereiser.

Thank you to Kevin Commins, Meg Freeborn, and Kate Wood from John Wiley & Sons for providing the platform and support, being gracious and patient, and reminding me I have deadlines and a conscience.

Finally, we thank family, friends, and anyone we missed.

On behalf of Larry Kochard and myself, with great appreciation,

CATHLEEN M. RITTEREISER
December 18, 2009

About the Authors

Cathleen M. Rittereiser informs and educates institutional investors as a writer, speaker, and consultant. She chaired the Markets Media Eye on Endowments and Focus on Foundations symposium and edited the *Markets Media Annual Review and Outlook for Endowments and Foundations*, a magazine published in January 2010. Rittereiser is the co-author, also with Larry Kochard, of the book *Foundation and Endowment Investing*, published by John Wiley & Sons in January 2008.

An alternative investments marketing executive with more than 20 years' experience in financial services, Rittereiser has held positions with leading asset management, research, and brokerage firms. Her hedge fund experience includes stints in marketing and business development for Alternative Asset Managers and Symphony Asset Management. She began her career with Merrill Lynch.

Rittereiser received an AB from Franklin and Marshall College in Lancaster, Pennsylvania, and an MBA from New York University's Stern School of Business.

New York Times technology columnist and author David Pogue chose three of her submissions for his book *The World According to Twitter* (Black Dog & Leventhal, 2009). A New York City resident, she can be found on the Web at www.cathleenrittereiser.com.

Lawrence E. Kochard, Ph.D., CFA was appointed chief investment officer at Georgetown University in June 2004. In addition to serving as CIO, he teaches investment courses for the McDonough School of Business at Georgetown. Previously, Kochard was managing director of equity and hedge fund investments for the Virginia Retirement System (VRS) and adjunct professor of finance for the McIntire School of Commerce at the University of Virginia. Prior to joining VRS, he was a full-time faculty member at UVA. Before his return to academia, his background was in corporate finance and capital markets, concluding with Goldman Sachs. He currently serves on the board of Janus Capital Group and as chair of The College of William & Mary Foundation Investments Committee.

Kochard holds a BA in economics from the College of William & Mary, an MBA in finance and accounting from the University of Rochester, an MA and Ph.D. in economics from the University of Virginia, and is a CFA charter holder. He is co-author, also with Cathleen Rittereiser, of *Foundation and Endowment Investing* and is married with four children.

Evolution of the
Hedge Fund Industry
and Investing

CHAPTER 1

The Truth about Hedge Funds

From Misunderstood Investment Vehicle to Household Word

f you read the business press, watched television, or eavesdropped on a congressional finance committee hearing at almost any point since 1999, but especially in 2008, you might define hedge funds in several ways:

- Mysterious, secretive, risky pools of capital managed by swashbuckling, cowboy investment managers.
- Lying, thieving, Ponzi-scheming criminals.
- The cause of the whole breakdown of the financial system.

Alexander Ineichen, a leading research analyst and author, has said, "The reputation of hedge funds is not particularly good. The term 'hedge fund' suffers from a similar fate as 'derivatives' due to a mixture of myth, misrepresentation, negative press, and high-profile casualties."[1]

Ineichen made a similar observation in another publication: "There is still a lot of mythology with respect to hedge funds. Much of it is built on anecdotal evidence, oversimplification, myopia, or simply a misrepresentation of facts."

But in that instance, he asserted a hedge fund definition that is simpler and more germane to serious, sophisticated investors: "Hedge fund managers are simply asset managers utilising other strategies than those used by relative return long-only managers."[2]

While the term *hedge fund* is used broadly, it is often used to describe a vehicle with a 1 and 20 fee structure. In our book *Foundation and Endowment Investing*, we summarized hedge funds as follows:

> *Hedge funds are private investment vehicles structured as limited partnerships with the investment manager as the general partner*

*and the investors as limited partners. "Hedge funds" is not a tra-
ditional asset class but rather an amalgam of investment managers
and traders who are compensated by a performance fee, have an opportunity to invest in any number of strategies across various asset
classes, and use return-enhancing tools such as leverage, derivatives,
and short sales. The defining characteristic of hedge funds is their
goal: to generate an absolute return over time with little systematic
or public equity market exposure.[3]*

This chapter will further define and describe hedge funds, provide historical context behind their rise to prominence, and discuss issues facing the
industry and investors in the future.

HEDGE FUNDS IN THE SPOTLIGHT

Hedge funds have become part of the collective consciousness not just because the media can easily exploit misinformation, but also because they
have grown as an investment allocation in institutional portfolios. They
now comprise a larger percentage of portfolio asset allocations and investment industry assets under management and influence most market trading
activity.

Institutions Spur Hedge Fund Growth

Foundations and endowments led institutions into investing in hedge funds
in the mid to late 1990s. At the end of 1999 total hedge fund assets under
management were estimated at $450 billion.[4]

Writing *Foundation and Endowment Investing* in mid-2007, we said,

> *The main reason hedge funds have received so much attention in
> recent years is their performance during the equity market down-
> turn of 2000–02. At that point, ten-year average returns ending
> December 2006 beat both the US Public Equity (Russell 3000) and
> Bonds (Lehman Aggregate), by 200 and over 400 bps per annum,
> respectively.[5]*

Observing the success foundations and endowments experienced in
hedge funds and the ability hedge funds had to perform in adverse market conditions, pension plans began allocating to hedge funds in greater
numbers. Broader acceptance of hedge funds among institutions represent-
ing much larger pools of capital fueled the growth of hedge funds.

Greenwich Associates reported that by 2007 45 percent of all U.S. institutional investors had invested in hedge funds, accounting for 2.6 percent of total institutional assets and close to double the number reported two years earlier. European and Japanese institutions had embraced hedge funds even sooner than those in the United States, with U.K. and Canadian institutions lagging.

The velocity and size of the growth in assets meant that by mid-2008, $2 trillion was estimated to be invested in over 10,000 hedge funds. At the end of 2008 hedge fund assets under management stood at approximately $1.8 trillion.[6]

Hedge Funds Are Here to Stay

In *Foundation and Endowment Investing*, we wrote, "Although many individual funds have underperformed, as a whole they (hedge funds) truly have provided an absolute return due to a neutral exposure to the equity market."[7]

Despite the extreme market upheavals and hedge fund losses since then, that statement still largely captures the reasons why hedge funds have become so important and why investors want to understand them and learn how to invest in them.

More investors need to know about hedge funds, because more investors have either invested in them in some way—even if only through a company pension plan—or will decide to invest in them. Since hedge funds play such a large role in the markets, investors that have not or will not become hedge fund investors need to know how hedge funds impact their existing portfolio.

WHAT IS A HEDGE FUND?

Hedge funds are almost easier to define by what they are not, rather than by what they are. Put another way, they are best defined at every level—from philosophy to legal structure—by what they are relative to traditional long-only investment strategies.

Philosophy

Hedge funds differ from long-only strategies at the philosophical level in terms of their investment objective, manager's skill, and approach to risk.

Return Objectives   One way to compare long-only investment strategies to hedge funds is by their investment objective. Ironically, long-only strategies seek relative returns. They aim to perform better *relative to a benchmark*, usually within their own asset class. In a very simple example, a long-only strategy investing in U.S. equities is managed to perform better than the S&P 500. As a result, a long-only fund can lose money, but if it loses less money than the benchmark, then it still is considered to have outperformed. In that same example, if the S&P 500 drops 40 percent in one year, as it did in 2008, a long-only strategy that falls 38 percent in that same period has done well.

Hedge funds seek *absolute returns*. They aim to make money regardless of market conditions and to beat the risk-free rate.[8] Hedge funds balance profit seeking with loss avoiding by identifying and exploiting investment opportunities while managing risk to protect against the loss of principal.

Manager Mindset   Hedge funds are considered skill-based strategies, meaning they depend on the skill of the individual manager to earn returns.[9] Because the managers tend to invest a significant amount of their own money in their funds, they have incentives to make profits and thus approach risk management much differently.

Investment professionals describe the differences in terms of alpha and beta. Beta is the return generated from the allocation to an asset class or exposure to a risk factor, which could be implemented passively, such as in an index. Beta is the return from the market. If the S&P 500 is up 10 percent in a year, an investment fund benchmarked against the S&P 500 that has returned 10 percent has delivered market beta. Alpha is the excess return generated by active investment managers above what could have been generated by investing in a passive exposure to a particular asset class.[10] Using the same example, if the investment fund had been up 12 percent when the S&P 500 had been up 10 percent, the 2 percent of excess return is considered alpha. Hedge fund managers focus on reducing beta and increasing alpha.

Risk Management Approach   The difference in risk management philosophy between long-only and hedge fund strategies is, at the core, the purest definition of hedge funds. As stated previously, in trying to achieve absolute returns, hedge funds manage their portfolio to profit both when market conditions are good and when they are poor. They do not try to lose less money than everyone else during a downturn; they try not to lose money at all. They employ *hedging techniques*, typically pairing long and short positions against each other, in order to manage the risk in their portfolio. Hedge funds hedge.

Hedge fund managers care about total risk, or as described by Ineichen, "the probability of losing everything and being forced to work for a large organization again." Long-only managers look at risk relative to their benchmark. An S&P 500 index fund is seen as without risk; taking action that deviates from the benchmark portfolio construction is seen as adding risk.

In an extreme example, if the S&P 500 somehow dropped to $0.50, a long-only fund would not be taking risk if it continued to replicate the index portfolio construction. It would be taking active risk if it deviated from the benchmark construction, even if that action resulted in losing less money. If such calamitous conditions actually were occurring, a hedge fund manager would be actively buying, selling, and hedging the securities in the portfolio in an attempt to preserve capital if not earn a profit. In their approach to risk and its impact on performance, hedge fund managers hate to lose money, period, and focus on protecting the portfolio from downside risk. A long-only manager does not like or want to lose money, but if the fund loses less money than the benchmark, it has managed risk well.[11]

The approach to managing volatility, represented by the standard deviation of returns, is another important distinction between long-only and hedge fund risk management philosophies. Hedge funds focus on achieving risk-adjusted returns or getting the best performance possible relative to the amount of capital at risk. The Sharpe ratio measures risk-adjusted return.

$$\text{Sharpe Ratio} = \frac{\text{Performance} - \text{Risk Free Rate}}{\text{Standard Deviation}}$$

Managers strive to achieve a Sharpe ratio of 1 or better.

To give a very simple example, a long-only fund benchmarked against the S&P 500 will have the same level of volatility. If the volatility of the S&P 500 is 25 percent, so is the volatility of the fund. If that fund returns 15 percent on 25 percent volatility it will have a Sharpe ratio of 0.6. An equity long/short manager with the target return of 15 percent would use hedging techniques to attempt to limit the volatility of the portfolio to 12 to 15 percent for a Sharpe ratio between 1 and 1.25. In that scenario, the long-only fund has taken double the risk to get the same return. The hedge fund would have to return less than 7.2 percent to match the risk-adjusted return of the long-only fund. Over the long run the total compounded return is much better when risk-adjusted return is factored into portfolio performance.[12]

One of the great ironies of hedge funds versus long-only funds is that they are perceived as risky, yet hedge funds manage and control risk and deliver a less risky investment to their investors.

Investment Structure and Techniques

The main area of difference between hedge funds and long-only funds is the structure of the investment vehicle and the types of investment techniques that hedge funds are allowed to employ within that structure

Almost any description of a hedge fund starts with the phrase "Hedge funds are an investment vehicle that...." This description has more to do with the hedge fund legal structure than its investment techniques. A long-only fund is described as "a long-only fund." Hedge funds and long-only funds are both investment vehicles. The hedge fund vehicle lacks constraints and gives the hedge fund manager more freedom.

Hedge fund managers can employ various specific, individual investment techniques that are more risky on their own. When employed incorrectly by less sophisticated investors, these techniques can be catastrophic to a portfolio. The ability to use these techniques is probably the source of the belief that hedge funds are extremely risky investments. The paradox is that some of these "risky" techniques allow hedge fund managers to reduce the risk in their portfolios.

The following list shows the key investment characteristics and specific investment techniques employed by hedge funds.

Broad Mandate: Hedge funds offer investors access to a wide variety of investment strategies and risk exposures not typically available through traditional investment classes and investment vehicles.

Multiple Asset Classes: Historically, hedge funds have focused on long and short investments in equities, fixed income securities, currencies, commodities, and their derivatives.

Limited Risk Exposure: Hedge funds are generally managed to limit exposure to broad market risk, unlike traditional funds, which typically are fully exposed to general movements in underlying stock or bond markets.

Leverage: Hedge funds are typically leveraged in that the value of the long positions may exceed, in certain circumstances substantially, the investor's capital in the fund.

Shorting: Hedge funds have the ability to short securities, mainly stocks, in order to combine with long positions to hedge risk and to earn return.

Uncorrelated: While not an investment technique itself, by utilizing these various tactics, hedge fund returns are largely uncorrelated to other markets.

Regulation and Ownership

Hedge funds are structured as private investment partnerships due to their regulatory and ownership statuses. Compared to long-only funds, particularly mutual funds companies, hedge funds are lightly regulated as it pertains to their investment mandates. The regulations imposed on hedge funds apply mostly to protect investors, such as minimum net worth requirements and forbidden marketing practices. The following lists important regulatory characteristics of hedge funds.

Regulatory-Related Characteristics
- Funds are offered privately and not sold or available to the general public.
- Investors must be qualified:
  - High net worth individuals and institutions.
- Funds are not required to register as an investment company under relevant Investment Company Act laws.
- Funds can be domiciled offshore.

Hedge funds have an ownership and performance incentive structure rarely seen in other investment vehicles, even though investors find it to be one of the most important and appealing characteristics of hedge funds. They appreciate the structure and incentive culture, because it aligns the manager's financial interests with theirs. The most common ownership and fee structure characteristics[13] are highlighted in the following list.

Ownership Characteristics
- Firms are professional investment management firms.
- Funds are structured as private partnerships.
- Managers typically own a large stake in the firm and serve as the fund's general partner.
- Fund managers and personnel invest a significant or meaningful portion of their liquid net worth in their own funds.
- Hedge funds receive a share of the fund's profits based on its investment performance.
- Funds give investors periodic, but usually restricted or somewhat limited rights to redeem.

The performance-based fee structure drives the ownership and incentive compensation practices of hedge funds. A long-only fund usually charges a straight management fee, typically a percentage of the underlying assets. Hedge fund managers impose a management fee and a performance fee, typically percentages known affectionately by the industry as "2 and 20."

In other words, hedge funds will charge a fee ranging from 1 percent to 2 percent for the assets under management and will then take 20 percent of the profits from the fund's return. Performance fees are usually paid on the amount of performance that has accrued in the one-year period following the investment. They are usually calculated against a "high-water mark," meaning that a manager must earn back any losses before it can take the performance payment. The sizeable performance fees make owning a hedge fund and sharing in its profits particularly lucrative. Unfortunately the challenge of earning back losses over a high-water mark frequently leads a manager to close shop and leave the investors high and dry instead.[14]

Asset Class or Investment Style?

Investment professionals debate whether hedge funds are asset classes or not. The President's Working Group on Financial Markets (PWG) says no:

> Hedge funds are investment vehicles that allow investors to gain exposure to a wide range of investment strategies. They do not represent a single asset class but rather a type of investment vehicle.[15]

On the other hand, Ineichen makes the case for classifying hedge funds as a separate asset class:

> Return, volatility, and correlation characteristics differ from those of other asset classes such as equities, bonds, commodities and natural resources, real estate, and private equity. In addition, it allows separation between liquid asset classes (e.g., equities and bonds) and less liquid asset classes (e.g., real estate, private equity).

His strongest argument for treating hedge funds as a separate asset class is that doing so helps to calculate and demonstrate that adding hedge funds to a portfolio can increase its efficiency.[16]

At the same time, he says that it makes sense why some view hedge funds as simply a style of asset management.

> Absolute return managers are asset managers who define return and risk objectives differently but manage money by investing in traditional asset classes—equities, bonds, currencies, commodities, or derivatives thereof. They recruit staff from the same pool of talent as do other money managers and offer their products to the same client base.[17]

Over time, this debate will most likely subside as institutions have begun to evolve their asset allocation approach toward treating hedge funds as an asset management style, not an asset class.[18]

Misunderstood No More

Some individual hedge fund strategies are risky, mysterious, and complicated. Unfortunately, over the years that reputation has overshadowed all hedge funds and led qualified investors to miss out on the portfolio diversification and return enhancement benefits.

Simply, hedge funds are investment vehicles that seek to achieve absolute returns. The funds are managed by entrepreneurial investment professionals motivated by ownership of their firm and a share in lucrative performance fees. These managers rely on their investment and risk management skills and the broad investment mandate and tools of the hedge fund structure to create investment strategies that capitalize on opportunities in various markets while protecting capital. If done correctly, the hedge fund approach should result in positive performance, lower volatility, and little correlation to the markets. The broad investment mandate and the level of risk inherent in certain hedge fund investment techniques has caused regulators to restrict the pool of potential investors to wealthy individuals and institutions, because they are seen as being able to handle the risks. They invest in hedge funds because the ownership structure and 2 and 20 performance fee incentives align their interests with those of the manager. The risk-adjusted return profile and low correlation of hedge funds make them function in an investor's overall portfolio as a diversifying asset class.

Ineichen claims that the hedged style of investing has been around since Joseph tried to buy his wife Rachel in biblical times. The relative return style of investing most investors know through long-only funds is a somewhat recent phenomenon that may be (or deserves to be) short-lived.[19]

In modern times the earliest hedge fund managers weren't so much mysterious as they were obscure. Alfred W. Jones gets most of the credit for creating the first modern hedge fund and for establishing the structures that remain in use today. He would probably be quite surprised at the reputation, size, and impact of the industry segment he originated. The next section chronicles the recent history of the hedge fund industry—dating back to Mr. Jones, not Joseph—to determine how and why the industry got where it is today.

ORIGINS AND HISTORY OF HEDGE FUNDS

Most hedge fund experts trace the origins of the modern hedge fund to Alfred Winslow Jones (1900–1989) and the equity investment partnership he started in 1949. Using techniques such as leverage and short selling, Jones sought to maximize returns while minimizing market exposure by taking both long and short positions in securities. He referred to it as a "hedged fund."

An American born in Australia in 1900, Jones had an eclectic background. He graduated from Harvard in 1923, became a diplomat as Hitler rose to power in Berlin in the 1930s, and earned a doctorate in sociology from Columbia University in 1941, before becoming a journalist writing on nonfinancial topics for *Fortune* and *Time* magazines.

His experience researching and writing an article on stock market technical analysis entitled "Fashions in Forecasting" for the March 1949 issue of *Fortune* inspired him to become a professional investor. That year he formed the A. W. Jones & Co. general partnership with four friends. Jones contributed $40,000 of the firm's initial $100,000 and saw his investment gain 17.3 percent in its first year.

Jones used leverage, to enhance return, and short selling, often in tandem. Believing stock selection drives return, he used short selling to capitalize on price drops in overvalued stocks and to control risks in the portfolio. Jones would tell other investors that questioned the use of short selling that he used "speculative techniques for conservative ends."

Jones invested all of his own money in the partnership, because he thought investors should not be taking risks with their capital that he would not be willing to take, and thus aligned his capital and interests with those of his investors. When he converted the general partnership to a limited partnership in 1952, he added a 20 percent performance fee.

The first investment manager to combine the use of short selling and leverage in a portfolio, Jones also pioneered the concepts of aligning his interests with investors and sharing in profits from performance. He tended to leverage the portfolio 1.5 to 1 ($1.5 invested for every $1 in capital) and ran 110 percent in long positions and 40 percent in short positions. The equity long/short hedge funds of today barely deviate from that model.

In the early stages of their investment careers two investors with household names today, Warren Buffett and Barton Biggs, managed money using the Jones model. His investment style remained obscure, however, until *Fortune* magazine reappeared in his life, and made Jones the subject rather than the reporter of an article. In 1966, Carol Loomis (still a reporter for *Fortune* in 2009) wrote "The Jones Nobody Keeps Up With" for the April issue. In the article, she introduced Jones and what she called his "hedge fund" to the investment world. At the time Jones was outperforming the best performing mutual funds over a 5-year period by 44 percent and over a 10-year period by 87 percent, *after the 20 percent in fees was taken*. Readers did not care what the investment style was called; the spectacular performance inspired investment managers to launch hedge funds and by 1968, about 200 were operating.

Market downturns in 1969–1970 and 1973–1974 took a toll and most hedge funds failed. An estimated 30 funds with a total of $300 million in capital existed by 1971. Managers began starting hedge funds again after 1974. Most were small private firms running equity long/short funds, what hedge fund investors today would probably call "two guys in a garage with a Bloomberg terminal." By the end of the 1970s, approximately 100 hedge funds toiled in obscurity relative to the rest of the investment industry, but had numerous opportunities to exploit market inefficiencies.

During the 1980s the next wave of hedge funds came to the forefront, led by managers considered legends today, including Julian Robertson, George Soros, Michael Steinhardt, and Jack Nash. They made money in bull and bear markets, capturing the attention and assets of European investors. Another article about an individual hedge fund manager raised the industry's profile again when Julie Rohrer profiled Julian Robertson for the May 1986 issue of *Institutional Investor*.

The bull market of the 1990s gave newly wealthy money managers and traders the impetus to leave larger firms to start their own hedge funds. Simultaneously, managers began starting hedge funds using new types of portfolio construction techniques or investing in markets that had not been used by hedge funds before. The type of hedge fund available became more diverse; previously about 90 percent of hedge funds were macro or equity long/short styles. With more types of strategies available, hedge funds became less correlated with each other, making it feasible for investors to combine individually risky hedge funds to create more risk-controlled portfolios.

Endowments and foundations then began investing in hedge funds even though they were still perceived as an unconventional investment. Hedge funds of funds began forming and growing, setting the stage for the influx of institutional investors that have made hedge funds the most prominent and influential form of investing today.[20]

Hedge funds have become a household word.

CONCLUSION

Investing in hedge fund strategies is no longer unconventional and is no longer the province of the superrich. Large pension plans invest in hedge funds, while absolute return mutual funds have come to market. Although hedge funds have grown in prominence and popularity with investors, hedge fund misinformation and misunderstanding has grown too.

The growth of hedge funds has created a more challenging investment environment for hedge fund investors and managers. This proved particularly true in the market crises of 2008. But thinking about hedge funds over the long term, we stand by this statement in *Foundation and Endowment Investing,*

> *Providing talented managers with a larger supply of capital helps make all markets more efficient, creating fewer security mispricings and arbitrage opportunities. Accordingly, future returns will likely be lower than they have been in the past.*[21]

Similarly, Ineichen says, "As the hedge fund industry matures, becomes institutionalized and mainstream, and eventually converges with the traditional asset management industry, this rent (return) will be gone."[22]

Even so, hedge funds are a household word because they are here to stay. They became popular because absolute return investments can provide excellent, risk-adjusted return with low correlations to the markets and other funds. While the returns may be less attractive in the future, the role they play in diversifying investment portfolios will remain important. Investors will benefit from learning more about hedge funds and from getting insights and advice from accomplished hedge fund investors.

This chapter gave an overview of hedge funds, what they are, and how and why they have become important. The next chapter outlines the standard best practices for investing in hedge funds and will provide context for the advice from the subjects in Part Two.

CHAPTER 2

The Investment Process

Best Practices of Successful
Hedge Fund Investors

Hedge fund investors and their fiduciaries must establish an investment process that is consistent with their investment objectives and skills. Although any investor should conduct thorough due diligence of all potential investments, it is an extremely important consideration for someone investing in a hedge fund.

As hedge funds have become more prevalent and institutional, so has the industry. Several industry associations have endeavored to educate investors and establish standards to support their efforts to lobby regulators. The regulators themselves, primarily in the United States and United Kingdom, have also convened task forces, issued recommendations, and produced educational material to ensure that investors understand the risks and conduct thorough due diligence when investing in hedge funds.

Employing leading hedge fund researchers and authors, or committees of institutional investors and hedge fund managers, these groups have released extensive professional white papers and policy reports that serve as an incredible resource for hedge fund investors. To provide an introduction and broad overview of the hedge fund investment process, this chapter will highlight key points of two of those works, *Principles and Best Practices for Hedge Fund Investors*, by the Investors' Committee to the President's Working Group on Financial Markets, and *AIMA's Roadmap to Hedge Funds*, from the Alternative Investment Management Association.

PREPARING TO INVEST IN HEDGE FUNDS

Before instituting a hedge fund investment program, qualified investors should be convinced that doing so will improve the risk and reward profile of their portfolio and help them achieve their overall investment objectives, typically diversification. Investors should also be certain that they, with their advisers and staff, have the knowledge and capability to handle all aspects of building a hedge fund portfolio.[1]

Investors should then determine their investment objective for the hedge fund component of their portfolio. In other words, they must consider the stand-alone contribution they expect hedge funds to make in addition to diversification. Investors more concerned with diversifying the overall portfolio and seeking to limit risk tend to prefer nondirectional or market-neutral absolute return strategies. Investors seeking diversification and potential for greater returns tend to choose directional hedge fund strategies.[2]

IMPLEMENTING THE PROCESS

The two main components of the hedge fund investment process are manager selection and portfolio management. Manager selection includes the research, monitoring, analysis, and decision-making tasks that are employed prior to allocating capital to evaluate and select individual fund managers and to understand the investment strategies. The portfolio management component uses the same skills to determine the optimal allocation sizes and mix of hedge fund managers to construct a portfolio of hedge funds. Once implemented, investors must monitor their portfolios in order to manage risk and assess performance, a process that continues for as long as the investor remains invested in hedge funds.[3] Depending on the investor, identifying, selecting, and monitoring managers could be a constant activity, such as in an institutional hedge fund of funds, or it can be more opportunistic.

Manager Selection

Experts believe manager selection is the most crucial element of the entire hedge fund investment process. Due diligence is the most crucial element of the manager selection process.

Beginning with Due Diligence   The report *Principles and Best Practices for Hedge Fund Investors*, by the Investors' Committee to the President's Working Group on Financial Markets, a task force consisting of institutional hedge fund investors, was issued January 15, 2009. It defines due diligence as "the process of gathering and evaluating information about a hedge fund manager prior to investing in order to assess whether a specific hedge fund is an appropriate choice for the portfolio."

Because hedge funds have less transparency and more complexity than more commonly known investments such as mutual funds, information that could help investors make an independent investment decision is not readily available or accessible. The report goes on to say, "Therefore, the unique and complex nature of hedge funds requires a level of due diligence above and beyond what is required for more transparent investments that are strictly regulated."[4]

Effective due diligence combines qualitative research and judgment with quantitative analysis to evaluate the reputation and character of the manager and his team and to determine the strength of the fund as a business.

Researching managers involves gathering information about individual hedge fund managers through meetings and other personal interactions, networking and speaking with other investors, and reviewing answers to standard due diligence questionnaires. Other steps include contacting references, conducting background checks, and verifying service provider relationships.[5]

Evaluating the fund as an independent business entity by determining the quality and robustness of its operations, infrastructure, and service providers is also important. Investors should also review and understand the fund's legal documents, especially investment terms; assess financial stability using credit reports; and assess business viability by analyzing its investor base and assets under management over time.[6]

Due Diligence Guidance *Principles and Best Practices for Hedge Fund Investors* provides a comprehensive set of guidelines for effective hedge fund due diligence. The report serves as an excellent resource for investors seeking an in-depth education in effective hedge fund investing.

The authors assert that the due diligence process should be tailored to the needs of the investor, since a "universal guide" is not germane to every situation, and they present the case for developing a strong due diligence questionnaire. "A well-tailored due diligence questionnaire (DDQ) may serve as a useful tool to aid investors in understanding a hedge fund's opportunities and risks and provide structure to the overall due diligence and monitoring process."[7]

The DDQ "should contain probing questions regarding the material aspects of a hedge fund's business and operations," and at the minimum, should cover the essential topics in the sidebar entitled "DDQ Topics."

DDQ TOPICS

Process: What is the manager's investment process?
- Markets and instruments
- Advantage or "edge" over other managers of alternatives
- Risk tolerance

Performance: How has the fund performed historically?
- Explanation for periods of particularly strong or poor returns
- Prior experience and track record of the manager
- Use of leverage

Personnel: Who will manage the fund?
- Participants in investment decisions
- Manager(s) of back-office functions such as accounting or cash and trade reconciliations
- Length of experience individually and as a team
- Portion of employees' own assets invested in the fund
- References to substantiate their character and skills

Risk Management: How does the manager assess and manage risks?
- Market risks
- Liquidity, counterparty, operational, and other risks that could adversely affect investment returns and the overall business
- Disaster recovery and business continuity plans

Third Parties: What third-party service providers do they employ?
- Administrators, prime brokers, auditors, legal counsel
- Counterparties
- Process the manager uses to select third parties
- Structural or contractual relationships that may cause conflicts

Structure: Is the hedge fund a partnership, corporation, or other entity?
- Limits on investor or manager liability
- Large investment management enterprise or "boutique" firm

Domicile: Is the fund domiciled onshore or offshore?
- Legal, regulatory, and tax regimes of the jurisdiction where the hedge fund is domiciled
- For offshore funds, can managers fulfill all obligations (e.g., regulatory filings or taxes) that may arise?
- Characteristics of the judicial system governing the assets and laws that would apply to investor claims

Legal Matters and Terms: What are the fund's fees and other material terms, such as liquidity, limitations on investments, and leverage?
- Use of "side pockets," segregated pools of illiquid investments
- Regulatory bodies with oversight or where the manager is registered
- Impact of taxes on the fund, firm, or investors

Compliance: Are risk-management and regulatory compliance policies documented?
- Presence of a chief compliance officer

Source: Adapted from *Principles and Practices for Hedge Fund Investors*

While the working group advocates the use of a carefully constructed DDQ, one "is never sufficient on its own to enable a hedge fund investor to make a fully informed investment decision." The committee recommends that investors pursue other avenues to get the information they need and argues against using unmodified industry-standard DDQ templates, such as those published by the Alternative Investment Management Association or the Managed Funds Association. The group reiterates that the DDQ should be "adapted to the specific needs and objectives of the investor."

The committee also recommends that the DDQ be tailored to the hedge funds and managers being considered, setting the stage for the next part of the manager selection process, strategy evaluation.[8]

Evaluating Investment Style and Performance   While the aforementioned steps in the due diligence process pertain more to evaluating the people and business management of individual hedge fund firms, investors must also understand a hedge fund manager's investment strategy and process in order to evaluate the investment performance. When an investor decides to conduct further due diligence on a manager, the process enters a monitoring period. Effectively analyzing historical returns and assessing current performance relative to the markets becomes more important to the process.

Understanding Markets and the Strategies   In *AIMA's Roadmap to Hedge Funds*, Alexander Ineichen writes, "To truly understand a manager and a manager's value-added, we must first understand the sector in which they are operating." In order to be successful, hedge fund managers must be able to adapt to changing markets and expertly manage risk while doing so. Therefore, investors that understand the dynamics of certain markets and strategies and also engage in a continuous review process can identify shifts in market conditions and better appreciate and assess a manager's performance in response to those changes.

Ineichen goes on to say that investors must "determine the sources of risk and return in each strategy. This involves dissecting the strategies into their component parts and applying market knowledge to determine how a hedge fund operating within that strategy has the potential to make profits and what risks are being taken in order to achieve the returns."[9]

Engaging in the process of identifying the risk and return drivers of a strategy improves investors' ability to differentiate and compare managers. At times the performance of certain managers in the same type of strategy may differ from others because "certain aspects of these drivers will have more influence than others on the future performance of the manager and must be emphasized." Sometimes nonmarket factors such as a fund's liquidity and level of assets under management may impact the performance of one manager versus another. The more an investor knows the strategy, knows the market, and knows the manager's investment process and structure, the more he can use that knowledge to his advantage in the manager selection process.

Strategy and market knowledge also helps investors understand the impact of other forces, such as increased capital flows, that will impact investment performance. Ineichen says, "Infusion of capital always changes [the] characteristics of [an] opportunity set. The opportunity set is never unlimited. There are capacity constraints. Inefficiencies tend to disappear if more capital chases the same inefficiency. However, what is often overlooked is that a flood of new capital creates new inefficiencies itself."[10]

Hedge Fund Strategies   Because hedge funds are rooted in the idiosyncratic skill and style of the manager, each hedge fund is unique and does not easily fall into a specific, narrowly defined style box. Nonetheless, most hedge funds can be grouped into categories based on their bias to the market. Strategies can then be typed based on the market or instrument used to execute the strategy or on the portfolio construction methodology. The following list, adapted from Ineichen's *AIMA Roadmap to Hedge Funds*, shows the hedge fund categories and key characteristics of the funds within those categories.[11]

Hedge Fund Categories and Characteristics

Category	Relative Value	Event Driven	Directional
Description	Strategies have little or no directional market exposure to the underlying equity or bond market. These strategies tend to profit by capitalizing on differences in market price of one security relative to another security in the portfolio and construct positions to have little market exposure. Market-neutral strategies fall into this category.	Strategies that seek to profit from corporate events such as mergers or restructurings. Merger arbitrage is tied to announced mergers and is similar to relative value strategies in that it lacks directional bias. Investing in distressed securities involves buying the low-priced securities of a company in distress and profiting from an event such as a bankruptcy resolution or turnaround.	Hedge fund styles that profit from directional moves in an underlying market or economic and political shifts
Types of Strategies	Equity market neutral Convertible arbitrage Fixed income arbitrage	Merger arbitrage Distressed securities	Global macro Equity long/short Systematic trading
Expected Returns	9–12%	10–14%	13–16%
Target Volatility	2–5%	4–7%	8–14%
Typical Leverage	High	Medium to low	Low
Liquidity	Medium	Low	High

Dividing funds into general categories and further defining them by type and characteristics helps hedge fund investors achieve diversity when constructing portfolios of hedge funds.

Portfolio Construction and Management

When hedge fund investors construct portfolios they balance bottom-up manager selection with top-down strategy diversification based on their objectives for the portfolio. Some investors, typically enterprises such as hedge fund-of-funds organizations, may construct narrowly biased portfolios focused on a region, market sector or strategy type. Traditionally investors based their investment and portfolio construction decisions solely on the outcome of their qualitative due diligence. With more techniques and technology available to them, today investors can benefit more from quantitative analysis when making these decisions.

Risk Management   An important objective of the portfolio construction process is to manage the risk of the overall hedge fund portfolio. Investors need to select managers and strategies that mitigate predictable risks, while also looking toward the future and making assumptions about the probability and possibility of less predictable scenarios, to try to protect the portfolio from those risks. When constructing portfolios, investors need to diversify and hedge risks. Diversifying involves combining strategies that are highly likely to be uncorrelated during periods of extreme market stress, even if they are correlated at other times. Hedging means investors offset risks by combining strategies that are negatively correlated.

"Most hedge fund investors use the full spectrum of diversification potential," says Ineichen. Encouraging all hedge fund investors to do the same, he says:

> The more volatility that is accepted through adding market directional risk to the portfolio the more the hedge fund portfolio resembles long-only portfolios that have, by comparison, low Sharpe ratios, large drawdowns, higher percentage of negative months and little to no asymmetry between positive and negative returns. In other words, the essence of portfolio construction is to utilise all available opportunities to diversify risk and use available optionality to hedge unwanted risk.[12]

The advent of sophisticated risk management technology has given hedge fund investors more robust tools to calculate and analyze relevant statistics and more awareness of the risk implications of various portfolio construction scenarios. The ability to quantify risk enhances the overall portfolio construction process and increases the likelihood that the portfolio will withstand unforeseen risks.

Portfolio Monitoring Is Essential   Investors that want to "buy and hold" should avoid investing in hedge funds, because investors need to monitor their portfolio actively after the initial hedge fund investment. Even when investors have conducted thorough due diligence and believe they understand the risks and rewards of the individual strategy and its function in the overall portfolio, they need to review and determine the effectiveness and consistency of the manager and the strategy. After any lock-up period expires and investors gain the right to redeem, they should deliberately consider doing so as part of their ongoing monitoring process.[13]

Manager Selection and Portfolio Management Intersect This quote from the President's Working Group report stands out because it could describe both the initial manager selection process or the ongoing manager monitoring process: "Ultimately, investors must determine whether a manager's results are due to luck or skill and, therefore, whether results are repeatable over time."[14]

Similarly, in describing the process of selecting managers Ineichen encapsulates the entire hedge fund investment process:

Manager identification and evaluation is probably the key to success. Investing in hedge funds is essentially a people and relationship business. By allocating capital to a manager or a group of managers, the investor expects to participate in the skill of the manager or managers and not necessarily in a particular investment strategy or a mechanical process.[15]

As an example, he says that an investor that chooses to invest in a convertible arbitrage manager isn't trying to just be a participant in a classic form of trading. It is a complicated investment strategy and the opportunities change over time. "The investors' expectation is to participate in inefficiencies and opportunities in the convertible bond (CB) market where a skilled and experienced manager has a competitive advantage over the less skilled—that is, the rest of the market."[16]

CONCLUSION

This chapter provided a broad overview of the hedge fund investing process based on the thorough work of leading investors, researchers, and trade associations.

The hedge fund investing process breaks down into two main components, manager selection and portfolio management. Hedge fund investors and researchers attribute success to superior manager selection, a process characterized by lengthy and extensive due diligence to determine the quality of the personnel and the business practices of individual hedge fund managers. Manager selection also involves the investor gaining a thorough understanding of the strategy and the hedge fund manager's idiosyncratic execution. Once investors have identified good-quality individual hedge fund managers, they construct diversified portfolios from among three main categories of hedge funds, using a combination of qualitative and quantitative analysis. Investors then engage in an ongoing process of monitoring their portfolios to ensure that managers execute their strategies consistently and successfully.

This introduction to hedge fund investing should provide readers a strong base for gaining additional insights about the investment process from the comments of the leading hedge fund investors profiled in Part Two.

CHAPTER 3

The Hedge Fund Investment Landscape

A Snapshot in Time

This chapter provides a brief summary of the market conditions hedge fund investors were experiencing at the time of their interview. The information encompasses the period when investors still reeled from the aftereffects of the financial crisis of 2008 until hedge funds began to recover. It provides a context and sets the stage for the top hedge fund investor profiles in Part Two.

THE FINANCIAL CRISIS OF 2008

Hedge fund investors and managers faced many challenges in the aftermath of the 2008 financial crisis. When we began interviewing the subjects of this book in the first half of 2009, the worst was over, but investors still had to deal with the repercussions.

Marcel Herbst and Georg Wessling of Harcourt AG, writing in their firm's magazine *swissHEDGE*, summarized the circumstances aptly:

> *To say that the hedge fund industry looks back on a very difficult 2008 is an understatement. Starting in the second half of 2008, in an environment of both falling and failing markets, the vast majority of hedge fund strategies suffered unprecedented losses, resulting in the worst year on record for our industry. The industry today is much smaller, has fewer participants, is greatly de-levered, and faced with a more institutionalized and critical client base. Deep and lasting structural changes have occurred, and the restructuring of our universe is still ongoing.[1]*

At the end of 2008, hedge funds had declined an average of −17.7 percent while the average fund of hedge funds lost an estimated −21 percent. Aggregate hedge fund assets under management peaked at close to $2 trillion and ended the year at approximately $1.2 trillion. Adding insult to injury, hedge funds proved to be highly correlated with the global equity markets. A comparison between the HFRI Index and the MSCI World Index showed the correlation to be .90.[2]

Looking on the bright side, the estimated $300 to $400 billion of capital hedge funds lost seemed almost inconsequential compared to the estimated $28 trillion lost in the global equity markets. Hedge funds outperformed most traditional benchmarks, beating the MSCI World index by 20 percent in 2008,[3] while the S&P 500 fell 38 percent.[4]

Over the long term, hedge fund investments continued to demonstrate superior absolute and relative returns compared to long-only investments. In the period from January 1990 to January 2009, the compound annual rate of return of the HFRI Fund of Funds Composite Index was 8.1 percent and the HFRI Fund Weighted Composite Index was 11.8 percent. Meanwhile global equities compounded at approximately 4.2 percent and bonds at 7.0 percent.[5]

The president of index publisher Hedge Fund Research (HFR), Kenneth Heinz, stated that not only had hedge funds outperformed the S&P 500 since 1990, they had done so with less risk, measured by standard deviation.[6]

The fact that hedge funds achieved relatively better performance than long-only strategies failed to impress many hedge fund investors. For the most part, hedge funds failed to deliver absolute returns, preserve capital, or justify high fees.

For those and other reasons, investors aggressively redeemed from hedge funds. Net redemptions amounted to an estimated $43.5 billion by October 31, 2008, compared to net inflows of $194.4 billion for 2007. HFR president Heinz said 2008 was "the worst year in terms of performance and capital flows that we've seen."[7]

Strategy Performance

Almost every type of hedge fund strategy lost money in 2008, regardless of the underlying market or asset class. As one might expect, HFR reported that short selling strategies—a very small percentage of the assets in hedge funds—rose 31.4 percent.[8] Only two of the more common strategies performed well. Global Macro strategies returned 5 percent and Commodity Trading Advisor (CTA) funds delivered 14 percent.[9]

Equity long/short funds usually earn the bulk of their positive returns on long positions, but they lost money in 2008. Many investors had gone into equity long/short strategies after hedge funds withstood the 2002 bear market. Back then, the overall market fell 22 percent and hedge funds were flat to slightly negative. However, there was also greater dispersion among stocks in 2002, meaning that stock selection made a difference. In 2008, the majority of stocks dropped regardless of their quality or future prospects.[10]

Herbst and Wessling at Harcourt took equity market beta into account when analyzing equity long/short returns and found "that the losses realized by equity hedge funds are predominantly explained by beta."[11] Other popular strategies had even worse returns on average than equity long/short funds. The Dow Jones index for convertible arbitrage strategies showed losses of 50 percent, and distressed funds lost an average of 37 percent.[12]

The Harcourt analysts could not place the blame for such poor returns in those and other event-driven and relative value strategies entirely on equity market beta. To the extent a fund outperformed others in its strategy group, they attributed it to a focus on the most liquid markets, limited use of leverage, and avoidance of the most crowded trades.[13]

Financial System Exacerbation

A number of macro and other external factors, largely created by and tied to problems at banks and brokerage firms, contributed to poor hedge fund performance in 2008. In short, hedge fund managers had to "de-leverage" their portfolios, often as a result of margin calls, and did so by selling assets, leading to increased selling pressure. Having less liquidity and facing more investor redemptions, many hedge funds restricted redemptions, a practice referred to as "gating."[14]

The Harcourt team of Herbst and Wessling summarized and described the most important financial system problems that affected hedge funds:

De-leveraging: Due to severe losses from sub prime exposure most investment banks had to cut their balance sheets substantially. This led to tighter credit conditions for hedge funds (reduced credit lines, higher credit costs), as well as to unwinds of their trade books. As a consequence, hedge funds were forced to cut their balance sheets as well (although their leverage was not particularly high compared to earlier periods like 1998). Unwinds of trade books at banks and hedge funds led to a pronounced and indiscriminate selling pressure across the board; funds which were strongly exposed to so-called "crowded trades" have been hit most by this sell-off.

> *Counterparty risk: In their role as prime brokers, investment banks are the most important counterparty for hedge funds, frequently subsidizing funds' infrastructure: they provide credit lines, custody of assets, and act as counterparty for various OTC derivative transactions. The default of such an important counterparty has far-reaching consequences for funds, which can consequently encounter substantial losses. Yet, hedge funds have managed this risk quite well and losses directly linked to the Lehman default have been limited.*

> *Government intervention: Governments and government agencies have taken several actions aimed at stabilizing financial markets. This includes the rescues of Bear Stearns and AIG, the nationalization of the mortgage agencies, as well as the short selling ban on financials. The first two interventions had a negative impact on fundamental managers which had expected default for the respective banks and agencies. The short selling ban significantly reduced the hedging opportunities for many hedge funds strategies in a negative market environment.*[15]

Madoff Fraud

In the midst of all these problems, in December 2008, Bernard Madoff, a renowned trader and the purportedly successful manager of a large hedge fund, was arrested for fraud. Facing redemptions from his investors, Madoff had confessed to his sons (also his business partners) that the fund did not exist. Friends, family, and institutions lost an estimated $50 billion in Madoff's Ponzi scheme. He pleaded guilty to the crime in mid-2009 and was sentenced to 150 years in prison.

POSTCRISIS OUTLOOK

Industry analysts anticipated that hedge funds would suffer along with the rest of the market in the short term, but would recover faster. Limits on leverage and the amount of financing available would put a damper on returns in some cases, but opportunity for returns existed. Fewer hedge funds and investment banks meant surviving hedge funds faced less competition and more opportunities to purchase undervalued assets.[16]

Observers expected investors to either initiate or increase allocations to hedge funds, because funds had achieved some of their objectives—to outperform the overall market—and long-only opportunities remained limited and volatile.[17]

Industry Issues

The poor investment performance of hedge funds seemed likely to have more ongoing implications for the business of hedge funds, especially regarding terms and conditions. The following summary is adapted from a UBS research note written by analyst Alexander Ineichen.[18]

- **Fees:** It appeared likely that investors would have more negotiating power with managers and greater likelihood of paying discounted fees on existing or new commitments. The majority of hedge funds were open, including prestigious funds that had long been closed. Those with high-water marks were attempting to find ways to stay in business and earn partial fees while meeting their obligations to recover losses.
- **Gates:** Redemptions were high in 2008 partly for technical reasons, as many contractual gate provisions were "stacked" instead of "level." The stacked structure means "first in, first out" and gives investors an incentive to submit notices early for fear of being too late. Many investors over-redeemed as a result. Level gates treat all equally if they meet the deadline, eliminating any fear of not getting a fair share. Most hedge funds were expected to implement the level gate structure in the future.
- **Lock-Ups:** Previously hedge fund investors justified lock-ups if the underlying asset warranted a longer commitment and tolerated them in general. When investors needed to, they redeemed from funds with more generous and liquid lock-up provisions, so those managers were hurt the most.

As frustrated as investors were by lock-ups and gates, Ineichen expected more managers to implement such provisions to secure their capital base even for liquid market strategies.

An increased interest by investors in managed accounts also stemmed from concerns about lock-ups, but was also tied to the desire for more portfolio transparency for risk management purposes. The likelihood of increased hedge fund regulation remained a concern, but it had taken a back seat to more pressing economic and systemic concerns. The Madoff case raised questions about the abilities of regulators, since the SEC had missed numerous warning signs, and led investors to focus more intently on operational due diligence.

Conditions for Top Investors

In the months after the financial crisis, when we interviewed the leading investors profiled in this book, "risky assets" ranging from equities and credit, to energy, to "illiquid Asian physical real estate" rallied. The rally showed a "reversal of the acute risk aversion" investors had displayed in late 2008 and early 2009, but economic growth forecasts had not reversed and remained depressed. Developed economies had the most limited prospects, but even the most promising emerging market economies had low growth expectations. Those primarily export-driven economies were hurt by the reduced demand and limited credit of their trading partners.[19]

At the fund level, beta-driven strategies had the best performance record in the first half of 2009. The HFR Global Hedge Fund Index turned positive, up 7.2 percent by July 31, 2009, after losing 23.3 percent in 2008. A high-volatility environment allowed funds to achieve performance without excessive leverage. At the same time, the financial system seemed to have stabilized, reducing fears of systemic risk. Analysts expected hedge funds to continue to perform well under those conditions.

Net capital inflows to hedge funds had increased between May and July of 2009, although hedge funds continued to close. The limited number of new hedge fund launches had little success, indicating that hedge funds that survived the crisis were likely to get bigger and stronger as the recipients of the new allocations.

CONCLUSION

This chapter provided a view of the hedge fund investment landscape at the time we interviewed the top hedge fund investors profiled in Part Two. The description is meant to provide a snapshot of the economic, market, and industry conditions they faced at the time, in order to put their comments in context.

These leading hedge fund investors offer a variety of different backgrounds and perspectives on investing in hedge funds, including their response to the current environment. Their profiles bring together theory and reality as they discuss how they apply the principles detailed in Chapter 2, given the market conditions described in this chapter.

Through the stories of the top hedge fund investors profiled in Part Two, investors will learn about the experiences and strategies that made them successful and glean lessons and advice that will help them navigate the hedge fund landscape in the future.

Top Hedge Fund Investors: Stories and Strategies

CHAPTER 4

Author of the Hedge Fund Investing Story

Richard Elden, Founder and Former Chairman, Grosvenor Capital Management

As a Chicago newspaper reporter in the late 1950s and early 1960s, if Richard Elden had discovered the story of someone with a life and career similar to the one that ultimately unfolded for him, he most likely would have regarded it with skepticism. The story of a reporter who becomes a leading hedge fund investor and a pioneer in the industry would seem to defy what one would expect.

Elden is the founder and former chairman of Grosvenor Capital Management, the nation's first fund of hedge funds, which he launched in 1971. He retired as chairman after spending 34 years with Grosvenor. Then, after helping Carl Icahn launch an activist fund in 2004, Elden, together with two other partners, started a fund of activist hedge funds in 2006.

Prior to founding Grosvenor, Elden had been a reporter for the International News Service (INS), the City News Bureau of Chicago, and the *Chicago Sun-Times*. Next he was a financial analyst with Science Research Associates (SRA) and a securities analyst with A.G. Becker & Co., Inc.

He also has a distinguished educational background, including a BA from Northwestern University in 1956, and an MBA from the University of Chicago Booth School of Business in 1966. He completed the Harvard Business School's Owner-President Management Program in 1997. He has been on the investment committees of the University of Chicago, the Field Museum, the Museum of Contemporary Art, and the Francis W. Parker School.

BACKGROUND

Elden credits his experience as a journalist with giving him the reporting, fact checking, and analytical skills—and skepticism—that would make him a successful hedge fund investor. "The lessons I learned while being a reporter were listening, interviewing people, analyzing what they're saying, and checking for consistency. Being able to write—I was writing eight hours a day—helped me to be more analytical and critical in reading managers' letters and interviewing people."

His journalism career began in 1953, when, still a student at Northwestern, he traveled to the Soviet Union with a group of college newspaper editors. Except for one New York City lawyer, he and his colleagues on the trip were the first Westerners to enter the USSR since 1947. Their story made front-page news, capturing the attention of editors and eventually leading Elden to his first press job with INS.

After INS, he went to the City News Bureau of Chicago, the basic training ground for local reporters (also a setting of the classic 1928 Hecht-MacArthur play, *The Front Page*). "The motto of the City News Bureau was, 'If your mother tells you she loves you, check it out,'" he recalls, noting that this gave him a healthy dose of skepticism.

It was "the best training in the world. Essentially I've been a reporter for 55 years, the last 38 applying my reporting skills to checking out money managers. To me, it's just an extension of reporting." Following his final journalism stint, five years with the *Chicago Sun-Times*, Elden had job offers from *Newsweek* and the *New York Times* but decided to go to business school instead.

Soon after starting at the University of Chicago in 1964, he met his eventual partner, Frank Meyer (Chapter 5). "I was 31 and getting an MBA. He was 21 and getting a Ph.D. in statistics, so you know who the smart one was," Elden recalls. While Meyer's expertise in statistics and Elden's fact-finding skills "totally complemented each other," several more years passed before they actually became partners. In the interim, Elden took his first job after business school as a financial analyst at SRA, today a division of McGraw-Hill.

"Out of the blue," he says, a friend, David B. Heller, called and said, "I know you've been a reporter and like to ask questions" and offered him a job as a securities analyst at the firm A.G. Becker. His mandate was "to find two or three stocks that had the potential to produce high returns." These "special situations" were "long-only" investments that were highly correlated with the overall stock market.

A business school classmate introduced him to the work of Edward O. Thorp, a mathematician who had written a best-selling book, *Beat the*

Dealer (Random House, 1966), about using the technique of card counting to win at blackjack in Las Vegas. Thorp took on the stock market next in *Beat the Market* (Random House, 1967). Elden studied the book and learned about Thorp's warrant hedging technique.

"At that time, a number of stocks had related warrants." By buying, for example, Sperry Rand stock and selling short Sperry Rand warrants, he had achieved a 25 percent annualized rate of return. "That's better than trying to pick individual stocks, where you're subject to overall market risk," Elden says, adding, "not only did Thorp's market-neutral strategy produce better absolute returns, but also better risk-adjusted returns."

The insight led Elden to start Grosvenor Partners (later renamed the Grosvenor Multi-Strategy Fund) in 1971 with two concepts in mind: first, to invest with external money managers, and second, to utilize market-neutral investment strategies. Although Grosvenor was the first fund of hedge funds in the United States, it was preceded by a fund of funds launched in Geneva in 1969 (Leveraged Capital Holdings, managed by Georges Karlweis).

"In 1971, hedge funds looked very different from today's model," Elden recalls. Although there are no reliable statistics, one source has estimated that there were no more than 30 hedge funds in existence and the largest had $50 million under management. The aggregate capital of all hedge funds combined was probably less than $300 million. "Generally, the few people who established hedge funds were a self-selected group of elite investors such as Cumberland, Convertible Hedge Associates, Steinhardt, Fine and Berkowitz, and George Soros's Quantum Fund. Each fund had started with less than $10 million."

Elden started with his own family's assets and a handful of individual clients, including a lead investor, Irving B. Harris. Harris "had recently sold his company to Gillette for $20 million and went on to become a major philanthropist."

From that start in 1971, Grosvenor pursued warrant hedging and convertible bond arbitrage. Frank Meyer joined Elden in 1973. Together, they managed Grosvenor for 13 years. The firm began finding new types of investment opportunities: long/short equities (the original A.W. Jones model), commodities and futures, merger arbitrage, and strategic block investing. Over the years, the Grosvenor Multi-Strategy Fund has outperformed the S&P 500 stock index with significantly less volatility, and the firm remains a powerful force in the industry under the leadership of Michael J. Sacks.

Despite the tremendous growth and significant changes in the industry, Elden retains the same investment objectives he espoused in 1971, namely: "Look for talented managers, who can produce good returns, take modest risk, and who are essentially hedged."

INVESTMENT PROCESS

Elden bases his investment philosophy on his objective of maximizing long-term, after-tax, risk-adjusted returns and seeks strategies with consistent returns and low correlations to the market. He cautions investors, "Focus on the power of compounding and the risk of negative numbers, which affect compounding."

He learned the impact of negative performance numbers early in his career. "The fund had an 8 percent loss in 1973, just two years into its life. But the loss had nothing to do with the bear market at that time; rather, it was a fraud by Equity Funding, an insurance company that was one of the biggest growth stocks, owned by many institutions. It turned out that the company's managers weren't writing the insurance polices, but rather were simply making them up. The assets did not exist," Elden says.

At the time, it was the largest fraud in U.S. corporate history. Several of the hedge funds Grosvenor had invested with owned the convertible bonds and had sold short the stock. Thus, while they were hedged, they did have a modest net exposure that resulted in a loss. The lesson: While a fraud by an issuer of publicly traded securities was a rare event, it nevertheless is an additional risk.

That early experience helped to make Elden risk-averse. His philosophy became "Maximize risk-adjusted returns subject to low correlations to the markets—and keep compounding." As a result, "For any given level of returns, we took less risk than other people."

Manager Selection Guidelines

When Elden and Meyer began investing in hedge funds, their investment process consisted mostly of interviewing money managers. Decisions were "really based on our interviews with these people. We didn't have a formalized process, but we did our homework," he says, adding that they learned early that most hedge fund managers could be quickly categorized.

"You could tell some were brilliant, unusual, and talented, like Ed Thorp and his partner, Jay Regan. Others clearly were not impressive, so you dropped them from consideration immediately. A third group required more work, more digging."

Between Meyer's analytical approach and his own dogged reporting style, Elden says, "We usually got to the key issues and found out a fair amount about the managers. It wasn't until years later that background investigative report services came into use. We did our own digging, talking with people and checking managers out with the people we knew."

When selecting investment managers, Elden uses a "parameters test" that includes reviewing and evaluating such quantitative aspects as the size of the investment staff, number of positions in the portfolio, amount of assets under management, and number of clients. Then he studies the firm's culture, an exercise he believes that few hedge fund investors do, or do deeply and frequently enough.

Evaluate Skill   In tennis, errors are either forced or unforced. That is, they are caused either by the superior play of the opponent or by the poor skill or decisions of the player. Elden applies the latter, "unforced error" concept in his analysis and tries to separate those types of mistakes from the forced errors the manager cannot control. He also tries to determine whether the unforced error is apt to be repeated in the future.

An unforced error in a hedge fund is a risk when a manager "puts himself in a position to be put in a bind" by saddling the fund with:

- Excessive leverage
- Too much concentration in a small number of investments
- Illiquid holdings

There's also the mismatch of assets and liabilities, when a fund has illiquid assets and allows investors to withdraw quarterly or annually. This mismatch led some funds to suspend redemptions in 2008, making it a recent and glaring example of an unforced error.

Favor a Classic Hedge Fund Model   "Hedge funds are a superior investment model. Equity long/short is superior to long only, because the manager has two sets of opportunities, less market exposure, and primarily makes money based upon stock selection, not market direction. It's a better model."

Moreover, "Hedge funds take different kinds of bets than traditional long only managers," he says. "Although the long component of long/short equity funds is similar, many hedge fund investment strategies involve completely different approaches, convertible arbitrage, merger arbitrage, macro-investing, distressed debt, etc."

Elden believes the classic hedge fund business model also provides an advantage. "You attract more skilled managers in an industry segment that pays premium fees, and have a structure that creates the right incentives." The combination of the investment model and the business model, he claims, "provides a superior approach to investing."

He stresses however, that in creating the right incentives, it is crucial that the manager have a significant portion of his (or her) net worth invested in the fund to help ensure a proper alignment of interests with investors.

See Characteristics Others Miss   Elden's experience has taught him to be wary of certain manager flaws and to focus on fund characteristics that other investors often miss.

> Fund Size: The size of a fund can be a positive or a negative. "There is a trade-off between managers starting with a small asset base and one or two generalists, versus firms with a large asset base and a team of specialists. There are pros and cons to each one, and it's not clear that one is inherently better than another. A case can be made for either approach."
>
> While the performance of a fund can be adversely affected by too large a total amount of assets under management, large size is not always a negative factor. More important is whether a manager's primary objective is performance or simply gathering assets.
>
> Pedigree or Apprenticeship: Elden will consider investing in start-up and early-stage hedge fund managers if they have "a great pedigree." He cites Lone Pine, a firm founded by Steve Mandel. "An exceptionally talented person, with the right philosophy, and the right approach." Mandel started his firm after gaining experience as a highly regarded retail analyst at Goldman Sachs and then working for Julian Robertson at Tiger Management.
>
> Several successful hedge fund managers started their funds after stints working with Robertson at Tiger and have become known as "Tiger Cubs." Elden mentions Tiger Cubs in general as the type of new manager he would be more likely to consider. In addition to Mandel, this group includes Andreas Halvorsen of Viking Global Investors and John Griffin of Blue Ridge Capital.
>
> "If the person has a really first-rate pedigree, realistic expectations, and puts together a talented team," then Elden will be more likely to invest in the early days.
>
> "Pedigree, or apprenticeship, is far more important than people realize. They don't give enough weight to where a manager was and who his mentor was."

Manager Due Diligence   To elicit accurate information and get helpful insight about managers during the due diligence process, he uses his standard reporter's interviewing tactics and backs them up with systematic background checks. Elden considers the Grosvenor Capital Management manager due diligence process "best in class." The Grosvenor method combines quantitative and qualitative analysis and includes investment due diligence as well as noninvestment due diligence.

When evaluating hedge fund managers, he finds it especially helpful to spend personal time with them. For example, Elden went hiking in Aspen with one manager. "Way up in the mountains he wore a T-shirt and shorts, nothing else. It poured. Most hikers would carry a poncho. After the hike I concluded that I would never invest with him. He was totally oblivious to risk."

Investors also should try to uncover and understand any "hidden bogeys" or underlying objectives of a prospective manager that may jeopardize or motivate performance. One famous hedge fund manager quietly yearned to have his own wealth keep pace with that of another, more famous manager. Another found inspiration in trying to climb back to his pre-divorce net worth. To determine a manager's underlying objectives, Elden asks, "What motivates him? How competitive is he? How smart?"

A key question for investors is whether the manager has a competitive edge. If so, is it sustainable? Elden says that today, "it's really hard to have an edge, since so many people are doing the same thing." Nevertheless, some managers do have a competitive advantage.

The detailed interview remains his most important tool to "really understand managers, what they're like and what they do." Elden believes that investors must not leave a single stone unturned. When checking references and "nonreferences" (the people you find from your own research), if you call a person you do not know, "you'll get a perfunctory answer." Elden would instead "find somebody who really knows the manager and visit them in person and find out what they really think. That's important."

Many investors tend to outsource their noninvestment due diligence:

- Investigative specialists conduct "a very thorough search" and background check. Such firms have the expertise to discover false information, litigation, and regulatory violations.
- Legal experts check the documents thoroughly.
- Back-office due diligence experts can tell you whether you ought to reject a manager because his back office is not up to speed or because there may be cause to suspect a fraud.

Risk Management Evaluation Elden began evaluating hedge fund risk management skills long before today's sophisticated monitoring systems became prevalent. His classic approach not only works, but also seems simple and sensible. To evaluate a manager's approach to risk management, he collects and analyzes data on the extent of change, over time, of various metrics: volatility, exposure, performance attribution, concentration, and leverage.

"There's a difference in the risk management mind-set between CTAs and stock pickers. Most equity managers have a micro attitude. If the stock is cheaper now, they'll say it's a better buy now than it was before and will hold it in the portfolio. CTAs or macro managers have a different approach. If something goes down in price, they're out in two seconds. They couldn't care less about value, they're managing the portfolio risk."

Elden cites Bruce Kovner (Caxton Associates) as "an outstanding manager of risk," and Paul Singer (Elliott Associates) as "a terrific risk manager." While he admires both, he says, "They're totally different in their approaches to risk, but each has an approach that is suited to his own investment strategy."

With his "kick the tires" approach to evaluating risk management, he remains the inquisitive reporter. Elden is concerned about two factors: first, permanent impairment of capital or second, being forced to sell (or cover a short position) at distressed prices.

He quotes Frank Meyer on the difference between "airplane risk and automobile risk":

- The probability of an airplane crash occurring is very low, but if a crash occurs it will probably be a disaster.
- The probability of an automobile accident occurring is much higher, but if an accident does occur, it's not likely to be very serious.

An example of airplane risk would be Long-Term Capital Management, which, in 1998, was down 90 percent. An example of automobile risk would be a long/short equity fund that is down 10 to 15 percent.

Portfolio Construction

When building a hedge fund portfolio, Elden believes that selecting the right types of investment strategies is as important as selecting the right managers. "People don't focus on it, but which strategies to include and which strategies to exclude is a crucial decision."

Strategy Selection   Elden's fund of funds portfolio tended to include:

- Equity long/short
- Convertible and merger arbitrage
- Distressed securities, bankruptcies
- Global macro investing

His fund of funds portfolio generally excluded:

- Regulation D securities
- Market-timing strategies
- Quantitative strategies

However, those decisions change over time as new opportunities appear and others diminish.

Activist Managers Elden and Meyer started investing with activists like Carl Icahn and Coniston more than 25 years ago. "When you invest with activists, you really need diversification for two reasons: (a) the funds are concentrated, and (b) they tend to be long-only or long-biased."

Elden identifies two types of activist managers:

- Operational activists: They focus on the income statement, cutting costs and increasing profit margins.
- Transactional activists: They focus on the balance sheet: recapitalizations, repurchasing stock, selling a division or even breaking up a company.

The successful activist manager needs to be a good:

- Stock picker (to find the undervalued stocks)
- Businessman (to decide on and execute changes to improve a company's performance)
- Salesman (to convince other shareholders that the proposed changes will enhance value)

Few people have the skills needed for activist investing, Elden says. "It's a small universe. Of eighty activists, there are twenty that are worth considering."

Risk Allocation To construct a portfolio, he says, "You want to have risk-based allocations. The greater the risk, the smaller the allocation; the less risk, the larger the allocation."

Historically, portfolio construction was based on the low correlations between managers. Although it was an effective tactic for many years, it did not work in 1994, 1998, or 2008 when most managers were highly correlated with one another. Since then, funds of hedge funds have tended to look for managers with lower volatility, rather than low correlations.

Desire to Exit Affects Performance The newest phenomenon in the hedge fund industry is the "exit strategy." In the 1990s, Tiger, Odyssey, and Steinhardt all liquidated their funds and went out of business with zero terminal value. Then, in 2004, Highbridge Capital was sold to JPMorgan Chase for $1 billion. It was the first major sale of a hedge fund to an institution.

Since then, several other firms have been sold or done initial public offerings of stock.

The possibility of creating a saleable enterprise has affected hedge fund managers' attitude toward performance, risk, and managing their businesses, Elden says. "We have seen product proliferation, and a focus on gathering assets, things that are not necessarily in line with their investors' interests. Sacrificing performance to have lower volatility, a steadier stream of revenues, and to have greater value if they want to sell to a major institution or go public has had a major impact, and it will continue to do so."

Diversification   One of the principal advantages of a fund of hedge funds, Elden points out, is diversification, a tool that is referred to as the "last free lunch" in investing. Specifically, diversifying across investment strategies and among managers using the same strategy reduces the risk of the portfolio, without reducing expected returns. Although this approach has not protected portfolios in extreme circumstances, it works well in most normal markets. While the individual hedge funds have a fair amount of volatility on a monthly basis, the composite, or fund of funds, is fairly stable on a monthly basis.

At the same time, Elden cautions investors to avoid overdiversification. "A lot of funds of funds are overdiversified. Having fifty or sixty hedge funds in a fund of funds is not necessary. Fifteen to twenty-five funds is plenty."

Asset Allocations   There are limits to how much control a fund of funds manager has in determining allocations to the underlying securities. He points out that there are three levels of asset allocation, not all of which he can influence:

1. The fund of funds allocates to both single-strategy and multistrategy funds.
2. The underlying multistrategy funds have a mandate to move in and out of substrategies and change allocation targets as conditions warrant.
3. The underlying single-strategy funds, although limited to a single strategy, vary their net and gross exposure.

As a result of this phenomenon, Elden would hold some cash to be opportunistic. "Stay in touch with your managers in order to know what investment opportunities they're seeing," he adds.

Transparency   As hedge funds have increased in complexity and the number of strategies utilized has risen, transparency has become a key issue. Even so, certain prominent hedge fund firms thrived without offering any transparency. Elden describes the Medallion Fund, managed by James Simons, as "a classic example of nontransparency." Medallion, which always operated very secretively, stopped taking new investors in 1993 and several years ago went private.

Today, however, "the opaque model is less acceptable," says Elden.

Although Elden expects hedge funds to provide more transparency, he does not expect full transparency will become the norm. Nor does he advocate it.

"Funds should be willing to provide 'intelligent transparency'—by asset class—gross and net exposures by sector, by region—and leverage and liquidity," he says. "You don't need position-level transparency." Investors need "just enough information to let them accurately assess the risk and liquidity."

HEDGE FUND INDUSTRY

Over the last 40 years, the hedge fund industry has had phenomenal growth for one reason, Elden says. "Generally speaking, hedge funds have produced superior risk-adjusted returns. Not only has the absolute performance been good, but the returns, for the most part, have had a relatively low correlation with the equity markets." He attributes the outstanding performance of top-tier hedge funds largely to three factors:

- Manager skills
- A superior investment model
- A compensation structure that attracts talent and aligns the interest of the investor and manager

"Essentially, hedge funds have been transformed from the original A.W. Jones model to the point where they represent the cutting edge of the investment management business."

Funds of Hedge Funds

Elden believes the role of funds of funds has become more crucial than it was when he started Grosvenor in 1971. "With the increase in globalization and specialization, hedge funds have adopted additional, more complicated investment strategies. Moreover, with greater complexity and the risk of fraud, there is a much greater focus on thorough, in-depth due diligence."

Investors choosing to invest with a fund of hedge funds should understand the culture of the fund of funds in the same way that they would evaluate that of a single hedge fund.

Elden also believes investors should look carefully at two indicators of manager selection skill:

- Blow-ups: "How many hedge fund blow-ups has the fund of funds experienced? Why did they happen? What did they learn from them?"
- Top-tier managers: "How many top-tier hedge funds did the fund of funds miss and how many did they invest with?"

He anticipates that "there will always be a role for smaller funds of funds that focus on newer, emerging managers." But he thinks such funds "will not satisfy the larger institutional investors." Elden says that the advantages of an institutional firm like Grosvenor make it difficult for small funds to compete for those investors. Those advantages include:

- An experienced, professional management team
- A large team of investment specialists with the skills and experience to analyze and understand more complex investment strategies
- Thorough, in-depth due diligence
- Transparency and voluminous collateral information
- The ability to negotiate better terms with hedge fund managers

Reflections on the Industry

Reflecting on his experience in the hedge fund industry, Elden says, "I never would have expected to see this kind of size. It is way beyond anything I ever dreamed of when I started. The exponential growth has been incredible."

Elden identifies two important characteristics of large and successful hedge funds: The most successful macro managers, "Bruce Kovner, Paul Tudor Jones, and Louis M. Bacon, have unusually capable people overseeing the business operations." Most hedge fund managers "need to have better and stronger business partners," if they want to pursue an institutional model.

Second, in pursuing multiple investment strategies, it's often necessary to add not just one person, but also a team of people with specialized expertise. "Depth is important."

Best Characteristics

In managing money, self-confidence and curiosity are major assets. But arrogance can be a major problem. To manage money successfully through all kinds of market environments requires a certain amount of humility.

Someone once told him, "In selecting hedge fund managers, the three most important criteria are character, character, character." Elden says investors can and will "find some of the best and the brightest people. They have had great records, are on top of all kinds of things, and have lots of interests."

However, one has to avoid managers who are "taking too much risk or operating beyond their core competence."

INVESTIGATOR, INVESTOR, INSPIRATION

By applying his inquisitive mind and investigative skills to understanding hedge funds, Richard Elden inspired the growth of the industry and participated in its evolution over the last 40 years. Not content to just observe and report the hedge fund story, he helped write it. A quintessential reporter became the quintessential hedge fund investor.

The City News Bureau motto that inspired Elden now inspires a new motto for hedge fund investors: If Dick Elden tells you how to invest in hedge funds, check them out, then do it.

CHAPTER 5

The Predictive Value of Performance

Frank Meyer, Founder and Former Chairman, Glenwood Capital Investments

Frank Meyer began investing in hedge funds in the early 1970s, giving him a perspective on hedge fund investing and the evolution of the industry few investors share. Among his many accomplishments, Meyer is best known for founding Glenwood Capital Investments, a fund of hedge funds, in 1988.

After receiving a BA and MBA from the University of Chicago, he began and ended his brief academic career as a statistics instructor in the Booth School of Business. Meyer then joined A.G. Becker & Company to redesign their pension performance measurement service, and while there, learned of an obscure and intriguing investment called a hedge fund. In 1973, he joined Grosvenor Partners, the fund of hedge funds started by Richard Elden (Chapter 4) in 1971. Meyer was a partner in the firm and co-manager of the funds until September 1986.

Meyer detoured into private equity as a general partner of a leveraged buyout firm, Knightsbridge Partners, but the crash of 1987 made him realize he preferred to invest in hedge funds.

Meyer started Glenwood Capital Investments, LLC in January 1988 and remained affiliated with the firm until resigning as chairman in January 2004. In the interim, the Man Group, plc, an investment advisor based in England, purchased Glenwood in October 2000 and ran it as a wholly owned subsidiary until 2009, when it was consolidated with other Man Group subsidiaries.

Meyer has been a managing partner of several investment entities and registered securities broker/dealers and has served as an outside director for several companies. He remains involved in hedge funds as a private investor and as a member of the advisory board for SkyBridge Capital, a New York–based hedge fund seed investment firm.

BACKGROUND

Frank Meyer graduated from the University of Chicago after completing a program that compressed bachelor degree and MBA studies into a five-year period. Having grown up with both of his parents teaching humanities, he thought he wanted to be a teacher too, although his area of expertise was finance and statistics.

As he continued in the university's Ph.D. program and after teaching for several years, he realized a career as a professor did not suit him. "It was the wrong path in terms of my psychological makeup. Once you reached the top of the heap in teacher ratings that was it. The thought of teaching mean, median, and variance year after year wasn't that appealing."

Nor did writing articles appeal to him. "There were no word processors. I had to bring articles to the typing pool. Mine had subscripts, superscripts, and sub-superscripts. It was horrible. I pitied those poor people."

Nor did his articles appeal to others. "The thing that tipped it for me, I brought an article home and my mother used it as a coffee trivet."

Meyer attended the University of Chicago when the economics and finance academics were building the body of work and forging the prestigious reputations that would influence economic and market theories for generations and result in several Nobel laureates. He took classes from "a wonderful group of teachers," including Eugene Fama, Merton Miller, and Milton Friedman. "Any failures I may have had in academia are certainly not due to them, but probably in spite of them."

Another, less well-known professor, Harry Roberts, sparked Meyer's interest in business statistics and offered him the instructor position he remembers as "a great opportunity, but one that solidified the fact that I was not academic material."

Facing reality, Meyer thought about what he could do. "I had spent many years going down a path and the first thing I had to do was admit that it was wrong for me." He decided to seek an opportunity that would use as much of his education as possible.

A friend brought him into A.G. Becker, a financial services firm that offered a performance measurement service for pensions. Becker would help assess whether a pension plan was properly managed compared to other plans of the same size by calculating various plan statistics and providing periodic reports and quarterly and annual reviews.

Becker hired Meyer to apply current academic research to improve the existing product and to develop new products. He spent three years analyzing corporate pension plans and occasionally studying the private portfolios of wealthy individuals.

"These things called hedge funds" in the private portfolios intrigued him, because the performance "wasn't necessarily better or worse, but it was much more consistent and uncorrelated to market indexes."

Asked to evaluate the operations and process of a convertible bond manager, Meyer concluded it took advantage of an inefficiency that "was bound to evaporate in a few years."

In retrospect he says, "That's what happens when you leave academia and go into the real world, you come out with all kinds of blind spots, like a gambler that figures out a gambling system and then goes to Las Vegas. When you meet the real world, you discover that many inefficiencies that are assumed away only in academic articles actually make a significant difference."

His interest in hedge funds led Meyer in 1973 to join his business school friend Richard Elden at the fund of hedge funds he had founded two years previously, Grosvenor Partners.

Early Days of Hedge Fund Investing

When Meyer first joined Grosvenor Partners they invested primarily in convertible bond hedging strategies, broadening into other types of strategies around 1979, a move that ultimately positioned the firm to grow. What is now a multibillion-dollar institutional fund of hedge funds was a small firm catering to individual investors at the time Meyer joined the business.

"I don't think we had any institutions. In the early days institutions shied away from hedge funds. They violated the prudent man rule in a number of states, because then the rule was driven on a security by security basis and you could be sued if you made an investment that was not prudent."

Meyer explains that because convertible hedge fund strategies were generally long one security of Company X and short another security from Company X, by the prevailing definition, one of these positions had to be imprudent, typically the short side. As a consequence the strategy violated the prudent man rule.

Subsequently, the work of William Sharpe and Harry Markowitz considered prudence in the context of the entire portfolio. Their individual research contributions became the basis of prudence under the revised statute, replacing the security-by-security approach.

Until the change, Grosvenor continued to concentrate its investments in convertible arbitrage hedge funds strategies. Despite Meyer's earlier predictions, the strategy could capitalize on inefficiencies, because it was typically a much harder strategy to start.

"There weren't too many convertible arbitrageurs, because computerized databases didn't exist. Managers had to have file cabinet after file cabinet full of prospectuses, so if somebody offered a security, they had to check what was in the files to know the exact terms. Computer power was very expensive. What you had in the early 1970s was a fraction of what you can now buy from Dell for less than $200. The barriers to entry were very substantial."

Computer Power   Meyer's own experience with computers while at the University of Chicago illuminates the difference between the early days of hedge funds and today.

"Everything was submitted on cards. When they came back and told you the program didn't work, the first question was, 'Were the cards warped?' You would then have to run them through again. If they weren't warped, then you had to really do work.

"Programming was very, very inefficient. Machine resources were precious. You had to write in high-level computer language, Fortran, Cobol, sometimes Assembler. If that didn't work you would have to write in machine language of zeroes and ones.

"Getting time on the university computer was also expensive. The university had pricing algorithms, so you had to have a big research budget. As a student and later an instructor, I did not have much of a budget."

Meyer got around the expense with his own pricing algorithm arbitrage. "I figured out how the pricing algorithm worked. The computer would poll the index register to see if data was there, if it was, they'd charge you." He wrote an Assembler program that constantly took his data out and "increased my budget."

These experiences gave Meyer an aversion to computerization that continues to this day. "To minimize my time in front of a screen, my secretary reads all my e-mails."

Private Equity

Meyer was a partner at Grosvenor until 1986. "Every so often you need to do something different," so he teamed with former Beatrice Foods executives to form a private equity partnership focused on leveraged buyouts of smaller companies. Their purchases included two bakeries, a distributor of screws and adhesives, and a franchiser of barbershops. He found the experience interesting because he could "once again see the inefficiencies of the marketplace" in the real world.

For example, the adhesives distributor was a subsidiary of a larger Washington, DC company that needed to raise money. "A case of corporate neglect; they bought a company and ignored it. Consequently, the president's golf game was better than it needed to be. When the parent needed cash, it looked at all the subsidiaries to see what could be sold."

When Meyer and his partners took over, he says that they "made one simple change that turned the company around. We gave employees 20 percent of the equity in the company. Sales doubled or tripled, I don't remember exactly, but it was a substantial difference."

The barbershop franchiser, Super Cuts, gives another example of inefficiencies. Two barbers had developed standardized hair cutting and training techniques, making it easy to franchise the concept. The inexperienced founders aggravated franchisees by raising prices and sold the rights to additional franchises to another organization. The existing franchisees sued, making it impossible for the second organization to sell new franchises. To fix the situation, Meyer and his colleagues bought back the franchise sale rights, mollified the franchisees, and installed new, cost-conscious management.

Private equity fills a void between floundering public companies and people with good ideas. "If a public company does well, because of the way the market operates, people get focused on short-term earnings reports and companies sacrifice the long term for the short term. It makes sense for a private person to buy it, clean it up without worrying about earnings reports and analysts, and reintroduce it to the public market when it has been fixed."

Meyer believes private equity serves a valuable function in the markets, because while investors want liquid assets and want to own shares they can sell or buy at will, they become overly focused on the short term. Companies are not run efficiently for the long term, providing opportunities to fix them. "Opportunities generally contribute an economic benefit."

His experience in private equity gave Meyer an appreciation for the work involved and for the role it plays in the markets. "It is not just about the concepts, it's hard work in terms of execution." It also gave Meyer an appreciation for more liquid hedge fund portfolios, because "you get the benefit of broad diversification and the flexibility to adapt the portfolio to changes in your personal situation."

Meyer had continued to invest his money and excess partnership cash in hedge funds. When the stock market crashed in 1987, "I knew the private companies were worth one third less, but the partners acted like nothing had happened. I realized I was not designed for illiquid investments and hedge funds were more appealing."

In January 1988, he and two associates started Glenwood Capital Management, a hedge fund investment advisory firm and fund of hedge funds.

HEDGE FUND INVESTOR

Meyer gained valuable insight from his visit to private equity. "Private equity experience really brought home to me the importance of how the manager runs his business."

He adamantly believes a manager's ability to run his business has an impact not just on the viability and longevity of his firm, but also on his ability to invest successfully. Many hedge fund investors do not make the quality of the manager's business management skills such an important factor, but from Meyer's perspective they downplay it to their detriment. It is a core principle of his hedge fund investment philosophy, influencing his decision to invest and his moment to redeem.

Selecting Good Business Managers

When evaluating managers, investors need to understand that a hedge fund manager is responsible for running an investment portfolio and a small business. Meyer assesses the manager's capability on both counts before making a decision to invest. This premise is very important for hedge fund investors because of the nature of how most hedge fund businesses begin and the origin of many funds from inside larger organizations.

In the typical scenario, a person talented at managing money decides he wants to leave an organization and go out on his own. Investors know the person can manage money. "You don't know to what extent [the] manager's abilities are tied to being part of the larger organization and don't know how they're going to do running their own organization."

Meyer says that a new hedge fund manager coming from a large firm has usually only had to decide what securities to buy or sell. Starting a fund forces a person to make decisions about accountants and marketing and to work on contracts and legal agreements. It means running a business. If a person is able to do that and raise money, investors then need to question his ability to grow.

"Is he going to be good at expanding the organization? Is he going to be good at delegating? Maybe he initially does all his own research, but may have to hire people. Does he know how to calibrate them?"

Meyer reinforces the point. "Looking at a manager that you're going to give money as a passive investor, I don't care what the strategy is, the manager has to succeed in carrying out two key tasks: He has to run the money, and he has to run the business."

Based on his experience, Meyer reinforces his point for a good reason. Managers typically get better and better over time. Theoretically they should, because they have seen more markets and made more trades, but yet they often stumble. "Usually they stumble for a business reason."

Meyer believes strongly that "past performance is not necessarily indicative of what you can expect in the future." He says, "It's very true for many reasons. One of the main reasons is as a manager progresses in size and the organization matures, he faces different business challenges, things he's never seen. Your question as an investor should be, 'Can he meet these challenges?' If you think he can't, you pull out; if you think he can, you stay with him."

Unfamiliar business challenges always have an impact on the investment portfolio. "If you just look at the past track record, a fantastic track record may not continue if the manager is coming up against difficult business hurdles."

For example, a maturing firm may have employees with no ownership stakes who may leave to start their own firms. "Maybe that's part of a plan and the manager is going to replace them with younger people. Maybe he doesn't want to give his people that much buy or sell authority. That could be good or could be bad. The point is [that] you as an investor have to focus on it."

Meyer uses the manager's business management acumen as a gauge throughout the life of the investment, including when to terminate. Reverting to statistics terminology he says, "The predictive value," for deciding "when to leave a manager, is best determined by focusing on how he runs the business."

Should an investor help a fund manager having business problems? When he faced such situations, Meyer would always give advice. He did not judge whether the manager followed it, but he would ask himself, "Is he heading to the rocks or not?" If he thought the manager could not overcome the next set of business hurdles, he would usually redeem from the fund.

Selecting Good Portfolio Managers

"Past performance is not indicative of future performance," a statement that particularly applies when assessing investment performance. "Look at periods where a manager has done well in the past. What are the characteristics? How are they different today? Are these differences positive or negative? Say he ran $100 million, now he runs $300 million, is that a plus or a minus?"

Investors should learn the answers to many such questions. "Did the manager perform well on more or less money or with a larger or smaller team? Did he perform well at a firm like Goldman Sachs, where he could rely on colleagues?" Investors should evaluate each response based on its importance to them. Meyer reminds investors to follow up with, "Was that a plus or a minus?"

While he admits the pluses and minuses investors can assign are subjective, when they add them all up, they will be able to form an opinion of whether the manager can maintain the past record.

"Avoid looking at the past track record." Meyer says that statistics can be misleading because investors will "extrapolate them out and think the performance is going to continue."

For instance, "A manager can take enormous risks and if the business does not stumble, he looks conservative by most statistical measures. The performance has been great relative to others, but on the other hand it could be the result of taking large risks."

Meyer agrees his method can be summarized as a qualitative review and analysis of the quantitative performance. "What generated that performance is often seen best in qualitative ways."

Quantitative analysis does provide useful information in some instances. He measures the variability of past returns because he finds the statistic to be a good predictor of the variability of returns in the future.

Meyer does not, however, consider the variability of returns a good measure of risk. He offers the example of a man walking along a cliff. "If he does not fall off, he is considered prudent by most statistical measures. He will have a good Sharpe ratio, so he's done pretty well. If he falls off the edge, he was foolhardy."

Elaborating, he says, "Risk is exposure to an unfavorable outcome. Statistics typically do not measure the exposure, but after the fact, did he succeed or not at avoiding the risk? Did the bad outcome occur or did it not? That is not a measure of risk, but rather a description of results."

When evaluating the risk profile of a manager, rather than looking at the variability of returns, Meyer considers the inherent risks of the investment strategy and assesses the riskiness of the enterprise. "Too much money, under- or over-staffed, issues with employees, there are a lot of other factors that determine our risks as investors."

Blow-ups occur for a number of reasons such as fraud, excessive leverage, and excessive risk. But if investors want to avoid them, they should heed the lessons he has learned working in private equity and being a hedge fund investor since the 1970s.

"The main thing investors do not do is look at the business side of the manager's operations. They focus more questions on the portfolio, not enough on the business."

Selecting New Hedge Fund Managers

Because he placed much less weight on track record than most other investors, Meyer was more willing to consider newer or start-up hedge fund managers. "At any point in the Glenwood portfolio, we had many managers that were early stage, with Glenwood as one of their earliest investors."

Meyer seeded new managers, putting new hedge funds in business by investing money in the fund and taking a stake in the business. The seed investor then has an active interest in whether the fund succeeds or fails as a business. In that case as the primary investor, "you give as much input as you can."

Seeding has become more formalized over time, and several investment firms have funds dedicated only to seeding new hedge fund managers. (Ted Seides of Protégé Partners, Chapter 12, has seeding as an important component of his investment fund. Meyer himself is on the advisory board of SkyBridge Capital, a New York–based hedge fund seeding firm founded by former Goldman Sachs executives Anthony Scaramucci and Scott Prince.)

Meyer describes two types of hedge fund seeders: "The first gives money and says, 'Okay, go do it on your own.' The second gives money and talent. By sharing talent and experience they try to help this person grow his first, and hopefully only, money management organization. In that form of seeding you're actively trying to make the manager better."

Investment firms that specialize in hedge fund seeding have to fight the perception of having adverse selection built into their investment process. Adverse selection stems from a belief that hedge fund managers willing to share a percentage of their company or fees tend to be lower quality. Meyer avoided that problem by not specializing in seeding and by carefully choosing and understanding the needs of the manager.

Meyer describes investors who just want to give money and leave the manager alone as "passive seeders." He says this form of seeding "tends to work if you're going after a group of people that have worked well together in the past. It's like developmental drilling in the oil business."

Succeeding at Seeding   In those early days all seeding tended to be "active seeding." Meyer would invest money, but also help recruit talent, advise the managers on their portfolios, and help them with their business.

"If he has it all together he doesn't really need you." Meyer would ask himself, "What is it that this manager needs that he doesn't have right now?"

Using the oil business analogy, he compares backing a hedge fund manager going out on his own to wildcatting. Since that is more difficult than backing a known entity, Meyer says, "The key thing is sizing up the manager. You can't make him talented, you can only ask, 'What does he need and can I supply it?' Often it is not just money, but helping them through the legal process, helping them raise money, helping them build an organization, and those are the things you have to put in. It's not enough to put in just money."

Where seeders make a mistake, especially passive seeders, he says, "They think money is all that's needed; as a result they often don't succeed. It's not a question that the managers are better or worse. The flood of money coming from people that want to be passive tends to not give managers what they need to succeed. That's why it's been so difficult for so many seeders."

A LEGENDARY WILDCAT STRIKE

The almost legendary story of hedge fund wunderkind Ken Griffin is summarized on the website of his firm, Citadel Investment Group (www.citadelgroup.com): "While a student at Harvard, Ken Griffin developed his first convertible bond arbitrage model and traded from his dorm room. In 1990, one year after graduation, Mr. Griffin launched Citadel as a single-strategy fund."

Meyer seeded Griffin. By doing so, he helped create and launch what is now a diversified institutional financial services firm employing over 1,000 worldwide, with one of the largest and best-known hedge funds at its core, despite stumbling in 2008. How did he decide that Griffin was worth seeding? Meyer describes his decision.

"Citadel, at that time, was an individual, Ken Griffin, no organization, just one person. He managed money in college, had a fund for family and close friends, and was very young."

This was not developmental drilling; it was wildcatting, making the thought process more intense. "When you look at the manager, you ask, 'What does he need to succeed?' If he has everything, he would not need you, and he'll quickly find that out."

Meyer identifies flaws and determines whether they are fixable. Twenty-three years old at the time, Griffin was too young to gain the confidence of investors and needed Meyer's help with raising money, credibility, legal advice, and mentoring. Being too young was a "fixable flaw," so Glenwood backed Griffin.

What led Meyer to believe Griffin would succeed despite his youth? Running a convertible arbitrage fund like Griffin's required skills in programming, economic analysis, organizing, and marketing.

A manager is usually great in some of those skills and not great in the others. Griffin was "very good at everything."

In addition, Meyer observed that even at that young age, Griffin already had a history of being in business, having started an educational software company as well as his dorm room fund. "He was entrepreneurial and practical. He turned weakness into strength."

For example, Griffin needed to borrow stock to do convertible arbitrage, so he went and met personally with the heads of stock loan departments. Meyer says they found Griffin, still an undergraduate, so intriguing they loaned him stock "at rates comparable to the Feshbach Brothers* and protected him from being called.

"He made being a college student in a tiny dorm room a strength."

While Meyer thought Griffin's skills and personality gave him good reasons to invest, it was important that he also felt Griffin was a decent and honorable person.

Meyer sees a lesson in his experience seeding Ken Griffin. "Get rid of biases, such as never looking at a manager who doesn't have a five-year record or who hasn't worked for a major firm. You can get blinded by the past and by prejudices, but you have to look at things as objectively as you can."

---

*In 1990, Feshbach Brothers was a well-known $1 billion short-selling specialist hedge fund. It closed in 1991.

Portfolio Construction Process

After identifying funds with potential for investment, Meyer conducts further due diligence. In general, he believes the due diligence process protects investors, because if they can find and identify problems—including fraud—then they can keep from making a mistake. Because Meyer has such strong manager selection principles, the due diligence process helps him determine the likelihood that a manager will perform well at managing both an investment portfolio and a business entity. Although it can be complicated, he believes the best way to ferret out that information is to check references extensively.

Due Diligence Reference Tactics   "You have to do a lot of reference checking. For example, say the manager comes from a big organization. What did the organization do for him? To what extent did he contribute? You have to check with other people that have come from that organization." But, he asks, "Why should anyone tell you the truth? It's a litigious society; what I say can only hurt me." Because of that he says investors need to have robust and thorough methods to check references.

At Glenwood they kept records of every person they ever interviewed, compiling information on their education and employment history in an electronic database. "If a manager said he worked at Goldman from 1987 to 1993, we would go into the database to search for people [who might] know the person."

Meyer offers a roundabout, but useful tactic for extracting better information from a cautious reference. "Try to find a person that knows the reference. Tell your contact you want them to ask the reference person about the money manager, but say, 'I don't want you to violate his or her confidence.' Then ask your contact to tell you after talking to the reference if he or she said anything that would make you not want to invest in the money manager."

The reference is more likely to tell your contact worthwhile information than they would tell you, the investor. "You don't want to betray the person, but you have to get around the issue that reference checking is so ripe for litigation."

Investors can check certain information easily and directly, like calling the university the manager attended to confirm he graduated, but Meyer finds few real, objective sources of information, so investors have to be really careful and thorough when conducting these checks.

"People don't have to tell you things," he says and gives the example of one hedge fund where he was invested. "Excellent CFO, we had met with him, a very capable man of high integrity, and he sees fit to leave without having another job. That indicates this manager has problems, and we pulled out right away. The manager could tell stories about problems he faced in the investment portfolio, but in reality the organization was crumbling."

Strategies to Avoid   When constructing a hedge fund portfolio, Meyer shies away from hedge fund strategies tied more closely to the economy than to specific companies. He names global macro in particular as a strategy dependent on economic news and trends and the manager's subjective analysis of how people will react to certain events. He explains his viewpoint with an example.

"Market is going down a little bit. Is this the beginning of the end? If that's the case, the sensible thing to do is sell everything." The same scenario can lead to completely opposite conclusions. "Is this a temporary decline? If so, then a natural conclusion is to buy."

The macro manager in that situation is making a lot of subjective bets on situations that have more than one answer. "He could be a talented manager, but he could lose the talent or suddenly lose touch with the market."

Meyer would avoid those strategies because, "I couldn't really tell when he was likely to stop being hot. Not knowing when he'll lose it made it difficult."

Meyer now avoids "black box" strategies (industry slang for opaque, computerized, model-driven strategies), but invested in them when he was an active hedge fund investor. "I'd sign a confidentiality agreement to know what was in the model. With my knowledge of statistics, I knew enough to know whether the manager was in control."

He describes black box strategies in a similar vein as global macro, except with more randomness and mystery as to what might go wrong. "Black box strategies are based on the state of the world. Will the world change? If so, will the strategy still work? If it won't still work, how quickly will you notice? How much will you lose before you realize it's not working?"

Meyer gives an unusual example to make his point: "You run a black box strategy that earns a dollar six out of ten times and loses a dollar four out of ten times. God decides you are a mean, horrible person who deserves a bad punishment and switches the odds. You can lose a lot of money before realizing that the world has changed."

When evaluating black box strategies, investors should maintain high standards for making an investment because of the statistical challenge they present. "How soon is the manager likely to realize that the world is changing?"

Strategy Selection Considerations   Having invested in hedge funds since the 1970s, Meyer has met numerous hedge fund managers, seen a myriad of investment styles, observed extraordinary growth and felt its impact, all the while developing a perspective that makes him a better investor.

> On leverage: "Strategies with a high level of leverage all have one common risk, namely, the people that are lending the money may want their money back when it's not an opportune time for the strategy. Everyone has to pull back and prices go down. How bad is it going to be if you are forced to repay before it's opportune?"
>
> The risk of using leverage in ordinary versus extraordinary environments influences how investors can manage risk in the whole portfolio.
>
> On portfolio risk: "In a normal environment leverage in one strategy may be independent of leverage in another. In an extraordinary environment, investors must be aware they can be more highly correlated and ask themselves, 'How fully do I want to protect myself in extreme situations?'"
>
> Investors particularly need to consider leverage and market environments when trying to diversify risk using typical portfolio

construction methods. "If you do statistical analysis and optimize, you might give leveraged strategies more weight than if you recognize that in extremes, they may become more dependent or more correlated."

Industry growth has made the amount of money a hedge fund is managing more of a concern than when Meyer entered the business.

On industry asset growth and its impact on manager selection: "There were no mega funds. Initially you could only have 14 investors, and then laws changed it to 99 investors, and then amended it so a hedge fund could have 499 investors. As the number of investors you could have increased, you could become a bigger fund and or have more money under management.

"When prudent man rules changed to have a portfolio perspective, the single investor slots could suddenly be huge state pension plans that could give hundreds of millions of dollars. The size of a single hedge fund could be enormous.

"Look at the reasons to invest in funds. They can short, use leverage, and be nimble about going in and out of the market as the manager sees fit.

"Historically these were all seen as evils. Leverage was taking excessive risk, shorting was seen as market manipulation, being nimble was associated with churning. Those characteristics discouraged big institutional funds.

"As managers get bigger and bigger those advantages go away. As an outsider, it gets harder to get your hands around the business.

"For those reasons, and [because of] the hunger of new managers, I found that it was easier and more satisfying—all other things being equal—to follow funds that were newer and smaller."

While observing and participating in the growth and evolution of the hedge fund industry has given Meyer a perspective for making investment decisions, it has also given him a perspective on lessons learned and on the direction of the industry.

HEDGE FUNDS IN PERSPECTIVE

Discussing the growth and change in hedge funds, particularly the impact of institutional investors, leads to questions about the relative lack of market inefficiencies compared to the past and the potential for opportunity in the future.

Meyer agrees inefficiencies have diminished over time as more capital has entered the market. He says, "In the early days there were larger inefficiencies and with the passage of time, yes, certain strategies have become more efficient. CBOE [Chicago Board Options Exchange]–covered option writing used to be a great strategy, but now it is too efficient to be great."

Change Eliminates and Creates Opportunity

Now that short selling is "widespread," he says, "Some short selling opportunities have evaporated." Building on that idea, Meyer says of short selling, "It's a classic example of how the world has changed." He describes typical conversations with managers about their use of short selling in three eras to show the differences over time.

Short History of Short-Selling Conversations

1. Early 1970s: Inefficiency-Rich Short Selling: "We short stocks. We look for companies that are frauds and try to make other investors aware of it. We want people to find out, so the stock will go to $0. Performance is independent of market and diversified from the rest of the portfolio.

   "Taxes on ordinary income are 70 percent, so we don't cover the sales. We never realize the loss, it's all tax-free to you, and you get capital gains."
2. Mid-1980s—Early 1990s: Earnings Shorts: "We still do fraud shorting, but the opportunities are fewer. We maintain attractive short positions by doing earnings shorts. If we think the stock will have disappointing earnings, we'll short it. Right or wrong, we'll cover. It's a great additional source of income and doesn't really correlate to the market."
3. 2009: Long-Term Concept Shorts: "Short selling helps us protect against movements in the market. We look for fraud shorts, but they're very hard to spot. They tend to be in small companies and you run the risk of getting squeezed. More people are chasing earnings shorts. The stocks are hard to borrow if you get in at the moment before the announcement.

   "We have migrated to long-term concept shorts. If we think airlines are going to zero, autos are going to zero, we will short companies in those industries, or an industry index. A long-term bet, it offers some protection against the market, an additional source of profit, and helps stabilize performance."

The key point of this example, Meyer says, is that with the institutionalization of the industry, "The opportunity to make large money has gone down. More competition for stock and stock loans and crowded shorts forces managers to pay much higher fees and cuts into the returns."

Opportunity Optimism   The short-selling history seems like a pessimistic description of an efficiency death spiral brought on by too much capital, but he remains optimistic, because "financial communities migrate from one opportunity to another."

While Meyer does think many strategies have deteriorated due to excess capital and certain activities, especially shorting, have become increasingly tougher, he does not believe the influx of institutional investors makes hedge fund investing more or less attractive than earlier in history.

"Managers were going into the market and being nimble. Opportunities were greater with fewer people." Even so, he says that new opportunities have continued to materialize, such as new instruments like options and futures contracts that had never existed in the early years. In addition, "Computer power got cheaper and cheaper. Mathematical strategies that were never possible have now become very possible. It has leveled the field. Now [that] you can buy reliable data inexpensively, the barriers to entry are a lot lower.

"There are always opportunities. They occur differently. Opportunities that didn't exist in the past appear and other opportunities rotate and change." Referring to the 2008 financial crisis he adds, "In the current economic disaster there are real opportunities to take advantage of the wreckage. There are constantly more opportunities. The more turmoil, the more opportunity."

Opportunistic Hedge Fund Investing   Although Meyer believes hedge fund managers will remain nimble and seek out new opportunities as they arise, he says that hedge fund investors have less ability to nimbly move in and out of individual hedge funds in response to market conditions or to make short-term tactical bets.

Regarding style rotation, Meyer says investors have to consider, "How quickly can the style rotate back? If you're with a good manager now and you can redeem, could you get back in on time?"

Pulling out of a fund because of market conditions or a shrinking opportunity set makes sense sometimes. He redeemed from a specialized merger arbitrage fund because he thought it had limited future opportunities. Meyer thinks it is hard for investors to be nimble, and they must consider a timing-related redemption decision against the practical realities of hedge fund terms, operations, and capacity constraints.

"Can you be nimble so that you can get out and not leave with bad feelings, so that you can come back in relatively easily?" Rather than try to time decisions based on market conditions, Meyer played to his strengths.

"Identify talented managers. If you pick talented managers, they tend to adjust position sizes based on how the portfolio is doing."

Institutional Investors Will Influence More Change   Meyer believes institutional investors will push for more changes from hedge fund managers regarding terms and fees, in response to both the financial crisis of 2008 and greater awareness of their market power.

For a long time, "institutional investors accepted the terms that were offered because of the limited number of investor slots available." Institutional investors were accustomed to having their assets managed in separate accounts and held in custody at a bank. Hedge fund partnership structures and conditions like lock-ups were new to them. Meyer surmises that institutional investors "figured this is the way we have to invest if we want to go into this area."

As more investor slots opened up and money flooded into hedge funds, it became harder for investors to tell whether hedge fund performance was market-related (beta) or not. Investors were already questioning hedge fund structures and fees when the 2008 financial crisis hit, and some hedge funds asserted their contractual ability to suspend or limit investor redemptions. Then the $50 billion Ponzi scheme fraud perpetrated by Bernard Madoff unraveled.

Investors everywhere realized, Meyer says, "Illiquidity is something they should care about." He expects institutional investors to migrate toward organizational structures, like managed accounts, that allow the investor to control the assets instead of the manager.

"In a partnership, the manager controls the assets and valuation, so in a fraud like Bayou (where the schemers set up a fake auditing firm), the manager can run off with money. If a bank hired by you controls the assets and is doing the valuation, you won't see that happen."

In addition to investors shifting control of structures from managers to themselves, Meyer expects management and performance fees to fall. "Institutions will be much more particular about what they pay."

A Role for Funds of Hedge Funds

Although he resigned from Glenwood in 2004 and saw hedge fund performance falter in 2008, Meyer disagrees with those who predict the demise of the funds of hedge funds model.

"There will and should be funds of funds. It is hard to meet the minimum investment requirements of different managers. Even as minimums get lower, just like investors have advisers to pick stocks, they will need people to pick funds for them."

Meyer believes there will be a demand and need for funds of funds, because investors need to diversify their hedge fund portfolios to avoid having too much institutional risk from any one manager. Investors hurt most by the Bernard Madoff fraud learned an extremely painful lesson about the dangers of institutional risk. "Performance was steady and fantastic. Investors said the fund was like a T-bill. They had institutional risk with all their eggs in one basket."

Long before the Madoff case, Meyer had already changed his mind about the possibility that single multistrategy hedge funds could cause the demise of hedge funds of funds. "I thought for a while there might be more of a need for multistrategy hedge funds instead of funds of funds, but with one common owner, they have institutional risk. If something happens the whole fund can go under."

The institutional risk of multistrategy hedge funds vs. funds of funds became clear when Amaranth, a $9 billion multistrategy hedge fund, collapsed in September 2006. "They had a number of strategies and knew some better than others. The strategy the manager knew the least about, of course, is the strategy that put the fund under."

Although the idea of investing in a single multistrategy hedge fund with a single fee, in lieu of a fund of hedge funds with two layers of fees, appeals to investors, they need to realize the perils of institutional risk.

After Amaranth, and certainly after Madoff, Meyer says, "Investors will be more sensitive to it. That means watching and monitoring a diversified portfolio, so there will be a demand for funds of hedge funds."

Learning from Investment Mistakes

Underestimating the value of integrity is one investment lesson Meyer painfully learned from making mistakes. "I used to think if a guy was a bit of a shark, at least he was *my* shark."

While doing due diligence on a fund for Glenwood, he learned the manager had not been truthful about his academic record. As a fiduciary, he felt Glenwood could not invest in the fund, but he decided to chance it with his personal money and lost. He says, "What I've come to realize is that agreements are stacked in favor of the manager. If a manager doesn't have real integrity, it's a risk."

The most important decision investors make about a hedge fund manager is when to leave. "It's easier to pick a winning manager than to know when to leave a winning manager. The way a manager changes from being a winning manager to being a losing manager is that the world changes."

That moment can be difficult to determine, "unless you're watching the manager pretty intensely to look for warning signs." Now that he is retired,

Meyer says, "I'm making mistakes by not getting out as soon as I should because I'm not watching as closely."

The Outlook for Hedge Funds

Meyer believes the strength and resiliency of the hedge fund investment model will continue to prevail. He explains this by describing the two ways a manager buys stock.

"One manager buys and holds until the price adjusts. Compare him to a manager with multiple tools. He can borrow to add to his high conviction positions, he can short stocks he thinks will go down, he can be sheltered from market moves and earn a profit. If one person has more tools than another, which one has the potential to do better? The one that has access to more tools."

Meyer sees a "place for hedge funds that are really and truly hedging," despite the fact that some of those tools, like shorting, as he described it, "may become more expensive and more difficult to do."

Competitive Global Environment Requires Tools Globalization has increased mobility and opportunity, but has also increased competition. Meyer says that until fairly recently, most people grew, lived, and worked in their own country. Now, he say, "The world is much more open across borders. You can be born in the United States, live in London, be married to a German, and work for a Japanese bank."

Similarly, regulators and markets are not tied to one particular country as much anymore. "If the SEC becomes unreasonable or too aggressive, there's an alternative exchange in Germany or Switzerland that's ready to take on the business."

The ability to move and operate in different countries provides a natural check on regulation. Although, Meyer points out, "That's not to say that people don't want any regulation. You could start a bank in Belize. It has much less banking regulation than the United States, but I don't see people rushing to move their charters there."

Because one world brings more competition, Meyer says, "It makes more sense to invest having more tools rather than less." Therefore, the hedge fund style of investing will continue to grow.

LESSONS, OBSERVATIONS, AND ADVICE

Asked the advice he would give to individuals contemplating hedge fund investing, Meyer says there are two kinds of investors, personal investors who probably should be passive investors and professional investors who should make use of all the available tools, especially knowledge and experience.

"For personal investors like the owner of a widget business, it's very tempting to think you can make your own decisions, but the key is to know when to leave. My main advice to them is to rely on someone who is monitoring the investment full time, in a fund of funds or as an advisor."

Meyer thinks professional investing offers an attractive career. "There are always going to be people with wealth that need advice. There is steady demand and little chance the industry could be made obsolete.

"It's best to work for someone else first to learn how a business should be run. It's hard to learn in the abstract. Working for someone else is very advantageous."

Accidental Mentors

Meyer says he never had a specific mentor. "I figured out everything on my own. Most of what I learned wasn't from a person taking me under his wing; it was more just advice that someone happened to give at a certain period of time."

The greatest advice came from a Los Angeles lawyer specializing in white-collar vs. blue-collar crime. He told Meyer, "Blue-collar crime is always visible. The alarm rings, money is missing from the cash register, you know you committed the crime."

Conversely, "white-collar crime is an everyday crime. Every day you are shuffling paper. The day you commit the crime you just shuffled paper again and never really saw it happen."

The lawyer's point was, "People don't really realize that actions are not judged in the present, but they're judged in hindsight. They don't think about how things might work out if all the facts were known and put in the newspaper."

The lesson is, "Become objective, try to keep your objectivity. Think about how you would feel or how something would appear if it was broadcast widely."

Advice Can Be Wasted on the Young   Meyer and his wife have created their own college scholarship program, providing money and advice to help disadvantaged students through college. One year, the commencement speaker at a graduation ceremony gave advice Meyer still remembers. Unfortunately, the students probably do not.

The speaker, an alumna of the school, had obviously given her speech much thought and had prepared well. Meanwhile the graduates had other things on their minds. "There was a beach ball being bounced around. The graduates were ready to get out." Fortunately, Meyer paid attention and repeats her three most "spectacular" points.

1. **Objectivity:** The speaker told the students, "You will be put in situations where you will have to make decisions under pressure. If possible think about situations in advance in the abstract and that will help you make better decisions."

   As an example, she told them to think about what they would do if their boss asked them "to cook the books." She suggested that the stress of the situation could lead one to gloss over the ethics and do it, but "if you have thought about it in advance, you're less likely to make the wrong decision."

   Meyer has seen this in the failure of certain money managers. "They made the wrong decision and paid the price."

2. **Reputation:** "Work hard to build and maintain a good reputation. At some point in your career, you will need people to trust you. If your reputation is good, you will get that trust, otherwise you won't."

3. **Long Term:** The speaker advised the students to think about the long-term consequences of their actions. For example, graduates uncertain about what they want to do often decide to go to law school. "If you think of the long-term consequences, after three years, you could be in debt, maybe locked in to a career you don't really like. Most people don't look far enough ahead at different consequences."

Meyer offers advice about giving advice. "When I think more about what advice to tell people, I find the more particular the advice I give, it's poor. The more general and applicable in a wide range of situations, the better."

Thinking again of the graduation day speaker, Meyer remembers, "The people in careers knew it was solid advice. The older people in the audience were nodding their heads; it resonated."

The story shares great advice, but it also exposes Meyer's problem with giving advice. "Advice is like a relay race. When you give advice, you're passing a baton. The person has to present it in a way that it can be accepted, and the person who is going to receive it has to make certain they are set up so the person can give it."

Meyer knew the speaker had quality to give, "but she couldn't figure out how to present it and the receivers couldn't figure out how to accept it." A long pause follows.

"I tend not to give advice. Instead, I try to teach our students to make good decisions on their own."

PAST PERFORMANCE EQUALS FUTURE SUCCESS

Although Meyer seems to say that his best advice is not to give advice, an investor can glean much from just a smidgen of the advice, ideas, and lessons Meyer shares from throughout the course of his career. While he does not consider himself an industry pioneer, he certainly settled the territory, building two successful investment companies and launching one noted hedge fund. Meyer says past performance is not indicative of future success, but any investor who studies Meyer's performance is more likely to have future success.

CHAPTER 6

The Best Qualities of Limestone

James R. Hodge, President and Chief Investment Officer, Permal Asset Management Inc.

G rowing up in Marion, Indiana—also the birthplace of movie icon James Dean and "Garfield" creator Jim Davis—James R. Hodge knew he faced two choices when it came time to go to college.

"I could go to Purdue, which had ugly brick buildings, or Indiana University, with the nice buildings made out of the best limestone in the world."

Hodge entered Indiana University as an undergraduate business major just as professors were "getting into efficient markets theory." He says he was taken by the subject, and fortunate to have encouraging professors.

Since leaving Bloomington, the home of IU and the limestone quarries, Jim Hodge has risen to become the president and chief investment officer of Permal Asset Management Inc., a $20 billion fund of hedge funds firm he joined in 1987.

Hodge has responsibility for all facets of managing the fund of hedge funds portfolio including researching, analyzing, and selecting managers; constructing portfolios; managing risk; and monitoring performance. In addition, he is a director, alternate director, and the advisory board member of a number of independent offshore investment funds.

Prior to joining Permal, he served as the controller of Biolectron, Inc., a privately held medical products company, and as director of cost accounting for the New York Stock Exchange. Hodge received an MBA from Harvard Business School, a BS with highest distinction from Indiana University, and the CPA designation from the state of New Jersey.

BACKGROUND

One "very, very good" professor in particular mentored Hodge: Les Waters, his faculty advisor. "He convinced me I could get through the calculus course and wrote the letters to Harvard Business School."

Hodge learned a valuable ethics lesson when the professor refused to accept a gift from a grateful student. Even though no one would have known about it, doing so would have violated university policy. Hodge "never forgot" the integrity Waters displayed.

After graduating from Indiana University, Hodge "did things that didn't amount to much" and ended up working for his father for a year. "He was in the magazine business, selling subscriptions door to door." The exposure to sales helped him when he became a hedge fund investor.

"I know they overpuff and overstate their accomplishments. This experience comes in handy when I'm meeting hedge fund managers, and it doesn't surprise me when they overstate their record, or something like that; it's to be expected in the business world. You just have to know what to look out for."

Hodge attended Harvard Business School, graduating in 1979, and joined the New York Stock Exchange, "working for the government in some sense" upon graduation. Then, some "friends wanted to make me rich in the medical products business" and he joined a company run by a Purdue Ph.D.

Eventually Hodge was "out looking for a real job" and joined Banque Worms. This French conglomerate had a New York City office where Jean Perrette and Clifford Mallory presided over an investment portfolio that eventually became Permal. (The name "Permal" is taken from the first three letters of their last names.)

Their investments included "one little $200 to $300 million fund of hedge funds" and a number of private equity direct investments, "tiny things." After joining the organization in 1987, Hodge spent the next year helping to "shut down" these private equity investments. And afterwards, beyond the 15 people in the office, they "didn't have anything left except for the offshore fund of hedge funds."

This fund had eight managers and "a good record, thanks to one of the first three managers being George Soros." (Soros, the founder of Soros Fund Management, is the legendary billionaire hedge fund manager and philanthropist.) From that base, Hodge and his colleagues have built a hedge fund investment firm managing approximately $20 billion in assets.

"Being lucky three times" characterizes his history at Permal. The first had been "the foresight to invest with Soros in the fund."

The second was a distribution agreement with Merrill Lynch, which offered the Permal fund to its offshore clients. This arrangement initially "didn't raise a lot of money." But from 1989 to 1993, though, Permal "almost doubled the S&P 500 based on the performance of Soros and Steinhardt, and we soon got very popular in the Merrill system. They then wanted more funds with different focuses." Using the Permal trade name, from there the firm "grew pretty steadily."

The third bit of luck came in 2005, when Legg Mason bought the firm. "We got the seal of approval from a U.S. firm." According to Hodge, the show of confidence helped the firm grow to just shy of $40 billion in assets under management. The market conditions in 2008 resulted in assets under management falling to the $20 billion level.

INVESTMENT PROCESS

An early memory provides a good analogy for Hodge's investment philosophy: "[The] first time I went to a major league baseball game—I'm dating myself badly now—I saw Mickey Mantle hit a home run. The ball went a long way. I think in every field there are stars. In politics it's Obama; in golf, Tiger Woods. I think you have the same thing in investment management."

He believes there are "people that are just better at making money than the general person. The high fees of the hedge funds world can attract those managers. We all know stars can be difficult, temperamental. They quit, they blow up from time to time, but I like to have a lot of stars."

Hodge estimates the number of hedge funds at 10,000 at the peak and 7,000 after the financial crisis. Of that number, one "can find 100 to 200 that are well above average in their abilities and their returns. It's not likely that they'll be highly correlated."

From there a person can assemble what he considers an ideal portfolio: "One hundred managers at 1 percent allocation." With such a portfolio investors can "get a very nice set of returns, well above average, good returns, and have much less volatility as compared to market indices, like the S&P 500."

The best thing about small positions, Hodge says, "is that God forbid you have a blow-up or even worse, a fraud, at least it's only 1 percent of the portfolio."

Manager Selection

When selecting managers, he does so with the goal of finding star managers and then combining them in a highly diversified portfolio. His due diligence process starts with calculating all the "standard statistics possible." At one point they brought in noted academic, analyst, and author Roger Ibbotson to help them refine their statistical techniques.

"We caught Madoff with an auto correlation test. It showed that he was smoothing his returns. That came in handy, although we wouldn't have hired him anyway."

A separate team conducts operational due diligence and audits, an area he and his colleagues have strength in from earning their CPAs. They "do all the qualification, verifying two signatures needed to move money, finding out the relationships with prime brokers, accountants, lawyers, and calling to verify the auditor." He recommends getting the phone number of the auditors from another source than the manager as a double check against a fraud.

Fraud Identification Techniques　　When assessing the likely risk of a fraud or blow-up, Hodge says, "Attitude is key. You have to believe it can happen to you. You can have a blow-up. You can have a fraud. You have to be constantly vigilant and think it can happen to you."

He says investors "cannot know the future." Yet all hedge fund investors have "had money with managers we thought would be fabulous." Therefore they need to remember an important difference: "Performance is in the future. Fraud is in the past."

Hodge explains, "If a manager is a fraud, he's already a fraud when you meet him. We dig deeply into a manager's background, looking for any inconsistency." Managers tend to be "more willing to say something that's not true than to put it in writing."

For instance, a manager will verbally say he has a Ph.D., but the written documentation will say something completely different. Hodge cites the case of a particular Chicago-based fund manager. He remembers that this fund performed exceptionally well one year and had the highest Sharpe ratio, but eventually blew up in European arbitrage. According to the manager, he had a Ph.D. from the University of Pennsylvania, but the paperwork did not match up. Hodge avoided that disaster.

The desire to uncover as much truthful information as possible up front has driven Hodge and his team to take "Deception Detection" training classes led by former CIA members. They have also studied with specialists in "Microexpressions" to develop the ability to identify telling facial expressions that may indicate lying or a negative emotion. The trainers claim there are seven facial expressions common to all cultures. "[One colleague] got 9 out of 10 on the test. I'm not very good at it. I'm better at listening."

Hodge regrets missing one meeting when the training paid off. "In August 2007 when the stat arbs blew up, a manager showed the number one sign of lying in the United States." He answered yes to a question, "but couldn't control his head and shook his head. The question was, 'Would you invest in your own fund?'"

The former CIA agents aim to train them to "be like a human lie detector." In another recent experience, the training clearly demonstrated its value.

Hodge and his team met with "a young man who had worked at Soros. 'At' is the key word here. He talked with his hands and would move them up and down." The motions continued throughout the questioning until the Permal team reached an important question, one they had rehearsed in advance.

"We asked, 'At Soros, were you an analyst or were you truly a portfolio manager?' Suddenly the hands stopped going up and he immediately crossed his hands across the chest. He got very defensive. 'Of course I am,' he said, and we thought, 'Of course you aren't.'"

Such techniques help determine if they need to examine the manager further. A subject's responses may have subtler meaning. The trainers point out that even if a subject is not lying, not wanting to discuss a particular topic can be a red flag.

Manager Preferences   Hodge says of managers, "What we really like is somebody that has an identifiable and understandable edge." He offers the theoretical example of a long/short railroad stocks manager with important advantages. "He's got an office in the Sears Tower in Chicago and a really good set of binoculars. He says, 'I watch the freight yards and can tell who is loading up and who is not. If Union Pacific is busy, I go long. Norfolk and Southern looks slow, I short that.' That's very understandable; we like that."

He finds, "Edge is easiest to determine with long and short. You can understand what they do. If they tell you a story of why Ford is going to survive and why General Motors is going to fail, you can understand it with words. It might be wrong, but at least you can understand."

Pedigree matters. He estimates that two thirds of Permal's new managers previously worked for other managers. "We know them in some organizational sense." They feel comfortable with a manager leaving a firm like Kingdon to start his own fund, more so if Kingdon invests in the new fund.

Strategy Preferences   Permal mostly invests in long/short equity and global macro funds, because they tend to have the depth and liquidity characteristics their investors want. Hodge says they tend to avoid highly leveraged strategies like convertible arbitrage and relative value. "We don't really understand what the manager is doing especially well. Even if we do, we realize he's using a lot of leverage." He qualifies his statement, saying "not never, but we tend to stay away from them."

They have rarely invested in mortgage-backed securities strategies, due to similar concerns about leverage. He also tends to avoid the exceptionally complicated strategies, because he worries about the potential to manipulate statistical analysis and models.

Hodge will allocate additional capital to underperforming strategies he believes have bottomed. He mentions having added to a bank loan fund run by Mark Shenkman after the 2008 financial crisis. He wanted to add to another credit-oriented fund run by George Putnam III, but timing and liquidity issues stood in the way.

Despite his inability to make the investment, his experience with Putnam over time has given him a favorable impression. It reminds him of another characteristic he likes that can apply to certain strategies and managers.

"We don't always test it in advance, but we like managers that when we need money back, they send it. George is that way. No complaining; they get the money transfer and wire it back. That's a good test of whether everything is real."

Portfolio Construction and Management

Diversification is the guiding principle for constructing hedge fund port-folios. "The lesson of diversification has been reinforced over the years from seeing the various things that go wrong in the hedge fund business," Hodge says.

When he got started, there were fewer hedge funds managers, and they "tended to be clustered under the umbrellas of bigger managers—Soros, Tiger—you got everything if you went to a big manager." Now, he says, "The business became so profitable, managers set out on their own, so investors have to recreate that effect themselves."

Risk Monitoring   Hodge and his team attempt to mitigate portfolio risk with their statistical analysis and background checks before they select managers.

Once a hedge fund enters the portfolio, they "tend to use management by exception." They assign managers to peer groups, check their returns at least twice a month, and compare the returns against others in their group. If a manager is "substantially above or below the peer group, we will investigate. We may not necessarily call, but if we still can't figure out why there is a difference, we then get in touch with the manager."

They stick to the twice-a-month policy, but "if things are in really bad shape, then it's regular checks on how the manager is doing."

Every quarter, analysts update a dossier with the latest information for each manager. They check the files, read manager reports, and note any concerns or changes, such as in assets under management. Generally, they also speak to the individual hedge fund managers to review their portfolios and get market commentary.

"Analysts are encouraged to be brutally frank in what they say about the managers. I'll read notes that say something like (I'm exaggerating a little), 'I can't believe we hired this idiot.' I then think I will have to read that file carefully."

Hodge says that if the manager is doing poorly, "we try to get out very gracefully, over as long as a period of a year. However, if it's terrible, and we fear the money will be lost the next day, then we'll seize the money."

The slow and graceful exit not only "helps us keep a good reputation in the industry," it also "helps with performance. We're human beings and tend to be bearish at the bottom." Their approach helps them avoid taking all the money out "at what may be the bottom."

The scrutiny and subtle pressure on the manager can have a positive impact. "It focuses the manager on the situation, and sometimes they do turn it around and do better."

Manager Termination Unexpected surprises can quickly lead to termination. In one example from his earliest days at Permal, they invested in one manager they thought had an "identifiable edge." This former Mergers & Acquisitions investment banker and dealmaker had started a hedge fund to invest in likely takeover candidates. Given the manager's experience, the Permal team thought, "Well, he ought to know a few (takeover candidates) a least," and invested in the fund.

"Literally six weeks later, he came in with his portfolio, and it was entirely invested in Japan, because he thought Japan was going to run."

"We usually give a manager the benefit of a year." But in this case, Hodge remembers his colleagues telling the manager, "We'll talk about it after you leave, but this is unacceptable," and they fired him. Back then, Hodge was just "the guy taking notes," yet years later, the manager's actions still confound him. "This was an extreme example of style drift. We just don't like to be surprised."

If a manager "tells us they're going to change the style gradually, that's fine. For example, Soros started as a stock picker and moved to macro. Steinhardt was an equity block trader and became one of the best ever in trading U.S. bonds. They didn't surprise us with that."

Other surprises that will either derail a potential investment or lead to termination include the mismatch between verbal statements and written documentation. "A manager may well tell us he is the biggest shareholder, but the documents report otherwise."

Financial surprises like "charging travel to funds agitates us." Hodge adds, "Personnel change is a form of surprise, and in general we don't like funds to employ relatives."

Managed Accounts   Regarding separately managed accounts he says, "At the moment there is more talk than action in the industry."

Long/short equity funds are easier to implement in the separate account structure. Even though they "have a good operations team, it's harder with macro because of all the ISDAs (International Swaps and Derivatives Association counterparty agreements)."

Permal has long advocated managed accounts and has been using them very successfully for a number of years. Not surprisingly, it has found managers more accommodating since the financial crisis. "Managers are more eager to raise assets." The Madoff fraud has also made managers more responsive to investor demands for separate accounts and transparency.

"If there's any blessing of Madoff at all, managers just can't resist the argument that you want a separate account, because you know you'll have the assets."

In some strategies investors can lose more than the amount they invested, making managed accounts less desirable. "We think we handle that problem by setting up corporations to house the separate accounts." By using the corporation structure, "we don't think we can go below zero in a separate account."

The higher level of position transparency offered by a managed account is better for risk management. If they cannot get a managed account, he will "take what (transparency) we can get." With less transparent managers, they tend to analyze the fund as if it were a single stock. They look at the returns, volatility, and explanatory factors to see if they can identify or explain style drift.

Fees and Lock-Ups   Permal has "always been very good negotiators on fees. We've tended in general to pay less than 2 and 20. It's even easier now to do that. You can't ask for everything, but it's easier now to pay less than 2 and 20 and get a separate account."

He emphasizes getting better liquidity rather than better fees, another reason to have separate accounts, because they prevent gating.

Hodge has experimented with a new type of fee structure. He recently met with a manager, a specialist in African mining stocks, and discussed risk control with him. "Here's how we're going to control the risk," Hodge said.

"We will put in a tiny percent, like half a percent, and we'll assume you'll lose it all. Now, talk to us about how you'll make money."

Because his positions are illiquid, the manager needs a three-year time frame for them to pay off. Hodge invested the small amount for a three-year period, but will not pay an annual performance fee. He told the manager, "First make a lot of money for us." At the end of the period, "you sell everything." The manager will only earn a performance fee on the total profit he earns over the period Permal has its money locked up. If Hodge likes the manager's performance, he then has the option to invest into the main fund or re-up the investment.

Some managers are preemptively suggesting similar fee structures for their funds, tying the timing of the incentive fee to the liquidity of the investor. Hodge says, "Managers should not lock someone up for a year and take an incentive fee every month. It's discouraging to see managers that have done quite well and their investors do not seem to have ended above par."

Managing Staff

Permal's "extensive investor relations and marketing departments take care of clients." This frees Hodge and his team to concentrate on investments.

Their twenty-five investment professionals tend to have backgrounds as CPAs and several have MBAs. He likes hiring MBAs fitting the Harvard Business School profile, saying, "In general, they are people that can put numbers and words together meaningfully. They're not all one or the other."

Hodge prefers to promote from within, and has never hired a senior staff member from outside the organization. New MBAs or CPAs with a few years of work experience start as analysts. Many grow into portfolio management roles, while "some like to stay with numbers and become senior analysts."

The main thing he looks for from newer employees "is to see them working. We don't want them running into our office telling us how to run the place. Put your nose to the grindstone and crunch numbers." After a few years, he says humorously, "If I notice you're still here, I'll think maybe you can do something bigger in the organization." He will then start to promote them.

Hodge thinks of his entire team as partners, "some are more junior and some more senior," and they all talk and e-mail frequently. "I don't think of myself as a manager. I just go around and ask for what I need, 'Can you do this correlation for me? Can you find more information on the manager?' Those that give me what I need are the people that get promoted."

His approach is not "up or out." Competent employees will remain with the firm productively as part of the team. Just as he tries to exit gracefully from managers, he gives weaker-performing employees similar considera-tion. When the firm underwent layoffs after the 2008 financial crisis, Hodge made it easy for attrition to occur instead.

"We've all done things we're proud of in our careers. We didn't lay off people from the investment team." When cuts became necessary, Hodge recommended his staff evaluate their standing in the organization, and if they thought they might be vulnerable, "to think about what you might do. If you want to send your resumes out, there will be no repercussions."

HEDGE FUND EVOLUTION AND OUTLOOK

Over the years, changes to his hedge fund investment style have had less to do with lessons learned and more to do with the passage of time.

"How have things changed? Part of it is related to getting older, as opposed to learning." As Hodge has gotten older he is "not just focused on how much money a manager can make *for* me. I think about what he can do *to* me, a terrible disaster that can cost me my job."

The financial crisis of 2008, exacerbated by the Bernard Madoff fraud case, certainly justifies his fears.

Even so, Hodge largely agrees with predictions in the paper, *The Hedge Fund of Tomorrow: Building an Enduring Firm.* Published by the research firm Casey Quirk in April 2009, the study concludes that the hedge fund industry will continue to grow after a transitional period.

While attending a recent meeting of the IU Foundation, which manages Indiana University's endowment, Hodge learned it "remains firmly com-mitted to hedge funds." He believes most institutions will follow suit. "No matter how bad hedge funds were in 2008, they weren't as bad as the S&P 500." Since "institutions are in to stay, the industry will grow again."

He expects that for one to three years after the crisis, the industry will be "a smaller but much more profitable business." Equity long and short managers are like "a herd of cattle in a field of alpha. So many players are out, like the prop desks that copied all the hedge funds." Many funds had already outperformed the market substantially by mid-2009, a phenomenon he believes will continue for a while. "Then, of course, greed will overpower fear and the money will pour back in."

Changes

Of all the growth and change he has witnessed in hedge funds, Hodge says, "The biggest surprise is how big it's gotten. I'm told it's the only financial product that started as a high net worth product and then became institutional. It's usually the opposite. I think that makes it very different."

The shift from high net worth individuals to institutions has not only changed the size of the industry, it has also changed the expectations and needs of the clients. "To me, high net worth focused on how much money they made." The attitude toward someone like George Soros was, "as long as you're making 30 percent, and as long as it's legal, I won't bother you."

The requirements of institutions are "essentially the opposite. It's not that they don't care that you *do* make money, but they care about *how* you make the money. They're willing to give up the upside for the perceived certainty of understanding, for the sense of a repeatable process."

Hodge does not mean to imply any value judgment in that comparison. He understands the position of institutions. "I don't see what else they—the foundations, big donors, presidents of the universities—can do. I wouldn't want to be the one in there saying 'we had a large allocation to Madoff.' You want to be super, super safe."

Bifurcation

When picking managers, Hodge has a bias toward boutique firms, those with strategies based in "marketable" securities like equities. Others think of boutiques as managers in unusual asset classes like film finances or music rights.

"I think it's worth looking at esoteric ideas. Andrew Lo says that alpha quickly becomes beta, so one of the services to provide to investors is to be constantly looking for new ideas and judiciously putting some into portfolios."

Permal also agrees with Casey Quirk's definition of bifurcation. The study concluded that the hedge fund industry would not necessarily bifurcate between the larger, more traditional firms and the smaller, more esoteric firms; instead, the industry is far more likely to bifurcate in relation to liquidity and terms of funds.

Mentors

Hodge knows the value of advice from more experienced hedge fund investors. He appreciates this even more today, given how hard it was to find early in his career.

"When I started in the business, there were not too many people in general in hedge funds, or doing what I did. Larry Chiarello and Gary Gladstein invested in outside managers at Soros and were always very, very helpful. They didn't need to be, and they were quite helpful over the years."

Hodge remembers one such interesting experience. At his boss's behest, Hodge called Chiarello to request help on a project.

"Larry, my boss, had the idea that we should compare the managers we have in common with you and make sure they're doing as well for you as they are for us. Maybe we can use a five-year period." Chiarello replied, "Maybe you need to shorten that period. The average guy lasts only six months." Hodge says, "I think there were only one or two we had in common."

Frank Meyer, profiled in Chapter 5, is another hedge fund investor he respects. They came to know each other when Meyer introduced Hodge to some managers, including Ken Griffin of Citadel. The two men also share some personal friends and occasionally see each other at events. "Occasionally when I'm worried about something, I'll call Frank and ask him what he thinks, and get his opinion." Hodge calls Meyer "a class act."

He respects Meyer as a person and as a professional. "If you can teach statistics at the University of Chicago, you have to be pretty smart. He and his wife have personally sent a number of students to college. They pay for their entire education and get them into schools.

"Leadership by example is how he's been a mentor. That's what I try to do. I don't know if I've been successful. I get to work on time, I'm not abusive on expense accounts, and no matter how rich or successful we perceive the manager, I try to take the analyst with me. It is important that not only do they get exposure to these managers, but they also get to see how they work."

Hodge mentors in other ways. "I'm surprisingly good at getting people into business schools. I'm shameless. I will go through our database and call up managers that went to Wharton to ask for help."

A Model Mentor   Perhaps Hodge should not be so surprised by how good he is at getting people into business school. It may be another lesson he learned from his college mentor, Les Waters, the writer of "good letters to Harvard Business School."

The entry for Professor L. Leslie (Les) Waters on the Indiana University web site includes in the description, "He will especially be remembered for his teaching and his efforts to find good jobs for his students."

Waters influenced other former students too. A story about a sizeable gift to the Les and Mary Lou Waters International Experiences Program Scholarship from Hank Fahl, MBA '59, appears in the Winter 2008–2009 issue of the *Alumni Newsletter for the Hutton Honors College*. Mr. Fahl credits his long, successful career in the transportation industry to help from Professor Waters in securing his first job at Cummins Inc.

The article quotes Mr. Fahl. "I've always considered Les as my mentor, and he was really more than that. As a teacher, he was my guide to many employment opportunities. He was a counselor and a friend, particularly when I needed him most. These are the kinds of things you never forget."

IN PRAISE OF LIMESTONE

Fahl's words echo Hodge's and describe an ethical man that devoted his life, intellect, and influence to help students achieve their potential. Similarly, it seems telling that when discussing the reasons he admires Frank Meyer, Hodge specifically cited the Meyers' commitment to helping promising students attend college.

Considering the help, encouragement, and influence of Waters and the example of Meyer, it makes sense that Hodge would want to give back by sharing his knowledge and insights and helping the next generation of hedge fund investors reach their potential.

For all his experience and success, Hodge still keeps his nose to the grindstone and does not run around telling everyone what to do. He focuses on investments, lets others talk, and reveals himself to be accomplished, dedicated, and down to earth.

Indiana is known for its limestone, a strong, durable, elastic, and damage-resistant resource. An investor with the strength and durability to survive and thrive in over 20 years of hedge fund investing, Jim Hodge also has the elasticity and flexibility to continue to learn and grow, and the resiliency to avoid much of the damage inflicted by the financial crisis.

For the book *Early History of Indiana Limestone* (AuthorHouse, 2008), author Ron Bell compiled newspaper articles from the 1800s to piece together the story. One quote that describes the qualities of limestone could describe Hodge as well: "It is not only the best in point of durability, but also best in every sense of the word and exceeds any kind of test. It is flexible, elastic, resonant."

CHAPTER 7

An Asymmetrical Talent

Mark J.P. Anson, Managing Partner and Chair of the Investment Committee, Oak Hill Investment Management

Mark J.P. Anson, Ph.D., JD, CFA, CPA, CAIA, is the managing partner and chair of the investment committee of Oak Hill Investment Management. Previously he served as president and executive director of investment services at Nuveen Investments, Inc., an asset management company that in 2009 had over $140 billion in a diversified blend of investment products across multiple asset classes.

Prior to Nuveen, Anson was the chief executive officer of Hermes Pensions Management Ltd. With $160 billion in assets, Hermes is one of the largest asset managers in the City of London. In addition, he was the chief executive officer of the $80 billion British Telecom Pension Scheme, the largest U.K. pension fund.

Before joining Hermes, Anson was the chief investment officer of the $245 billion California Public Employees' Retirement System (CalPERS)—the largest pension fund in the United States. Prior to CalPERS, Anson gained experience as a trader and portfolio manager after working as a lawyer.

Anson received a scholarship to attend the Northwestern University School of Law in Chicago where he received his law degree with honors and served as the executive/production editor of the *Northwestern University Law Review*. He also received a scholarship to attend the Columbia University Graduate School of Business in New York City where he received both his Ph.D. and master's in finance, again with honors, as Beta Gamma Sigma, and graduated with distinction from St. Olaf College in Minnesota with a double major in economics and chemistry.

A member of the New York and Illinois state bar associations, Anson has also earned the Chartered Financial Analyst, Chartered Alternative Investment Analyst, Certified Public Accountant, Certified Management Accountant, and Certified Internal Auditor professional degrees. He holds the Series 3, 7, 24, and 66 NASD securities industry licenses.

Anson is the former chairman of the board of the International Corporate Governance Network and serves on advisory boards for the NYSE, Euronext, MSCI-Barra, the CFA Institute, and the International Association of Financial Engineers.

He is the author of four financial textbooks including *Handbook of Alternative Assets Second Edition* (John Wiley & Sons, 2006), the primary textbook for the Chartered Alternative Investment Analyst program. He has published more than 100 research articles on topics ranging from alpha and beta separation to corporate governance, and he serves on the editorial boards of several financial journals.

Anson received the Lifetime Achievement Award from *PlanSponsor*, the Distinguished Scholar Award from the Fulbright Foundation and the Institute of International Education, and Best Paper awards from both the *Journal of Portfolio Management* and the *Journal of Alternative Assets*.

BACKGROUND

As he practiced law in a "very proper—button-down shirts, three-piece suits, white collars—white-shoe law firm" in the late 1980s and early 1990s, putting together commodity pools, Mark Anson might not have predicted his asymmetrical rise to the top of the investment management world. Now a leading hedge fund investor, influential pension fund manager, award-winning author and academic, and managing partner of an asset management firm, he also might not have predicted the changes in the hedge fund industry that he largely had a hand in shaping.

"Back then global macro funds were commodity pools. The hedge fund society was the Managed Futures Association. Managed futures were the bulk of the hedge funds in the markets, global macro managers playing currencies and physical commodities." Working on related documentation, like disclosures or SEC and Commodities Futures Trading Commission (CFTC) filings, sparked his interest in hedge funds.

Anson then did a "180-degree turnaround" and became an equity derivatives trader at Salomon Brothers, with hedge funds the majority of the counterparties he traded against. He then joined Oppenheimer Funds to create alternative products and managed a natural resources long/short commodity fund.

Sitting at the trading desk one day, he received a call "out of the blue" from a recruiter for CalPERS, the California-based pension fund, that would change his life.

"She said, 'Would you be interested in a pension fund?' Honest and blunt, I simply said no. She said the client was confidential, but, 'What if I were to tell you it's the largest in the country?' I asked if it was in Sacramento. Without revealing the confidential client we both knew who we were talking about."

Anson told the recruiter, "Sure, I'd be willing to have a conversation, just to find out why you would target me and why you would want to talk to me." He soon learned that CalPERS was beginning to think beyond traditional asset allocation and wanted someone who could "bring new ideas to the table. Probably not realizing just how many different ideas I would bring to the table."

Anson joined CalPERS to build their alternatives program and "has been an investor and supporter ever since."

Experience Drives Quest for Transparency

Early experience had a significant impact on Anson as a hedge fund investor. Having had full transparency and knowledge of what his hedge fund clients did, he found the limited transparency investors received troubling.

He was "amazed at how little disclosure there was for investors, even going back to 2000 at CalPERS." Having been a lawyer and derivatives trader gave him a much better knowledge base, because he understood what hedge funds could do, but that made him more certain of the need for more transparency. This knowledge "helped a bit, because disclosure was minimal, so poor that I might use more rude vernacular to describe the lack of disclosure and transparency."

After encountering Jim Kelly, an executive with the hedge fund administration firm IFS, while conducting due diligence on a hedge fund around 2000 and 2001, Anson approached him with an idea.

"What if I could have managers report to you? Then you can turn around and make risk reports for me without revealing their positions."

According to Anson, IFS had not previously been asked to provide such a service to an investor, but it seemed logical to him. "They were already dealing with manager positions as an administrator." His request led IFS to create a new line of business, serving as a middleman between investors and hedge fund managers. Anson hired the company to aggregate hedge fund data and calculate risk exposures without revealing manager positions.

The process resulted in a report that gave Anson a snapshot of the risks in his hedge fund portfolio. "The ultimate goal was to get full transparency, but I realized that was too far a leap ahead for hedge fund managers at that time."

Funds generally would not give position transparency or risk levels to investors, and although he would have a good sense of their activities from his due diligence, Anson saw the need to have a more systematic view of the economic exposures across the portfolio. He also understood the hedge fund's perspective.

"CalPERS is subject to public pension information requests and California has its own freedom of information law, the California Public Records Act. So for good reason, hedge funds may be reluctant to share position details. I had to figure out a way to protect them and allow us access so we could be good managers." Inserting a middleman alleviated the manager's concerns and helped him get the information he needed.

At the time, Anson had not identified or documented the key tenets of his hedge fund investment thesis that he now calls *The Asymmetry of Alpha*, but he says, "I just had the intuitive sense, knew I wasn't getting as much information as I normally would like or had been privy to in the past, and I needed to figure out how to solve it."

HEDGE FUND INVESTOR

Over time, as Anson continued to analyze and invest in hedge funds, he identified four asymmetries in favor of hedge fund managers embedded in hedge fund management and investment practices.

- Asymmetry of Alpha: Hedge fund managers have much better information about their true levels of skill than investors do. In other words, they have an asymmetry of information about whether they deliver alpha.
- Asymmetry of Incentives: "My gosh, we could probably talk and write a whole book on that."
- Asymmetry of Risk Taking: Lack of transparency gives hedge funds an incentive to take risks that might not be consistent with what investors want.
- Asymmetry of Liquidity: Investors may not have the same investment horizon as a hedge fund manager.

The resulting thesis, *The Asymmetry of Alpha*, forms the basis of his investment philosophy and process.

Asymmetry of Alpha

The premise of the first tenet, the asymmetry of alpha, is that investors cannot forecast alpha, they can only observe alpha based on actual results. Once they have an actual hedge fund return stream, they can calculate how much of the return is attributable to manager skill and how much is attributable to systematic movements in exposure to the markets.

Anson wrote a paper "with the whimsical title *Sherlock Holmes and the Case of Alpha Generation.*" Paraphrasing the famous Holmes line from *The Adventure of the Beryl Coronet,* he said, "Once you eliminate the beta, whatever remains, however improbable, must be the alpha."

In other words, there is some skill (alpha) and some component of systematic market risk (beta) embedded in a hedge fund return stream. "The trick is to tease out what is the alpha and what is the beta."

Convertible bond arbitrage strategies provide a good example of Anson's analysis. The beta components of the return stream include interest rate risk and duration risk because the instrument is a bond, and equity risk because it can convert to a stock. Companies with "less than stellar creditworthiness" tend to issue convertible bonds, so there is credit risk. The embedded option creates volatility risk, while the lack of liquidity and registration requirements adds liquidity risk.

Anson also measured how current prices are influenced by past prices and found they "do not follow a random walk." After analyzing the beta components and price data against a convertible bond index, and using the traditional definition of alpha as the value-added from superior security selection skill, he found that "alpha is negative."

The average convertible strategy had negative alpha, but a positive Sharpe ratio, leading him to ask, "How are they adding value if alpha is negative?"

With further analysis, Anson concluded that convertible arbitrage managers were not seeking undervalued securities to buy or overvalued securities to short. Instead, they were breaking bonds into beta components, hedging out expensive beta, and "loading up on cheap beta." Convertible arbitrage hedge fund managers had almost no beta to equities or volatility. The hedge fund managers hedged or "sold" these expensive beta components but retained significant beta exposure to interest rate, credit, and liquidity risk (the "cheap" betas).

Managers who should have been searching for alpha were actually finding cheap beta, but the positive Sharpe ratio gave the impression that the search had resulted in the creation of alpha.

The asymmetry comes when a manager says, "I have a positive Sharpe ratio. I must have skill." But, Anson says, "When you parse it down, on average they don't have skill in selecting over- or undervalued securities. Their best skill is slicing and dicing convertible bonds into beta bits and being smart enough to hedge out the expensive beta."

In his view, convertible arbitrage is "not about alpha, it's about beta. They're not really providing you with alpha, they are providing you cheap beta."

Thus, the asymmetry of alpha means investors do not receive alpha, they receive beta, but unless they have transparency and the information they need to conduct the *ex post ante* analysis, the asymmetry of alpha will continue to favor hedge fund managers.

Asymmetry of Alpha Influences the Process

The results of his asymmetry of alpha analysis influence Anson's hedge fund investment process, including strategy and manager selection, and suggest that hedge fund replication or passive strategies may be a good choice in some investors' portfolios.

Passive hedge strategies are, he says, "likely to grow. Searching for cheap beta you can do yourself. You don't need to be charged 2 and 20. Why not go out and buy cheap beta?" Investors should and will question such high fees if they know they can generate beta return by themselves for a much lower cost.

Asked whether it is worth the effort to pinpoint a manager with skill in times when market conditions make beta returns attractive, Anson replies, "For instance, in early 2009, picking the right active manager was less important than picking the right beta to go after. Investors could have generated more return picking undervalued asset classes, [that is,] beta, than they could picking the right managers. Once beta gets to be more fairly valued, then active management becomes more important."

When markets get back to equilibrium, "manager skill becomes more important for generating excess return." When he is seeking skilled managers, the asymmetry of alpha analysis shapes Anson's manager selection process and helps determine performance persistence and strategy preferences.

Performance Persistence   An important element of the manager selection process involves assessing whether a hedge fund manager will continue to produce consistent returns over time. In his asymmetry of alpha analysis, if Anson determines that a manager generated alpha in the past, he then tries to determine if the process for generating that alpha will continue to be valid.

The likelihood of performance persistence often becomes easier to discern in the fallout from a crisis like that experienced by hedge funds in 2008. Policy changes and business retrenchments may remove tools a manager once used to achieve alpha.

"Many hedge funds employed leverage to get alpha in convergence trading, betting on the convergence of two similar securities and extracting alpha using leverage." The ability to use leverage decreased during the 2008 crisis and will continue to do so, Anson says. "Prime brokers are not providing as much leverage. Ratios of 10:1 or 5:1 are a thing of the past, maybe 3:1 or 2:1 going forward.

"Can they generate the same alpha with less leverage when we are going through a global systemic deleveraging? Probably not."

Even though such a manager's process might be valid, Anson concludes, "The new paradigm means that alpha cannot be leveraged to the same level as it once was."

Anson roots out a manager's ability to generate alpha consistently by asking, "What do you do?" as long as it takes until he believes he has the answer. The story of one hedge fund manager illustrates his point so well it has made Anson's list of Top Ten Hedge Fund Quotes.

An amusing compilation of statements Anson has heard from hedge fund managers over the years, the list combines elements of David Letterman's Top Ten List with the old television program *Kids Say the Darndest Things*.

ANSON'S TOP TEN HEDGE FUND QUOTES

Throughout the course of my career, I have spoken to hundreds of hedge fund managers. The responses to questions are not always what you would expect. So, I decided to compile my own Top Ten List of quotes from hedge fund managers to provide a humorous insight into the hedge fund industry. These quotes are not indicative of the whole industry. However, should you ever run across one of these quotes in your due diligence, proceed with caution.

NUMBER 10: "IF WE DON'T CHARGE 2 AND 20, NOBODY WILL TAKE US SERIOUSLY."

A new hedge fund manager passed through to raise money. The two principals had successful track records investing in traditional long-only securities, but they had not previously shorted securities. I inquired why these two novice hedge fund managers with no prior hedge fund experience should be worthy of a 2 percent management fee and a 20 percent profit-sharing fee. I received the above quote.

(*Continued*)

ANSON'S TOP TEN HEDGE FUND QUOTES (*Continued*)

Beware of hedge fund managers trying to justify their fees based on what they think the market will bear.

NUMBER 9: "WE CHARGE 3 AND 30 BECAUSE THAT IS THE ONLY WAY WE CAN KEEP OUR ASSETS BELOW SEVERAL BILLION DOLLARS."

In the middle of a manager's presentation, I asked what his fee structure was. He initially responded "3 and 30," which was followed by dead silence for about one-half minute until he came back with the quote above.

Beware of hedge fund managers that focus on fees first and client wealth second.

NUMBER 8: "WE ARE 75 PERCENT CASH BECAUSE WE CANNOT FIND SUFFICIENT INVESTMENTS."

This statement is bad on so many levels; it is hard to decide where to begin. First, this hedge fund manager billed himself as an equity long/short investor. The key word there is "equity," not "cash." His job is to find long/short investment opportunities in the U.S. equities market. Furthermore, the cash he had in his account had not been generated by short rebates held at the prime broker—it was capital that had not been put to work, for which I was charged 2 and 20.

NUMBER 7: "WE DON'T INVEST IN CROWDED SHORTS."

I cannot begin to count the number of times that I have heard this statement from hedge fund managers. "Crowded shorts" refers to a situation where a large group of hedge fund managers collectively short the same stock in expectation that it will decline in value. The shorting becomes crowded because all the hedge fund managers rush to their prime brokers and request the same stock to borrow.

The last to evacuate their short position as the stock price increases are "squeezed" and see their profits erode dramatically. This phenomenon is all the more exacerbated the more crowded the short position. But if no hedge fund manager invests in crowded shorts, we would not observe short squeezes, so this must be a figment of my imagination.

NUMBER 6: "I HAVEN'T SHORTED BEFORE BUT I DO HAVE MY CFA."

Again this is an example of an inexperienced hedge fund manager who came from the world of traditional long-only investments. While it is commendable that this new hedge fund manager had his Chartered Financial Analyst (CFA) designation, this alone does not qualify him to be an expert in shorting stocks.

NUMBER 5: "HEDGE FUNDS ARE BETTER INVESTMENTS THAN MANAGED FUTURES BECAUSE MANAGED FUTURES IS A ZERO-SUM GAME."

Aren't all alpha-generating ideas a zero-sum game? For every winner there has to be a loser. Regardless of whether the alpha-generating idea makes a profit for a hedge fund manager or a managed futures manager, someone has to lose money on the other side. This argument made by a hedge fund manager reflects a fundamental lack of understanding about the financial markets.

NUMBER 4: "WHAT'S A MASTER TRUST?"

A new hedge fund brought their top attorney, a partner from a well-known and respected Texas law firm. When I suggested to the lawyer that he might wish to consider a master trust and master feeder structure for the onshore and offshore hedge funds, his response was, "What's a master trust?" A hedge fund manager that intends to run both an onshore and offshore hedge fund better have his infrastructure in place before rushing forward *and* charging 2 and 20 without having thought through the business model.

NUMBER 3: "YOUR HEAD OF EQUITY DOESN'T UNDERSTAND OUR HEDGE FUND STRATEGY."

One fund was going to demonstrate expertise in convertible arbitrage, merger arbitrage, managed futures, equity long/short, and corporate

(Continued)

ANSON'S TOP TEN HEDGE FUND QUOTES (*Continued*)

governance. These are very different investment programs with very different risk profiles that require significantly different skill sets to perform well. This was that same group that did not know what a master trust was. (Anson was the head of equity and turned them down.)

They immediately drafted a letter to the chief investment officer of CalPERS with the opening line: "Your head of equity does not understand our hedge fund strategy." There was only one problem. The former CIO had resigned and I had been promoted to be the new CIO, and therefore, I was the recipient of their letter.

NUMBER 2: "BASICALLY I LOOK AT SCREENS ALL DAY AND GO WITH MY GUT."

One day about three years ago, while visiting a hedge fund manager in London, I asked, "How do you generate your trade ideas?" I never expected to get the response that I received above. While he may be a gutsy investor, there is simply too much process risk associated with this hedge fund manager to make a credible investment.

NUMBER 1 TOP TEN QUOTE: "HE WILL BE WITH YOU IN JUST A MINUTE, SIR, HE'S STILL MEETING WITH HIS ARCHITECT."

I went to visit a hedge fund manager and showed up promptly. However, I was kept waiting in the reception area. Finally, after 20 minutes, I asked the receptionist what the delay was and received the quote above.

This statement told me he was more interested in building his new house than he was in meeting with a potential client. Mark Yusko of Morgan Creek Capital calls this the "Red Ferrari syndrome." Simply, when a hedge fund manager begins to overindulge, it is likely he has become risk averse and will now worry more about the preservation of his wealth than capital appreciation. This is a red flag (or Ferrari), and it is a good time to cash out of the hedge fund.

Source: This list is published in expanded form as Chapter 11 of Mark Anson's *Handbook of Alternative Assets, Second Edition*, 2006. Reprinted with permission of John Wiley & Sons, Inc.

At the recommendation of another investor, he was conducting due diligence on the manager and his $300 million fund.

"Great team, did fundamental research, but it was just not ringing true. Looking at turnover, it was too high. Looking for a consistent pattern of trades, how they are generating alpha, but I can't put my finger on it. Throughout the day I kept asking more and more questions and they would tell me they did 'fundamental bottom-up research, use our best ideas,' but the story just did not ring true. Finally at the end of the day, I think out of sheer frustration or just to get rid of me, the manager said, 'All right, Mark, basically what I do all day is look at screens and go with my gut.'

"Apparently he had some skill at doing that, and I finally wore him down until he told me the truth. But how can you replicate that? Or have some assurance that there will be performance persistence? What if his gut gets indigestion?"

Strategy Preferences   Asymmetry of alpha can apply to the performance persistence of specific hedge fund strategies. Certain strategies give Anson more confidence they will generate alpha consistently over time.

"Fundamental long/short equity has that potential. In general, I tend to think those that do fundamental research and construct a long/short portfolio can be persistent, because good fundamental research can reveal nuggets of information."

The hedge fund manager he grilled so insistently, Anson says, "had too much turnover for a real fundamental manager. The team had strength, but deferred to him."

Even if he likes the strategy type, such red flags will lead Anson to question whether a strategy does have potential for performance persistence.

After the 2008 financial crisis, Anson expects equity hedge funds to perform better than others since they rely less on leverage. Similarly, he thinks a form of hedged strategy known as "130/30"* should be strengthened by "leverage being sucked out of the market."

Anson cautions investors not to rely solely on their perception that a type of strategy may have performance persistence. "You do need to wear out shoe leather, assure yourself that something that looks persistent, is persistent. You still need to ask the questions, to make sure that something that looks repeatable is really taking place or is backed up by a good team."

---

*Portfolios constructed with 130 percent long positions and 30 percent short positions should, in theory, have no market exposure. Such strategies should be less volatile and are perceived to be less risky than typical hedge fund strategies.

While he believes good quantitative managers exist, Anson tends to avoid quantitative strategies that lack transparency. More specifically, he says, "What I don't like and [something that] people complain about are the black box strategies. In today's world of frauds like Bernie Madoff and Bayou Capital, there's no call to be a black box."

In general, Anson advises, "Don't invest in what you can't see, no matter how good those returns are. If you can't see it, then you can't validate it. As a result, you have got to take a pass, even if returns are really good."

It takes discipline to decide against investing in a fund with returns that seem too good to believe, but those may be returns that really cannot be believed. "You may have to turn away from what might be a good opportunity." But he adds, "How can you possibly monitor the risks if it's a black box?"

Activist Investing   Activist investing is one strategy Anson is known to prefer. During his stint at CalPERS Anson developed an appreciation for the style and helped create an in-house activist investment program. He remains a proponent of activist management.

The CalPERS program capitalized on the corporate governance expertise of his colleague Ted White. The two teamed up "to try to make a buck off it" and wrote a business plan for the CalPERS Board to turn its shareholder activism into an investment program. The CalPERS board approved it for implementation in 2002. Anson estimates that today the organization manages approximately $5 billion of internal and external funds in the program.

Hermes, the wholly owned subsidiary of British Telecom that Anson served as CEO, ran three activist hedge funds focused on the United Kingdom, Europe, and Japan for the BT Telecom Pension and outside investors.

From his long activism experience, Anson has developed strong, pointed opinions about the characteristics that define great activist hedge fund managers.

"More than just taking a large stake in a company and shooting your mouth off, activist managers really have to be prepared to roll up their sleeves and work on a business plan with the board of directors. They must identify weak links, assess human capital, and bring in new people, like a new CEO or CFO. Activist managers have to be willing to use their large equity stake to make those changes and withstand pressure from the corporation, other shareholders, and political elements."

In summary, good activists take large stakes, get actively involved, work on the company's business plan—not their PR plan—and commit to seeing those changes through. In the activist portfolio, Anson adds, "turnover has to be low and the time frame has to be long."

Anson finds it easier to gain conviction about the ability of activist managers to generate alpha. "One reason is the smaller, concentrated portfolios. At Hermes we had five to fifteen positions, no more than seventeen at any one point." Smaller portfolios enable activists to provide more transparency to investors and, therefore, almost force the manager to be able to articulate the business strategy or game plan for every position. "There has to be a clear rationale and investment thesis for positions, not just investing only because the companies are undervalued.

"What makes great activists as compared to traditional long-only managers? A long-only manager buys undervalued securities, then sits back and waits for a catalyst to happen. An activist investor becomes the catalyst. The traditional long-only manager is an active investor, but a passive owner. An activist manager is an active investor and an active owner. That's the key distinction."

Bottom line, Anson believes alpha is clearer and more transparent in activist managers. For him to gain conviction in a particular manager he says, "They must demonstrate why they are an active investor, why they think the company is undervalued. They must also demonstrate why they are an active owner. Why are they going to be the catalyst?"

Asymmetry of Incentives

Anson describes the asymmetry of incentives as "hedge fund incentive fees and the free option." As he analyzes it, hedge fund profit sharing and carry fees actually function as a call option on the profit of the hedge fund for the hedge fund manager. In an article Anson published in the trade journal *Pensions and Investments*, he wrote: "Hedge fund and other alpha managers essentially have a 'free option' with respect to the performance fees generated from their alpha-generative products. Incentive fees of 20 percent to 30 percent are the norm for hedge funds and other alternative-strategy managers. This is the nature of a call option: to share in the upside if profits are earned but to bear no risk on the downside. In fact, given that hedge fund managers are paid a management fee in addition to incentive fees, alpha managers are actually paid to take the free option."[1]

To illustrate the call option comparison, Anson offers a simple example of the typical scenario: "If, at the end of a reporting period, the hedge fund manager earns a profit for the asset owner, he collects an incentive fee. However, if the hedge fund manager does not earn a profit for the asset owner, he collects no incentive fee. Mathematically, this asymmetrical relationship is the same as the formula for a call option first made famous by Fischer S. Black and Myron S. Scholes in their seminal paper on option pricing."[2]

Anson elaborates, "The hedge fund manager has a call option on the profits of the fund. If they increase the fund's value above the high-water mark, they get to share in the profits. Indeed, the high-water mark is the strike price." What should concern investors, he says, "If they have this call option, what can they do to increase the value?"[*]

In their options pricing research, Black and Scholes showed that increasing the volatility of the underlying asset was among the easiest ways to increase the value of a call option.

If raising the volatility of the underlying fund raises the value of the call option, then, Anson says, "hedge fund managers have an incentive to increase the volatility beyond what investors might want."

The similarity between asymmetry of incentives and option pricing also applies when hedge fund managers perform poorly. In options pricing theory, another way to increase the value of the call option is to lower the strike price. Anson has seen it happen.

"A hedge fund manager had a net asset value lower than the high-water mark. He stopped managing that fund, started a new one. With the new high-water mark now set to zero, the incentive fee call option is now at the money."

Every time managers get below their high-water mark, given the asymmetry of incentives, they either increase the volatility or start a new hedge fund.

Investors need to be aware of this phenomenon, Anson says. "When it's underperforming significantly, all he is really trying to do is reprice the incentive fee call option by lowering the strike price."

Anson expects the asymmetry of incentives to decrease as investors gain more awareness and understanding of how incentive fees work and as more competitively priced hedge fund products, such as 130/30 funds, enter the market.

"The 130/30 structure has reduced the asymmetry of incentives. Managers with a portfolio that is 130 long/30 short won't be able to command a 2 and 20 price. They will have to price consistently with 130/30 managers and charge a percent to a percent and a half."

Better understanding of incentive fees and more competition from "alpha extension" funds like 130/30 will put more pressure on hedge fund

---

[*]Anson demonstrates how to price this incentive fee call option in his original research article "Hedge Fund Incentive Fees and the 'Free Option,'" published in *The Journal of Alternative Investments* (Fall 2001) and in his textbook, *CAIA Level I: An Introduction to Core Topics in Alternative Investments*, Hoboken, NJ, John Wiley & Sons, 2009.

fees. "I see a much better alignment, much better understanding, and more investors becoming more critical and less willing to accept 2 and 20."

The 2 and 20 fee structure may have more to do with marketing practices, as Anson relates in one of his Top Ten hedge fund quotes:

"Once upon a time, a long-only manager that CalPERS invested with came to us with a 2 and 20 hedge fund. They had been charging us 80 basis points on their existing fund. I asked, 'What makes you think I will be willing to accept the higher fees?' The honest response: 'If we don't charge 2 and 20, no one will take it seriously.'

"Nowadays to charge 2 and 20, you have to be able to show why. No one deserves 2 and 20. Now you have to prove why you should get that. It's no longer a right of hedge fund existence."

Anson retains close ties with Kurt Silberstein, the manager of the hedge fund portfolio at CalPERS, and supports his efforts to revamp fee structures across the industry, a response to poor experiences with hedge funds in the financial crisis of 2008. One objective is to institute the "claw-back" provision commonly applied in private equity funds that allows investors to get paid back any performance fees they had paid on unrealized gains that do not actually come to fruition.

"As more hedge fund managers put up gates, establish liquidity hurdles, or basically put in lock-ups—terms more like those in private equity—then you should include the flipside of the private equity world like claw-back provisions on fees."

Although Anson believes that the 2 and 20 fee structure as a standard should fade away for a large number of managers, he says, "Some managers will be able to command a premium and will be able to get it. Some managers have legitimate skill and can add a lot of value. If they do, then we will have to pay for it."

Asymmetry of Risk

Asymmetry of risk stems from the asymmetry of incentives, because the call option characteristics of fee structures give managers an incentive to take more risk. "The manager may not be fully aware of why he's taking risk, but effectively he has an incentive to roll the dice."

Anson wrote in *Pensions and Investments*: "Money managers that share in the gains from their performance, but not the losses, have an incentive to take excessive risk. Because money managers do not bear the cost of their losses from their investment strategies, they may take more risk than the asset owner is willing to bear. Furthermore, asset owners only get a 'snapshot' of their portfolio at any point in time. The amount of risk that is embedded in the portfolio might not be transparent and the same issue applies for the investment process by which the portfolio was constructed. Furthermore, in a 'black box' scenario it is impossible to assess risk whatsoever: the more opaque the hedge fund manager, the more the asset owner is 'at risk' to risk."[3]

Investors need to be cognizant of these issues, because some risks may not be disclosed or readily apparent as in the example of the "black box." The problem with a "snapshot" of the portfolio at some point in time, Anson says, is that "it may be from the past, historic information that looks back. It is not forward looking." This is particularly problematic with the dynamic trading strategies of hedge fund managers.

At a minimum, an investor should know about the asymmetry of risk, because "you may not understand that you're giving the manager an incentive to take more risk."

Anson tends to have the most confidence in the risk-taking framework of the strategies he favors for other reasons, particularly equity hedge strategies. "Long/short equity based on fundamental research positions tends to have longer tenure in the portfolio and less turnover. You can have a greater sense of confidence of risks in portfolio." However, that may not always be the case, especially in volatile markets. "There is a lot of turnover risk today, but that may be different from risks you see tomorrow."

Some investment strategies seem to have clear, identifiable risks, but in some cases, "you may think you understand risk but you don't." Anson gives the example of merger arbitrage.

"In merger arb, a manager buys the stock of the target, sells the stock of the acquiring company. He will have long and short equity positions, typically in the same industry, with one offsetting another. You think you're 'probably pretty low risk,' that it might end in a draw. The fact is it's an insurance contract. The hedge fund is insuring to the market that the merger will go through. If that's true, they make money. If it breaks down, the hedge fund manager is on the hook for the losses."

With the merger arbitrage manager functioning as a de facto insurer of a completed merger and the fund serving as a de facto insurance contract, the investment becomes "a short put option. The biggest exposure of the merger arb manager is 'short put' exposure, not the equity long/short exposure." An investor may think that the strategy is probably low risk, but "that's because risk is not transparent. They're getting a different risk profile than they think they have and are not aware of the actual risk."

Due Diligence

The asymmetry of alpha philosophy creates a holistic approach that incorporates typical due diligence tactics throughout the entire process. Anson does conduct manager due diligence and offers advice about the thought process.

- Never take anything at face value: When managers explain their strategy, investors "must pick and probe and confirm that it's true." More often than not, it's the truth, but in many instances, that's not the case. "If it doesn't look, feel, or smell right, keep asking more questions."
- Always have the option to walk away: Anson gives the example of a well-known activist investor. While at CalPERS, he was authorized to invest $200 million with the manager and arranged to meet him first at the Parker Meridien Hotel in New York City.

  "He was telling us what a great activist investor he was. I asked for basic investor governance rights and he refused. I said, 'You say you're an activist investor and you advocate good governance, but you won't give governance rights?' He replied, 'If you don't invest I've got a lot of other people that want to.' Wrong response! I never invested with him. People thought I was pretty dumb, but if something doesn't feel or smell right, just walk away."
- According to Anson, there are now more hedge funds than mutual funds in the United States, so investors need not worry about walking away. "Historically third-party marketers and hedge funds of funds all claimed they had access to good managers. Access is no longer the issue. There are plenty of good hedge funds for all investors. When somebody tells me they have access now, I say, 'Great, have a nice day.'"
- Important characteristics of a hedge fund include transparency, good risk management and monitoring, performance attribution and client reporting capabilities.
- Managers should always be able to articulate their strategy, produce the underlying positions that support the strategy, and show they can adhere to it.

LESSONS, OBSERVATIONS, AND OUTLOOK

Because he allocated to hedge funds at CalPERS, Anson receives credit for being among the first, and certainly the highest profile, U.S.-based public pension plans to allocate assets to hedge funds. Their foray into hedge funds in April of 2002 led the way for other institutional investors and helped spark the explosive growth in hedge fund assets under management that took place between 2002 and 2008.

Implementing the CalPERS Hedge Fund Program

At the beginning of the CalPERS hedge fund program, it invested almost exclusively in hedge fund strategies related to the equity markets. Anson says they took that approach for a number of reasons.

"We understood equity risk, so we stayed within our comfort zone. We had a better sense of equity strategies." CalPERS also had its own in-house equity long/short portfolio. "We figured, 'why not learn internally?' and see what it means to go long and short." Having their own fund allowed them to learn firsthand while also building their external hedge fund investment program.

As they became more comfortable with investing in hedge funds over the following two years, they expanded into other strategies and built more of an absolute return portfolio, a program called RMARS.

"RMARS stands for risk-managed absolute return strategy. It was clear the strategies were focused more on risk control and less on yield. As we evolved we added hedge fund strategies to provide a broader portfolio that was less correlated to the stock and bond markets."

When Anson left CalPERS for Hermes, the portfolio had .2 beta to the stock market and close to 0 beta to the bond market. It served as a stand-alone investment and an alternative source of return. He stresses that the absolute return portfolio was not in a portable alpha program, a form of hedge fund investing using derivatives that backfired on many institutional investors in 2008.

Hedge Fund Investment Issues

CalPERS used consultants and funds of hedge funds to help it start its hedge fund investment program.

Funds of Funds and Consultants   "Hired Blackstone and paid them a good fee. We understood it as kind of like tuition for getting an education in hedge funds. We did that for about two years, until they felt we could stand on our own two legs."

By that point, CalPERS had more of its own resources to build the portfolio, essentially its own fund of hedge funds, in-house, so Silberstein took control of the program.

Anson endeavored to take the in-house fund, California Hedge Fund Partners, and market it to other institutional investors. "I really wanted to build out the fund and sell it to other pension funds. Working behind the scenes, I took it to the board to have a conversation about it." The board decided against the idea.

Sometime thereafter Anson received a call from an investor at another public pension plan. "We exchange pleasantries and then he says, 'I hear you're checking out a manager we're evaluating, what do you think?' I told him it looked good. I had more work to do and said, 'I'll let you know.' Great. Two weeks later he called again asking, 'Where are you on that hedge fund?' I asked him why and he replied, 'I'm going to my board and I want to tell them you recommended it.'

"At least it validated my fund idea."

Anson believes there are solid reasons for relying on funds of hedge funds. "There are some very good funds in the market. They provide tools that investors may not have, some very good risk and portfolio analysis and attribution analytics. If you don't have the resources or the internal staff, it's worth it to pony up and pay for the fund of funds and have them do it for you."

Terms and Conditions Regarding lock-ups, Anson says, "Hate 'em. If you're going to lock me up, I should get a claw-back on the other side." However, he loves them when "investors get the wobblies," that is, panicking and cashing out at an inopportune time. "I want to tell them, 'don't go wobbly on me.' I want to be with other investors that have the fortitude to ride it out."

Because of "the wobblies" and other issues like transparency and liquidity, Anson anticipates greater demand for separately managed accounts. "There are pros and cons. As a limited partner, you might get some additional advantages, but separate accounts are just subject to the risk of the portfolio. You're not at the mercy of a weak-kneed investor that will panic and crystallize the losses."

A larger number of separate accounts will likely create more stratification among investors, but he says, "Control of investments is a great issue. If you're the last one in the hedge fund, you're the one left holding the bag."

Hedge Fund Industry Outlook

Anson describes a paradox that will drive the investment management business in the years ahead.

"There is a paradox. We talk a lot about the separation of alpha and beta. We now have a much better understanding of what is alpha and what is beta, so we can achieve that separation." At the same time he sees "a convergence of long-only managers and hedge fund managers. Hedge fund managers are building long-only funds, while traditional long-only managers are building 130/30 products."

While alpha and beta continue to disperse further apart from each other, hedge funds that have been associated with alpha and long-only firms that have been associated with beta are "converging and moving into the same space." Therein lies the paradox. He expects this convergence/dispersion paradox to continue.

Investment management business models will feel the impact of the convergence/dispersion paradox and the preferences of investors. Anson anticipates that three models will prevail.

- Focused Manager: Boutique firms that do one thing and do it well, such as hedge funds and private equity or single-strategy long-only managers. Anson describes them as having a "high cost of human capital," high spending on staff, high costs compared to revenues. However, they have a high rate of innovation and can charge high fee premiums.
- Asset Gatherers: Firms with salaries and bonuses in line with market medians, but lower than boutiques, not innovators. These firms tend to rely on technology to scale. "They embed a lot of operating leverage into the system, hammer costs to the bone, and profit on scale."
- Multi-Boutique: Anson's previous firm, Nuveen Investments, operates in this manner. He describes the model as a combination of technology leverage plus focused asset managers that create innovation.

Although Anson believes all three models have staying power, he says, "If I had to place bets on the future, those that continue to innovate will continue to succeed as opposed to those that basically just process trades and steal ideas."

ASYMMETRICAL SUCCESS

In an investment career marked by innovation and leadership, Mark Anson has a track record of outstanding performance across a number of disciplines. Among the first chief investment officers of a significant pension to invest in hedge funds, Anson helped spur tremendous growth and change in the industry. Not only a successful investor, he has led two of the world's largest pension funds, runs a well-regarded asset management boutique, and remains one of the leading intellects on the subject of hedge funds.

Despite this record of accomplishment, he shows no sign of "Red Ferrari Syndrome," and admits to having some flaws, like being "a really bad golfer."

Summarizing his outlook on the industry, Anson says, "Firms that rely on talented individuals and focus on innovation will succeed in the end." Investors who rely on the advice of Mark Anson, an asymmetrically talented and innovative investor, thinker, and leader, will also succeed in the end.

CHAPTER 8

Early Endowment CIO and Entrepreneur

Louis W. Moelchert, Jr., Managing Partner, Private Advisors, LLC

During his 30-year tenure at the University of Richmond, Louis W. Moelchert, Jr., became one of the first endowment chief investment officers to make significant investments in hedge funds. Starting in the 1980s, his early commitment to alternative investments helped him achieve a top quartile track record among similar institutions. His strong track record, coupled with an entrepreneurial mind-set, led him to start Private Advisors, LLC in 1997.

Private Advisors, LLC invests approximately $4 billion of client assets in both hedge funds and private equity partnerships. As managing partner, Moelchert serves on the investment committees of all funds and oversees all investment products and professionals.

He served on the investment committee for the Virginia Retirement System from 1996 to 2000 and chaired it from 1998 to 2000. He was also chairman of the Commonfund Board of Trustees from 1993 to 1997 and served as a trustee from 1986 to 1998. Moelchert received his BBA and MS in accountancy from the University of Georgia.

BACKGROUND

Armed with two degrees in accounting from the University of Georgia, Lou Moelchert embarked on a career in higher education, serving as the chief financial officer or VP of finance at three institutions. Although he had a personal interest in investing, he had no professional investment responsibilities when recruited for the CFO job at the University of Richmond.

Thinking it would be "a pretty neat experience" to have responsibility for the "significant, or at least it was at the time," $50 million endowment, he joined the university in 1975.

Bruce Heilman, then the president of Richmond, had also served as a CFO before leading the institution, and he influenced Moelchert's management philosophy. Moelchert learned what he calls "the who" or "getting the right people in the right slots and not being afraid to make changes." Heilman handled hiring personally, "as opposed to using outside recruiters," meeting and interviewing Moelchert "on the spot" at a conference. Moelchert admired Heilman's "very direct" style.

The Commonfund was another "extraordinarily important influence," Moelchert says. "I give a tremendous amount of credit to George Keane. Clearly, the Commonfund was growing into the organization it became and he provided leadership. He was a tremendous investment visionary and highly entrepreneurial."

Observing how Keane and the Commonfund operated, in particular Keane's "open-minded approach to different kind of investments," helped him. Moelchert eventually served on the Commonfund board for 12 years, leading it as chair for 4 of those years. "It was an incredible laboratory for learning about interesting managers and getting exposure to the best, newest techniques."

As he learned more about risk, Moelchert became interested in hedge funds. "Early on I developed a differentiated view of risk. The traditional view of institutional investors was that hedge funds were different, opaque and really risky, and because of that, 'I don't really understand them.' It became obvious to me that the return patterns were differentiated from the return patterns of traditional investments, and that a portfolio of mostly equities, international, small cap, and fixed income was extraordinarily highly correlated and therefore much more risky."

He realized he could combine alternatives—with their different patterns of returns—with other types of assets and get a much less risky portfolio. "Not only was the portfolio less risky, but the returns were better." What he hadn't anticipated was how much better the returns would be.

After developing his ideas about risk, Moelchert began the process of educating the investment committee members, bringing in speakers with expertise throughout the financial markets to get them comfortable with hedge fund and private equity investments. They first allocated capital to alternatives in the mid-1980s, mostly in equity long/short hedge funds, since there were few other styles available at the time. Alternatives grew to become such a significant part of the endowment portfolio that "it got to the point that when I stepped down from the endowment, 70 percent of the portfolio was invested in alternatives, mostly hedge funds."

INVESTMENT PROCESS

Over the years, Moelchert has developed a structured process based on five guiding investment precepts:

1. **Asset Class Selection:** "First and foremost," Moelchert explains, "just as I developed a nontraditional view of risk, really as I reflect on it, it became more of a view about being in the right asset classes. The smartest investors I know believe being in the right asset class is at least as important as manager selection, if not more important."
2. **Understand the Investment:** Moelchert will only "invest in what I can clearly understand." Although he may make exceptions, if he cannot understand it, then he will avoid it. "This tends to lead me away from highly quantitative strategies. In my experience they work until they don't, and when they don't, they fail profoundly."
3. **Fundamental Research and Value Orientation:** He thinks managers who elicit value by conducting bottom-up, fundamental research "win over time." Especially for investors with a long-term view, he believes the strategy will outperform other strategies, making it "a safer place to be."
4. **Contrarian Asset Allocation:** As much as Moelchert believes it important to approach asset allocation with a contrarian viewpoint, he says, "I like to say it but it's easier to say than it is to do." The difficulty comes from "the huge herd mentality in institutional investors, the tendency to invest by looking through the rear view mirror. Everyone is susceptible, even me!" If they want to succeed, investors must resist the urge to focus on the past, because it is key "to look into a murky future and try to read the tea leaves, if you will, and bias the asset allocation toward things that are not popular at the time, things the world has overlooked." He reiterates, "It's easier to say than to do."

   Most investors have problems being contrarian. If they are "cognitively built that way," then they tend to be "early and lonely" because contrarian investments can underperform for a long time. Moelchert describes an example from his tenure at Richmond in the late 1990s during the dot-com boom. The committee wanted to "fire all the value managers and go into growth managers." He resisted that pressure, and eventually he was proved right when the dot-com stock bubble burst in 2000.

   He sees this as just human nature. "The way the world is built, people want to invest in what has done well. People try to extrapolate trends, think they will continue, but the investment world doesn't work that way." When investors see the herd mentality take over, they need to "go do something else, run for the hills, but it's hard to resist it."

Moelchert quotes the late author Peter Bernstein. "To produce alpha you have to take the risk of being wrong." He adds, "I made my share of mistakes over time."

5. **Avoid Leverage:** Like many of his contemporaries, Moelchert dislikes investing in hedge fund strategies that rely on high amounts of leverage. "Generally, we have a significant dislike of excessive leverage to make a reasonable rate of return. Some of the time it works, but when it doesn't you have a disaster on your hands."

Moelchert also makes a point of dismissing value at risk (VaR) analysis, calling it "a cruel joke played on the financial community." An event that affects the portfolio by two standard deviations or more is most important to prepare against and also most difficult to predict and calculate. Private Advisors uses quantitative risk measurement tools, but he thinks, "Anyone that gets comfortable and manages their life using VaR is making a huge mistake. As we found out this last year, it just didn't work."

Manager Selection

The 10-person hedge fund investment team at Private Advisors focuses its manager research and selection on up to 14 different types of strategies. It tries to pick managers based on their expectations for the future, rather than a manager's good recent performance. The group prefers managers who show an "asymmetry of upside potential" as compared to the likelihood of losses, and it continually refines and "tweaks" the process.

To source managers, the investment team relies on its strong network of contacts and supplements it by attending prime brokerage capital introduction events and "spending a tremendous amount of time in New York City and other money center areas."

The ongoing process produces a typical watch list of 150 managers, and the team conducts "incremental diligence on the most attractive managers." At any one time it will have 20 to 30 managers on a buy list, including managers that it has not yet invested in, but would "feel comfortable with moving forward."

Manager Characteristics　　Moelchert and his team look for hedge fund managers with a good long-term track record, but will make exceptions for managers with a great pedigree who may be leaving a larger firm. Either way, the manager must have a proven long-term process, generally in the aforementioned fundamentally oriented, research-driven strategies.

"Preserving capital in down markets" is a valuable skill, one he focuses on extensively and believes "is generally underappreciated by the investment community." Moelchert says, "I want to see managers preserve capital in down markets, rather than performing with or above the market in good markets." He likes managers who tend to be "lagging in a bull market, but significantly outperforming in a bear market."

A manager's educational background at reputable institutions is important, "but not everything." If the manager has institutional investing experience at good-quality organizations, "in particular, top-notch hedge funds, that provides some comfort."

While Moelchert may consider new managers from good firms more readily than others, he remains wary. "There's a tendency for new hedge funds to come out with all the best ideas of their old firm and none of the bad ideas. But the bad ideas tend to mature over time."

In that situation investors need to ask, "Will they be great portfolio managers when they're making the decisions?" Managers can act differently when they are "part of a larger machine and when someone else is making decisions about risk controls and asset allocation."

Moelchert not only wants to understand the strategy type before he invests, he also needs to understand how an individual manager produces returns in his particular fund. "If we can't clearly understand how the returns are produced, we just won't go there." Therefore, they will study individual trades and positions to make sure they are comfortable with the manager's approach.

Several members of the Private Advisors team will meet the manager numerous times throughout the long period of time it takes for them to make an investment.

When it comes to evaluating managers and their teams, Moelchert says, "If we do not have supreme confidence about the head person, we wouldn't invest. In certain instances, we had confidence in the head person, but saw continuing turnover at lower levels. It ends up being a dysfunctional organization if they don't have continuity and consistency." Some turnover is expected, but he likes to see "a consistent team that learns how to work together." Any fund "is more than the key guy, but clearly that is the starting place."

Due Diligence   Determining the quality of the people is the main objective of the Private Advisors due diligence process. They conduct extensive background checks to make sure there are not any "hidden issues." Reference checking involves contacting people the manager provides and those the Private Advisors team generates separately by networking. Moelchert says, "It's a people to people business. You want to make sure you have a clear understanding of the kind of person you are investing with."

If a senior investment professional leaves a manager, they will arrange an exit interview with the individual, "to make sure we're not missing something." The exit interview proves valuable, "particularly for affirming what we think, but maybe not everything is exactly right. It is helpful."

Investors need to prepare thoughtfully for interviews, because much of the time, "People tell you what you want to hear. If you don't ask the right questions, you won't get the answers."

Strategy Preferences Early in his hedge fund investing experience, Moelchert mostly favored equity long/short strategies. His appreciation for other strategies has increased over time.

Weak performance during the 2008 financial crisis bothers him less than it does other investors who may have gotten caught up in the "herd mentality." He explains, "We were in a period of time when most hedge fund strategies had the wind at their back." Investors had high expectations, so "hedge funds really disappointed. While hedge funds did underperform, they did outperform the market."

Market conditions since the 2008 crisis have bolstered his confidence in hedge funds. For one, he expects reduced competition for opportunities, because investment banks have eliminated proprietary trading strategies. Meanwhile, some hedge funds failed or performed so poorly they have exited the market.

Moelchert's optimism has a long lead-time. He sees "a runway for hedge funds that are doing deep due diligence." He means, "It takes earnings to power the equity market and it's hard to see equities do well for a long time." Equities will probably remain "range bound," and that "opens a wide runway for hedge funds that can go long and short and can trade. I just don't see where the earnings are going to come from."

He does not have a strong bias toward any particular market sectors; instead, his bias seems to be toward fundamental research-driven strategies regardless of the sector or asset class. Describing his view on credit he says, "While credit has moved a lot, there is abundant reason to think there is money to be made in credit, with managers that are doing great due diligence."

Historically Moelchert shied away from global macro strategies, but now, "Macro may have the wind at its back because the world has changed." He finds it more feasible "to make the case for those with good long-term track records."

Portfolio Management

Although Moelchert may think about investing in a less familiar strategy due to favorable market conditions, he does not construct a portfolio accordingly. He describes their approach as more like "an ongoing process of tactical allocation" and says they "don't believe in market timing. Making huge shifts is not smart."

In his view, having a well-diversified portfolio of hedge funds works best over the long term. However, he thinks investors "can make incremental shifts in allocation that can make a difference on the margins."

The investment team does "pooh pooh" value at risk, but before adding a strategy to the portfolio they will do extensive quantitative analysis to assess the risks of a particular strategy. Essentially, they combine quantitative and qualitative techniques "to assess how bad things might be if things go really bad."

Once they have assessed individual manager risk, they analyze the combined statistics of all the managers in the portfolio, including their correlations to each other. Moelchert acknowledges, "There are no guarantees that it will be right; you assess the best you can." Investors may consider adding managers with higher risk profiles to their portfolios, but when doing so, they should size the positions carefully.

The Private Advisors investment committee reviews all the information and approves the investments. Although he believes their experience working with a wide range of managers makes a difference, in the end, constructing a portfolio is a "blend of art and science."

Moelchert briefly describes methods and advice for the ongoing management of various aspects of a portfolio of hedge funds:

- **Monitoring:** The Private Advisors team spends a significant amount of time communicating with the managers of the 60 to 75 funds in their portfolio. They will meet in person at least four times a year to review performance, positions, and business conditions, and they speak with a representative of each firm at least monthly.
- **Termination:** Private Advisors will terminate a manager for style drift and will "guard against excessive asset growth," because it can dilute returns. Moelchert also worries about a variation on excessive capital, managers who have "called in rich," meaning they have made "so much money they don't have to work as hard."
- **Capacity:** When a fund reaches an optimum size, or its capacity, the manager may close or set limits on new investments. Getting capacity with a high-performing hedge fund has historically been a boon if you had it, or a problem if you did not. Post the 2008 financial crisis, Moelchert says, "Capacity is not an issue, but for the best managers it's always an issue." Even though "with the money that's gone out, it's not a problem now," his end investors appreciate it, so capacity remains an important component of manager selection.

- **Position Size:** While having the right to make additional investments in a good fund matters, investors must guard against concentration. "An outsized position with any manager is just not a good thing." His team caps their positions with any one manager at 7.5 percent of the portfolio.

Terms and conditions, like the length of the lock-up and the fee structure, also affect manager selection and portfolio management decisions.

Lock-Ups and Liquidity Moelchert expresses a contrarian view of lock-ups. "I honestly think the whole industry would be better off if everyone had longer lock-ups." Longer lock-ups are more conducive to a long-term investment horizon, but "the world has a short-term view." Otherwise, he would prefer longer lock-ups, but thinks the market won't permit it.

He advocates longer lock-ups primarily because he thinks many investors have "knee-jerk reactions" in difficult markets. He advises hedge fund managers and funds of hedge funds leaders to manage liquidity carefully, because "when they (investors) want their money back, they want their money back." He adds, "You don't want a call from a manager putting up a gate because there's a liquidity mismatch."

Keeping the liquidity demands of investors in mind, the Private Advisors team tries to find managers with "livable liquidity provisions." They have spent enough time in the market that Moelchert feels confident, "We can find managers we like with reasonable lock-up provisions."

Fee Structure The best managers will always get paid a premium, but overall "the hedge fund industry is running a little scared." As a result, some managers have offered the firm better liquidity terms and fee breaks.

Moelchert believes hedge fund managers should establish a hard hurdle rate because, "Paying hedge fund fees to get T-bill returns is not reasonable." It is reasonable for investors to have the ability to claw back returns. He has seen too many "one-way street" instances, when a manager closes a fund without earning back losses and soon opens a new fund for investment. Moelchert would not likely invest in the new fund, citing a classic reason: "Fool me once, shame on you. Fool me twice, shame on me."

LESSONS, OBSERVATIONS, AND ADVICE

Because his career as a hedge fund investor and asset management entrepreneur stems from his experience as an endowment chief investment officer, Moelchert shares insight and advice from each vantage point.

Becoming a Smart Investor

Although Moelchert never mentions the Bernard Madoff fraud, his advice definitely applies. "Do your own due diligence. Never invest just because somebody else is doing it," he says. The proverbial "smart guy" might have completely different investment objectives or completely hidden motives. Making an investment without doing the due diligence because the "smart guy" is doing so "is self-reinforcing." In other words, the decision may feed your ego, but it may not feed your family.

Moelchert repeats his advice to "size your positions properly." He says, "I used to believe I could have a big position with a high level of confidence," but now he knows, "You can't predict what you can't predict." That means for investors, "You can't have too big a position with any one manager. The penalty you pay for being wrong is not worth the return for being right."

Despite having some concerns about investors' mind-sets, he says, "Most clients are realistic about returns; they're not looking for you to shoot the lights out." Conducting your own due diligence and sizing positions properly offer the best protection against losses caused by excessive risk.

Getting a University Education

His experience as chief investment officer of the University of Richmond endowment continues to influence his hedge fund investment philosophy. Thinking back to those early days and "how I did things then versus now, I was shockingly unprepared to be doing this." He had numerous responsibilities as CFO, including "overseeing the campus police, food service, and maintenance. I learned on the job, it was guts and intuition, and talking to a few other institutional investors I respected."

Today, Moelchert says, "I don't know how anyone who doesn't have the right kind of background or experience, unless you have a fully competent staff, can pick managers." The number of managers and the level of detail have increased so substantially, the process has become "just daunting." The idea of pursuing it without resources is "mind boggling." He says, "Some consulting firms do an exceptional job, but it is really tough."

Having "the right people on the investment committee" helped Moelchert develop and succeed as an investor. "Too many people get on investment committees because they think it's fun or the right place to be." When he started managing the endowment for Richmond, "nobody got on the committee if I didn't want them. I went out and interviewed them. I didn't have full control, but it was close."

He found it "instrumental to put people with differentiated views" on the committee, because the "arguments with intelligent people about what we should or shouldn't do" were instructional and productive. Moelchert values the "great investment committees that worked well over time."

His long tenure at the university makes Moelchert among the few hedge fund investors suited to comment on the problems endowments faced in 2008. He says, "The endowment model is not broken." Instead, it proved itself compared to the traditional 60 percent equity and 40 percent bond allocation model. However, "One thing that many endowments failed to recognize is you have to be particularly cognizant of liquidity needs and being gated." Endowment investment officers and committee members have to balance two questions. "How do you get the income that you're required to pay out? How do you get the liquidity to take advantage of the opportunities in the marketplace?" Either way, they "will be a lot more cognizant of the liquidity needs."

Leading an Investment Team

His mantra for managing an investment team is "Delegate but don't abdicate." Moelchert characterizes it as a "modified management by objectives approach." For a team to be effective, all members must know their responsibilities, so he and the individual in a specific role will mutually agree upon its scope, responsibilities, and objectives. He will then delegate decisions, but reserves the right to have some veto power over investments that go into the portfolio. "I can think of one time in the last ten years that I have actually done that." He says you have to "let them make mistakes, that's how they learn. You can't build an organization by doing everything yourself."

Now that he leads a private investment advisory firm, Moelchert has a "deeper team" and the resources to aid in hiring the best people. Private Advisors applies similar criteria to hiring staff as they do selecting hedge fund managers and considers background, experience, and references.

Moelchert mentions G.H. Smart, an outside human resources consultant that "does an extraordinary job" eliciting information in independent interviews. Going back to the candidate's childhood experience, they discuss successes and failures, look for patterns of behavior, and evaluate the person's ability to perform well in the available position. G.H. Smart has also conducted a "360 degree" evaluation of Private Advisors and trained their private equity professionals to use these techniques on companies.

While they invest "a lot of time and energy" in the process, he finds it worthwhile. Identifying and hiring "A-level people raise the level of the entire organization." Apologetically, Moelchert describes their "No Assholes Policy." Adopted from another firm he admires, it means, "No matter how good you are, it's not worth it."

Insights from Private Equity

Certain asset classes, distressed debt, for example, lend themselves to being invested through either a hedge fund or private equity structure. The convergence of these two investment vehicles seems to have worked better for managers than it has for investors. Since they serve a similar clientele, firms that select alternative investment managers theoretically could handle both styles effectively, but tend to favor either the hedge fund or private equity mind-set. Private Advisors has been able to create funds across both alternative investment styles.

"The private equity business is tremendously additive to the hedge fund business." To take advantage of private company intelligence, they established a program called Private Insight. Through that effort, they help hedge fund managers conduct market research by accessing the expertise in the 500 companies in their private equity portfolio.

Moelchert provides a successful example. They facilitated a call between a hedge fund manager who had a short position in a defense contracting company and a private equity manager specializing in the defense industry. The private equity manager explained to the hedge fund manager that although he was right about the unprofitable company, it still had a high profile in the military contract process, including, he said, "high security clearance in the State Department." The private equity manager added, "Our suspicion is the company will be taken out." The hedge fund closed out the short position and "saved their clients something like eight or ten million dollars. The next time they had additional capacity, they asked us how much of it we wanted."

The Private Insights program enables them to be "a value-added investor to our managers over a long period of time, so if they have incremental capacity, we'll get it." It can have a positive effect on performance, and at the minimum, generates goodwill. "We have done over 100 of these calls; not all are as successful. When we rate them, three quarters of the participants find them meaningful." Moelchert concludes, "Private equity is a big deal. It highly differentiates what we do on the hedge fund side."

Positioning for the Hedge Fund Future

Moelchert shares his thoughts on the outlook for hedge funds. "While hedge funds provided disappointing performance relative to expectations last year, on an actual basis they did better than most investments you could have chosen." If investors analyze the market through "the rear view mirror," they may miss opportunities. "With less money in the marketplace, there is a tremendous opportunity for hedge funds to be more successful in the future than they have been in the past."

Since Private Advisors avoided the major problems of the 2008 financial crisis, Moelchert thinks the firm is well positioned for the opportunities ahead. Investors may not see it, but because of his tendency to be early and his long-term perspective, he believes hedge funds have the wind at their back.

Evolving from Endowment CIO to Owner

Moelchert does not just believe in being early, he lives being early. He joined the University of Richmond just as endowments began the process of transitioning from investment poorhouses to investment powerhouses.* Many grew their endowments by investing in hedge funds, with Moelchert being among the earliest to do so. He became the first CIO to lead his own independent investment entity, and although he did not act as an outsourced CIO, he foreshadowed an important endowment management trend and inspired the model University of Richmond uses today. He describes his evolution.

"I always had a high entrepreneurial bent. One day late in my career, I woke up. I was getting pitched by all these investment firms, and thought I knew as much or more than many of them did." When he told his overseers at the university he wanted to start his own business, they said, "Great, but we'd like you to continue to be the chief investment officer." Moelchert relinquished his CFO title, moved his office off campus, and started Private Advisors, but remained a salaried university employee in the chief investment officer role.

He voluntarily corrects a common misconception, saying, "Private Advisors never ran, nor does it today, run money for Richmond. I thought there were too many conflicts of interest."

As both pools of capital grew and responsibilities increased, the arrangement became unsustainable. Moelchert knew other endowments had begun hiring chief investment officers with more professional experience and higher compensation. He realized, "To continue to be successful in the future, the University of Richmond would have to change the way it thought about compensation of the CIO." Moelchert convinced the university to set up an independent endowment investment management company similar to those at Harvard and Stanford. He thought the new entity, Spider Management Company, "would help insulate the investment office" from university compensation practices. They "hired a highly competent, successful senior investment professional, and that's worked well."

---

*Described in Chapter 1 of Kochard, L.E., Rittereiser, C.M., 2008, *Foundation and Endowment Investing: Philosophies and Strategies of Top Institutions and Investors*, Hoboken, NJ, John Wiley & Sons.

Even though his own career moves presaged the increasingly popular outsourced CIO business model, he says he has "been shocked at how much of that has happened and how successful it has been." Some university investment companies will manage money for outside institutions, but most outsourced CIO firms are independently owned and operated. Spider Management is one of the few hybrid models, owned by the university and the employees. Moelchert states it "has raised $700 million from outside institutions."

Regarding commercialized endowment investment companies like Spider Management, he says, "There are a number of institutions with terrific investment committees. It can work, if they devote time and effort to make it successful." However, "on average most investment committees don't function well," leading to the "success of the outsourced CIO model."

The outsourced CIO model, Moelchert says, "probably makes sense for those that don't have the right combination of a great consultant, good internal professional, and good committee." If they do not have at least two of those pieces, they should consider outsourcing. Whatever model they employ, because endowments generally lack resources, he recommends they strive to create a sense of ownership among their investment staff.

Perhaps Moelchert missed a larger opportunity, but unasked, he simply says, "I have ended up okay."

The ownership mind-set resonates strongly for him. He says managers should "get people to think like owners." At Private Advisors more than 20 employees have equity in the firm. "It attracts the right people; you want them to feel [that] they have ownership." A firm needs more than owners; it needs experienced leaders. "As you grow, the less experienced people do more of the work," but importantly, at Private Advisors, "most decisions get made by the most senior people."

NOT TIRED OF PRODUCING EXCELLENCE

A search for Moelchert on the Internet returns a link to the autobiography of his University of Richmond mentor, E. Bruce Heilman. Just scanning *An Interruption That Lasted a Lifetime: My First Eighty Years* (AuthorHouse, 2008), quickly reveals why Moelchert respects and emulates Heilman. An energetic, entrepreneurial university executive, he recognized early the strategic imperative of a strong capital base. Heilman describes receiving a $50 million endowment gift—the same pool of capital Moelchert would manage when he joined the university—from pharmaceutical executive E. Claiborne Robins, along with tacit permission to offer higher salaries to attract talented people.

Heilman says, "It made a lot of difference in the quality of the people we were able to employ and in turn, those people made a great difference in our success." Naming Moelchert as a member, he pays tribute to a select group of these employees. "They were believers in the cause and committed to success."

Describing his management philosophy Heilman says, "I always kept in mind the admonition, 'First-rate people employ first-rate people, while second-rate people employ third-rate people.'" Although the two men share philosophies, ideas, and wording, Heilman clearly admires and respects Moelchert.

Taking a quote Moelchert said of him, "He demands excellence of himself first and secondly from those who are around him," Heilman adds, "One can demand excellence only from those who produce it."

In a 2009 speech to the Eastern Association of College and University Business Officers, Heilman quotes Kipling. Describing the importance of being able to "wait and not be tired of waiting," he makes the point, "The outcome desired often presents itself if we don't rush to force closure before its time."

After many years as a leading endowment chief investment officer, prescient hedge fund investor, and successful alternative investments entrepreneur, Moelchert could easily "force closure" on his accomplished career. But as much as he likes being early, such a move would be "before its time." Having identified the hedge fund opportunity early once before, he waits patiently for it to come again.

Like Louis W. Moelchert, Jr., investors who take a long-term view, identify opportunities early, and remain patient will produce excellence.

CHAPTER 9

An Ambassador of the Highest Standard

Christopher Fawcett, Co-Founder, Senior Partner, Fauchier Partners

C hristopher Fawcett brings more than a European perspective and a "classic formation and background" in business to achieve recognition as a leading hedge fund investor.

Co-founder in 1994 of Fauchier Partners, a fund of hedge funds favored by prestigious British institutions, Fawcett offers expert advice stemming from years of investment experience. He also represents the viewpoint of a true industry leader, earning that reputation from his years of commitment and service in two influential industry organizations.

Fawcett was chairman of the Alternative Investment Management Association (AIMA) from 2002 to 2008 and continues to sit on the AIMA Council as a director of the association. He is also a trustee of the Hedge Fund Standards Board Limited (HFSB).

Prior to Fauchier Partners, Fawcett worked for Euris SA, a French investment holding company, and for the Duménil Group. He gained securities industry experience with Morgan Grenfell, Industrial Technology Securities, a venture capital company he also co-founded.

Fawcett has an MA in law from Oxford University, an MBA with distinction from INSEAD, and is a qualified Chartered Accountant. He serves as a director of the CFA Society of the United Kingdom and of Mirabaud Gestion SA.

BACKGROUND

Earning degrees in law and business and training in accountancy gave Fawcett a "classic formation and background" for business leadership in the United Kingdom. After his stint with Morgan Grenfell, an investment bank historically associated with the U.S. bank J.P. Morgan, Fawcett joined a French investment holding company, Euris SA. While searching for a better way to invest its surplus cash, he found a promising investment vehicle.

"We were looking for ways to get enhanced return on medium-term cash, one to two years, and were willing to take some risks to get returns above government bonds. Somebody pointed us to hedge funds and they looked attractive."

At the time, the "quite volatile" markets fueled good returns, and legendary hedge fund managers like George Soros and Julian Robertson reigned. Fawcett "looked into" hedge funds and made his first investments in a fund of hedge funds and some single managers in 1992.

"Frankly, we invested based on reputation and past performance. The managers already had household names and smart investors. It seemed a straightforward thing to be doing. We went into funds of funds to get into smaller managers and closed managers and to get diversification."

Through his hedge fund activity, Fawcett met many new people in the investment community. One of them, Patrick Fauchier, approached him with the idea of starting a company to run hedge fund portfolios.

"Right from the start the concept was to add value in two ways, through manager selection and portfolio construction. I immediately sensed there was a gap in the market, primarily in Europe, because other people had other activities that could be distractions or conflicts. We decided on a straightforward format, simply investing on behalf of clients using a portfolio approach."

Fawcett formed his investment philosophy then, and it remains much the same today. "Personally, it struck me as being obvious at the time and still does. Some people are more talented investors than others and some work harder than others. If you get a combination of the two, then you have the potential for excellent performance."

Those talented and hard-working managers are also "scattered across the globe" in different locations and specialties. But it is not enough to find the managers. "If one is trying to identify people with above-average analytical skills, focus, and ability to work hard, you don't want them to be in a constrained structure." These managers should not be investing through "a long-only fund that seeks just to beat the benchmark, in practice, that is putting constraints on them. If you want access to top talent you want it unconstrained."

Furthermore, Fawcett says, "You also want them to eat their own cooking, to be co-investors." At the same time, while talented managers should have few constraints, they must also have the tools to manage risk. He believes this construct is essentially the classic hedge fund model.

"Personally, as an individual I saw it as just common sense. This was at the time when most assets globally were actively managed against a benchmark. I really think it's a bad format." Both inexpensive index tracking funds from Vanguard and hedge funds were in their early days. "Over the years they have grown very fast. With good reason, it strikes me."

Patrick Fauchier had a similar view based on his experience as a private investor. To make his point, he would repeat a typical conversation with private bankers, "You're down 15 and the market is down 18. You've done quite well." Explains Fawcett, "That goes down very badly with private individuals."

The concept of absolute return seemed "very obvious" to both men and they started their firm, Fauchier Partners, in 1994. The business grew slowly—it was "tough early on"—particularly with its base in the United Kingdom. "At the time there was a very minimal appetite for hedge funds. For institutions it was close to zero." Individuals received unfavorable tax treatment and neither partner had a "huge contact base." They began to grow with the addition of some family office clients.

Fawcett admits the firm had "decent performance, but not enough outperformance to get business purely because of it. We were risk averse and those were boom years. Our numbers probably looked a bit dull compared to others."

However, the firm grew large enough to hire analysts and then had "a couple of important breaks." Oxford University and some of its affiliated colleges became clients "in a very visible manner." Fauchier Partners created a special vehicle for the investment called the Oxford Fauchier Partnership and received "good attention" in the process.

The firm also formed a joint venture with BNP Paribas that "very much raised the profile and changed the nature of the business. We were able to bring on more people and improve our systems and improve the way we work."

Occurring in 2001, the two advances marked a turning point for the business, as "simultaneously money started flowing into hedge funds." Fawcett says, "Fortunately, we were getting ourselves structured as an institutional business at a time when institutions had more of an appetite for hedge funds."

Fauchier Partners capitalized on the circumstances, not by cashing in, but by reinvesting in the business. "We changed the business internally by bringing in some key individuals." Dan Higgins joined from Mercury Asset

Management, bringing "more recent experience of the equity markets." Clark Fenton came from the prime brokerage unit of Morgan Stanley, adding expertise in "vetting hedge funds as counterparties." They also hired David Woodhouse, an experienced accountant and auditor, to run due diligence.

Adding such talented personnel was "key to take the business to the next stage," in order to improve their investment process and relationship with investors. Institutions were asking more questions and "we wanted to know more about what the underlying hedge funds were doing."

Fawcett had become involved in the AIMA in 1998 and eventually served as its chairman. The experience influenced the decision to build a multifaceted, institutional-quality team. "AIMA had written a guide to sound practices and a standard due diligence questionnaire. I sensed personally how the industry was trending partly due to my involvement."

INVESTMENT PROCESS

The Fauchier Partners investment process begins with identifying exceptionally talented and motivated managers with good risk management skills and proper incentives. After selecting managers, they construct disciplined, concentrated portfolios and monitor risks using an in-house system. Fawcett describes the process, starting with manager selection.

Manager Selection

"We have always have been very focused on manager co-investment. This may be because we go back 15 years ago or more, when Steinhardt and Soros were large co-investors in their funds. We like the feeling that we are co-investing with a manager. Where the manager is not invested, it's not a hedge fund, but a product with a lot of fees."

This "extremely important" prerequisite "has a tendency to get overlooked." Fawcett believes that has happened because investors have gotten "mesmerized by techniques." The manager need not invest all his net worth, but Fawcett does expect the manager "to the extent he's able, to be a material investor in the fund. We want to avoid being invested in a product."

Asked if the requirement extends to other members of a fund's investment team, he says, "That's an interesting point. I would rather see a situation with not just one individual or not just the portfolio manager being invested." They prefer to see additional employees invested in their firm's fund and require the same of their employees.

"We eat our own cooking and invest in our own funds. Bonuses are partly deferred and are de facto invested in our fund of hedge funds. We felt it unreasonable to beat on managers on their co-investment, and thought that if people asked, we want to be able to answer it positively. Otherwise it's a bit hypocritical."

Fund Size Fauchier Partners considers the size of a fund's assets under management but does not adhere to specific size limitations or rules. It wants "managers running an amount of assets to be stable, with enough to cover overhead and have a team." However, the manager should not be "so big that he's not going to be likely to benefit from opportunities in his strategies. We don't think there's a predetermined ideal size."

Numerous industry observers, including subjects of this book, expect large hedge funds to get even larger as a result of the events of 2008. Fawcett has a nuanced take on the reasons it will occur and the types of large funds that will benefit.

"One of the observations of last year is that larger firms did not outperform. They may have underperformed, because it was so difficult, they couldn't get out of the way." As a result, Fauchier Partners "discovered an illusion" about investing in large funds. Investors thought, "If you were smallish in a big fund, you could get money back. Say I have $50 million in a $10 billion fund. No way did I think I would get caught."

Bigger funds were perceived to be more liquid, but "they were just as illiquid. Last year it was the quality of your co-investor." In other words, the ability for an investor to have liquidity in a large fund had more to do with how many others wanted liquidity at the same time. The benefit of "being small in a big fund was an illusion."

The financial crisis means, "A lot of funds are out of the game. They drew down too much, or gated, or had horrible performance." So not all large funds will get larger. "Those large funds that were okay last year are attracting a lot of money. They were okay and they feel big and safe."

The hypothetical example of a 10-year-old fund with $8 billion in assets that had flat performance is exactly the type of hedge fund he believes is growing. "Those managers are taking money in from funds of funds and those institutions that want to go direct." Particular beneficiaries include "large managers that were hard closed for many years and reopened because they had redemptions."

Maintaining Standards Given the estimated 8,000 hedge funds active in 2009, Fawcett and his colleagues find it challenging to select managers who meet their standards. He describes how their approach has had to evolve over the years.

"Going back to the way I initially looked at things in the early to mid-1990s, there were relatively few hedge funds. The average quality was much higher." The managers had a harder job raising assets and there were very few institutional investors. "The biggest funds were really big; some were huge." Fewer, better quality managers meant, "The manager selection process was easier."

Fawcett elaborates. "Less information paradoxically means it's easier to select. There is not much to work with." The other side of the paradox is that the proliferation of funds and availability of information makes it harder to choose. "More information, a deeper understanding of strategies; it's an embarrassment of riches; no, an embarrassment of choice and information."

To choose managers successfully, he says the investment team has increasingly focused on and improved at "identifying managers who have an enduring competitive edge, within their strategy and relative to the environment. Especially with newer managers, we have to believe they will keep their edge. For example, with long/short equity, the manager must have a better quality of research or a better feel of the market."

Portfolio Management Models Funds historically tended to be led by a gifted portfolio manager, like a Julian Robertson at Tiger Management. His former analysts have so famously learned from him and then started their own firms that they are collectively called "Tiger Cubs." Other firms will collectively make decisions as part of a team. Fawcett discusses his view of those models.

"One is not the right or the wrong model. As firms grow, they may farm money out to the analysts. You often get a portfolio with hundreds of positions, too many positions. It's sometimes done to retain analysts. This sounds pejorative, but they give them a 'bit of capital to play with.'"

That approach can work, particularly if the lead portfolio manager finds some outstanding ideas and makes them a larger position in the portfolio. It "seems to get into trouble when markets are difficult, because it is not as tight."

In the other model, the portfolio manager asks analysts for ideas, filters out the best, and uses them in the portfolio. Fawcett describes a third model where the manager focuses the analysts on certain sectors and he picks their best ideas. The difference between the second model and the third is that "idea generation is driven by the manager." He is "not judgmental, but we want to know which it is."

Strategy Biases Fauchier Partners' portfolios always have had a substantial allocation to equity long/short. "It remains liquid, with no pricing issues and little leverage. You can get your head round where performance is coming from and why a team is better than others."

The strategy struggles in extreme market conditions, like those in 2008. At other times equity long/short can do well or hold up, such as in 2002 when many managers profited from shorting technology stocks.

"By and large if one is looking for steady positive returns, a portfolio of pure long/short managers in a number of cases won't do it." Fauchier Partners counterbalances the portfolio by choosing funds that trade volatility, with a short bias and negative correlations. Global macro managers, for instance, "tend to be agnostic to long/short market risk."

He likes credit funds, specifically long/short credit. "Not leveraged, that doesn't deserve a performance fee. Managers that pick individual securities." In essence he favors the long/short equity approach applied to credit.

They avoid investing in quantitative strategies, having often found that the managers lack the communications skills needed to explain the already opaque proprietary models. "I'm not saying there's anything wrong with them. I'm not sure we can add value in selection."

Mortgage-backed securities arbitrage "has a nasty habit of going badly wrong every few years." They avoid it and other funds where securities are "marked to model" rather than marked to the market price.

Fawcett and the firm are "leverage averse." He says, "The returns from using leverage are not necessarily high quality."

Multistrategy Funds   Regarding multistrategy funds, Fawcett says, "On paper they look and sound great. The manager should be able to deploy capital rapidly. There is one top-level performance fee; winners offset losers. If managed separately, the performance fee on one would not be offset by the other."

Fawcett indicates the days when industry participants considered multistrategy funds a substitute for funds of hedge funds have passed. While Fauchier Partners has invested in them, he says "only a very few have met our criteria." He thinks multistrategy funds can and do have trouble retaining talent, because determining individual compensation is difficult.

In his experience, multistrategy funds may have one or two good managers, but he generally finds them to have "Jack-of-all-trades, master-of-none syndrome."

When they have met with heads of substrategy teams in multistrategy funds, say the manager of a convertible arb piece, he finds those managers "don't compare with a pure play in the same strategy in an independent fund."

In theory "a multistrategy fund should be able to come in and capitalize very quickly on opportunities. Very few succeed at doing that."

Multigenerational Firms   Some investors theorize that multistrategy funds have the best chance to create a culture and build a firm that will have longevity beyond the life and tenure of the founder.

"Fascinating topic," Fawcett replies. "It's a personalized business, a small group of people with exceptional talent and work ability, and large investors that also work hard. It is very difficult to pass on to the next generation. I hope it happens, but if we had a situation with a manager retiring, we would put the fund on alert."

He agrees that a multistrategy firm has more potential than others to create a multigenerational firm. Firms with "several hundred people may have developed a culture and are not overly dependent in one person. The chances of Och Ziff not being totally reliant on one individual, I think are greater than a small fund."

Global Macro Funds   Investors with portfolios dominated by equity hedge fund strategies may have the desire to diversify into global macro strategies, but often lack the skills and confidence to pick one. How does Fauchier Partners choose?

"Global macro is one of the most difficult strategies in which to source managers, where it is most important that there is a long track record." Otherwise, the investor could choose a manager who has what Fawcett calls "a coin-flipping syndrome." In that scenario, the manager happens to "flip the coin on the right side umpteen months in succession."

Few managers are right all the time, but a good macro manager tends to be right more often than not. Investors should ask themselves, "Is the trade expression good? Are they good at stop losses? Do they use options well? What is their edge?" More so than in other strategies, investors need to consider trading skill, because a macro manager can perform not just from having the correct views, but also from having the ability to trade.

Fawcett adds, "It's very difficult to tell when they're going to perform well and the quantum of their performance. No idea when it will happen." Therefore investors need to choose global macro managers who "can run risk properly and are capable of delivering strong, uncorrelated returns."

Cultural Divide   Fawcett stresses the importance of choosing hedge fund firms with a strong culture, saying, "There has got to be clear leadership." The definition of a strong culture may shift depending on location. He says, "There are interesting nuances between U.S. and London managers. In London most of the best, successful hedge funds are run by a couple of people, a duo."

The Financial Services Authority (FSA), the U.K. version of the SEC, may have influenced the dynamic, because it requires an investment management firm to have more than one person at the top. Fawcett says that U.K. hedge funds tend to be founded by two equal partners, "one on the portfolio and the other on the business," and such a management structure has "cultural implications." There are also fewer hedge funds in the United Kingdom, most likely as a result of the FSA requirements.

In the United States, the two-person structure occurs "much less. It is usually a dominant figure." Fawcett explains, "Even in small teams there is a culture," and investors need to understand and evaluate it. In a single-leader structure, "It's very important how compensation works. Is it partly formulaic? We don't think there is a right or wrong approach, but we need to understand what it is."

Similarly, Fawcett does not prefer one overall cultural style, but elaborates on the differences to help investors decide for themselves. Referring to his comments as a "generalization," he says, "European managers tend to be more investor friendly. This probably comes from their long-only and mutual fund background. They are used to reporting with a client focus. FSA rules permeate the approach. European hedge funds tend to be set up with more of a view to the investor reporting, access, and the sort."

Fawcett recommends that investors "look very carefully before they give the money." However, he asserts, "That is not a comment on hedge funds' ability." Investors just "have to do their homework relatively carefully. Check documents and expenses going through the fund." He finds the latter action "more prevalent in our experience" in the United States and suggests that fewer registration requirements may foster a less investor-friendly culture.

Different geographical locations account for very little difference in investment styles. With its headquarters in London, the city is a "natural place" for Fauchier Partners to source managers, but Fawcett says it "is not the only place.". They allocate mostly to U.S.-based managers and have found a number of managers to choose from in Asia.

Investing in New Hedge Funds Fauchier Partners learned from experience that they could permanently miss good investment opportunities if rigid standards forbade any investment in early-stage hedge fund managers. In order to avoid passing on good investments while protecting their underlying investors, they created a unique in-house early-stage fund. Fawcett explains how their philosophy and approach to new managers evolved.

When the firm started in 1994, it required funds to have a three-year track record before it would invest. "By 2000, the best were closed by the three-year mark. One didn't have the luxury of track record." In 2001 they created the Fauchier Partners Incubator Fund to allocate to new managers. Every client of the firm has it in their portfolio.

Fawcett describes it as "a little fund of hedge funds with no fees. Through that structure we will invest early in the life of a fund. One or two times we have invested at launch, but that is unusual."

Their approach benefits all parties. "Clearly it changes the relationship with the manager, the day we arrive with $5 to $10 million." It means they can scale into the positions. "We get to know them very well and the risk is spread very broadly for the benefit of all of our clients."

Fauchier will not "go in with a big ticket. In our experience, even managers with the most impressive track record in their previous incarnation have struggled."

Fawcett offers a number of examples of the types of new managers and specific adjustment problems. Proprietary traders usually have never dealt with clients or administrative burdens. Long-only managers "may be good stock pickers, but they have to learn to short and use derivatives." Managers coming from other hedge funds "may not have been the trigger puller." Although they "appreciate a manager's need to raise money early, there's a bit of learning to be done. We are extremely unlikely to go in early with a big ticket."

Fawcett favors long-only managers that take an extra step when transitioning to their own hedge funds. "In some instances a long-only manager joins a hedge fund group. With other people there with experience, he can learn fast." Hedge fund portfolio managers will say, "When a short goes wrong, it gets bigger and bigger in your portfolio; a long gets smaller and smaller." To Fawcett, "that is exactly the sort of the thing you would want to see the manager getting to know and understand" before going on his own.

Regarding seeding hedge funds in return for a stake in the business, he says, "Economic interest in the manager can no doubt be a good business, but it's something we don't do. We don't want clients invested in the fund and us having an economic interest in the manager." The Fauchier Partners business model prohibits such a scenario, because it could create a conflict of interest.

Quantitative Analysis   Much of the manager selection discussion focuses on qualitative analysis and decisions, but as the firm has evolved, the investment team has employed more quantitative tools.

"As a firm we have made a lot of progress in the last three years and have gotten more sophisticated." Under the leadership of Praveen Kanakamedala, the head of risk management, Fauchier has developed its own system, incorporating historical data and transparency from funds. "We are matching fund information with quantitative analysis and looking at discrepancies to see if there are problems."

Fawcett calls the system "a tool for talking to managers, a basis of discussion" and finds it useful when evaluating new managers. If a manager says, "I always hedge credit risk," and the in-house report shows sensitivity to credit, "then something's wrong somewhere."

The investment team uses the system to help construct portfolios, monitor managers, and understand performance. "We will look at exceptional outperformance and underperformance." The analyst team has most of the responsibility for the quantitative reporting, but the results have impact at a senior level. "Both the head of due diligence and the head of risk have a veto on the investment team."

Portfolio Management

In the portfolio construction phase of the investment process, the investment team first seeks strategies "that are risk reducers or uncorrelated." They then try to determine why the manager demonstrates those characteristics and why he will be able to do so in the future.

Fawcett says his firm also "looks for managers that because of the way they think, and the way they position the portfolio, make them good diversifiers." He offers a "straightforward" example. "An equity long/short manager with a low net, who tends to be early in shorting certain sectors and in getting out of crowded shorts, can be very uncorrelated."

They look at the portfolio as a whole and do not benchmark managers against an index like HFR. The managers in their portfolio "may be running a low net versus managers in the index with more long exposure. That may be great in an up market," but it does not relate to the fund's role in the Fauchier portfolio.

He offers a more specific example, "We may have a manager that's a good diversifier, a convertible arbitrage that hedges credit risk. If there is a boom in credit, he may underperform."

Other hedge fund investors in that scenario might redeem if the manager underperforms. Because they consider a fund's role in the portfolio, he says, "It's very difficult to disaggregate the portfolio and say, 'this is the manager and that's the allocation.'"

Their portfolios contain approximately 30 managers, with "some more aggressive portfolios" having 20 managers. The right number of managers "is an art as much as it is a science," but portfolios with a larger number of managers "show a lack of conviction. May as well buy an index. Twenty to thirty core holdings is a good number."

Monitoring Managers and Risk   Fawcett defines risk as "a permanent loss of capital," adding, "It's one reason we're leverage averse. If a manager gets pushed out by the prime broker at a bad point, it is very difficult to come back. It is a level of drawdown that is too difficult to recover," and much worse than underperforming a benchmark.

"Crowded trade risk is very real in hedge funds." Fawcett cites a well-known example, "Everyone is short Volkswagen." Such trades represent a large, hidden, and worrisome risk to hedge fund investors. "Broker-driven trades end up in a lot of different hedge funds. You suddenly find you have an exposure you didn't think you had."

Fawcett expects that an improving amount and use of transparency will help reduce that risk. By aggregating position information in reports, investors will identify such instances early.

Some hedge fund investors have begun implementing their own hedging techniques, such as overlays, if they identify unwanted exposure to a specific manager or strategy. Fauchier chooses not to hedge portfolios independently. "The problem is getting too much involved in active management. Who are we to make that decision? How would we know that the manager didn't do something different yesterday?"

Fawcett says they would "rather start with a portfolio where the risk of any one particular manager is low." If the portfolio includes "truly different managers, doing different things" and they still find too much exposure to certain risks, they would trim it through partial redemption.

While concerned about crowded trades, he also finds, "In our experience if a group of very good managers is doing the same thing, they're usually right." The short subprime trade, "the greatest ever, especially when you look at risk vs. return," offers a good example. However, when it began to grow too large in their portfolio, they trimmed it.

Summarizing their viewpoint he says, "We feel the managers should be managing risk themselves. We are monitoring risk, being aware of it, not allowing it to become excessive, and reacting accordingly. We draw the line at reducing; we do it through the managers."

Terminating Managers   "The single most obvious" reason Fawcett says they would terminate a manager is "if we have evidence the manager has been untruthful." The manager would face "almost instant dismissal." A manager who said or did something he "manifestly knew to be wrong" would very likely be subject to immediate redemption. "Let's call a spade a spade. The fact is he's lying to us. The odds of us staying are nil," because the behavior "says something" about the manager's integrity.

The firm may terminate a fund if it had selected the manager for a reason that no longer holds true. Examples include: "Managing far more assets than he said he would; the loss of key analysts; or we feel he's lost his edge."

At times it may just want to reduce exposure to a strategy. Terminating in those circumstances has "nothing to do with a manager and is not a negative comment on the fund." Occasionally it replaces a manager when it finds another "better at doing the same sort of thing."

Some hedge fund investors might find a better manager, and instead of replacing the previous manager would just add the new one to the portfolio. Fawcett prefers "the discipline of having a tight portfolio. There is a temptation to just add managers," but he believes "there's got to be competition for capital."

Terms and Conditions

The terms and conditions in limited partnership agreements have historically favored the hedge fund manager. Investors considered them the cost of doing business. As institutions increasingly invested in hedge funds, they began to question the conditions or sought changes. Mark Anson, profiled in Chapter 7, provides an excellent example. The perceived self-serving actions of hedge funds during the financial crisis of 2008 raised more questions and heightened demand for change. Fawcett offers his thoughts on these issues.

Transparency   "What seems odd to me is having transparency on a regular basis, but then not necessarily being able to get out on short notice. But the point of having transparency is to be able to monitor risk across the whole portfolio and understand what a manager is doing in his portfolio, rather than have a sort of invitation to rush for the door."

The Fauchier Partners team has seen transparency improve over the years and has never invested in "anything completely opaque." When he started investing in the early 1990s, Fawcett got much less information than he does today, and he expects continued improvement in the availability of data.

Although he has seen continued improvement in transparency, Fawcett says, "What's gone in the opposite direction is the notice periods. Lock-ups have gotten longer. I think that is a result of institutional investors coming in to hedge funds. They can live with longer notice periods and live with funds of funds with longer notice periods."

Liquidity and Lock-Ups   The Fauchier team believes, "The liquidity offered by the manager should be commensurate with the liquidity in the portfolio; i.e., we don't feel a plain vanilla, long/short equity manager should have a two-year lock-up. We can understand why an activist investor has long lock-ups."

The lock-up period they can accept has more to do with the liquidity of the type of strategy rather than the liquidity of the securities in the underlying portfolio. An event-driven manager may have positions in liquid equities, but they would not expect the fund to offer easy terms if the manager needs to hold the position long enough for the event to happen.

Fawcett encapsulates their stance as "looking at the co-investor risk relative to the liquidity of the portfolio." Investors need not have rigid rules for each strategy; they just need to make sure they question, understand, and accept the reasons given for having a certain lock-up period.

"If the manager has much longer liquidity than the strategy requires, why? Is it for business reasons? To some extent, a not-too-long lock-up is a form of discipline."

But, Fawcett points out, "Having a too short lock-up doesn't help." Investors could then have a manager with the "Sword of Damocles," living in fear that "one down month and the money will go out the door." A lock-up that factors in the objectives of the strategy, the liquidity of the underlying securities, other investors in the fund, and that falls in the middle of two extremes, is appropriate.

Fee Structure   Fee negotiations have become more commonplace, "case by case," in particular, with "portfolios that got in trouble in 2008 and managers with newer funds."

Fawcett believes hedge fund manager fees "should have a hurdle rate of LIBOR [London Interbank Offered Rate], but very few do." When he started investing in hedge funds in the early 1990s, fees were "1 and 15, 1 and 20, then became 2 and 20." He advocates a hurdle, because he finds it "odd" that a hedge fund manager can earn 5 percent on short interest and then be paid a performance fee of 20 percent, when the investor could get 5 percent of his return from putting the money in the bank.

Larger, established managers will continue to collect full fees, but he expects newer managers will increasingly have to make some fee concessions. He finds it somewhat surprising that "there doesn't seem to be as much of a discount as in other parts of the industry." Long-only managers offer extensive discounts to institutional investors, but in hedge funds discounted fees are still relatively high. They do not even offer tiered rates, or breaks on certain levels of assets.

Managed Accounts   Fawcett sees irony in the fact that "managed accounts are becoming popular precisely when transparency has improved."

The Fauchier team dislikes the idea of a manager having a few easily liquidated managed accounts while the rest of the investors in the main fund have much longer terms. "It's wrong for clients with the best transparency to have better liquidity. If all have the same liquidity terms, that's different."

Fawcett says, "It's unusual for high-quality managers to offer managed accounts." The firm has not historically used them, and while he "wouldn't say we'd never use them," they have no plans to do so. In his view, "We're going through a phase because of Madoff. They're fashionable."

For some investors, certain European regulations may justify managed accounts. However, "If you want a portfolio of the very best hedge fund managers in the world, a portfolio of managed accounts isn't going to get you there."

According to Fawcett, the performance of two HFR indexes supports his assertion. The investible index with managed accounts is consistently outperformed by the index that compiles information from all the major managers.

HEDGE FUND INDUSTRY OUTLOOK

Fawcett is a trustee of the Hedge Fund Standards Board, which has developed "comprehensive and demanding standards that hedge fund managers agree to adhere to when they sign up." His industry leadership, hedge fund investing experience, and European background give Fawcett a unique perspective on the direction of the hedge fund industry.

Regulatory Perspective

Fawcett's regulatory knowledge stems from more than 10 years of involvement with the AIMA, including 6 years as chairman and now as a member of the board. The AIMA serves the gamut of industry constituencies, including hedge funds, funds of funds, and service providers, and has been "successful in developing good relationships with regulators," including organizing a large annual regulatory forum.

The differences between the U.S. and U.K. regulatory systems have an effect on more than the business cultures of hedge funds. The FSA regulates the industry in the United Kingdom to such an extent that an asset manager "cannot manage any money without FSA regulations. The FSA approves key individuals, applying a 'fit and proper' test. Effectively, they won't allow a one-man band."

Fawcett thinks the United Kingdom is the only country that monitors the portfolios of the largest hedge funds, but not in an onerous way. "The FSA has drawn up a list of funds that are sufficiently large that they want to know what they're up to and to check for systemic risk. The individuals

managing those funds have an FSA relationship officer, much like an investment bank."

The FSA collects hedge fund positions data and monitors the prime
brokers to calculate aggregate hedge fund leverage and risk reports. Fawcett
judges it an "excellent system," explaining, "I'm not a lobbyist for the U.K.
regulatory system, but it has worked. As far as I have been aware, there have
been no troubles with U.K. funds. The FSA has a good grasp."

Directives   Fawcett cannot say the same for other countries or would-be
regulators. As one of the leaders of the AIMA, he became actively engaged
in contending a draft directive from the European Union entitled, *Proposal
for a Directive of the European Parliament and the Council on Alternative
Investment Fund Managers.*

"It is extremely bad for the European hedge fund business. It would
put a cap on leverage; require an EU custodian and administrator, and
oversight by an EU regulatory body. Managers couldn't market a Cayman
Fund."

The AIMA was actively involved in commenting on the directive and
pushing for revisions. Describing the EU proposal as "opposite from the
U.S.," Fawcett says, "My own guess is we'll end up somewhere between
these two extremes. All hedge funds will have to be registered somewhere
and the key risks in the largest hedge funds will be monitored."

Having observed a number of U.S.-based hedge funds collapse during
the financial crisis, capped by the revelation of the Madoff fraud, Fawcett
politely expresses perplexity at the lack of regulatory action.

"If a very big hedge fund had gone bust, there could have been nasty
consequences. I would have thought regulators going forward would want
to know what hedge funds are doing. I would have thought they would
want to monitor leverage." He clearly hopes, and says he thinks, that "it
will happen on a more systematic basis."

Lessons of the Financial Crisis

Fawcett comments on the Madoff fraud in general from the perspective of
a hedge fund investor.

"It is fruitless to say one can never get caught out." When there is a
fraud, the documents are usually fraudulent as well, so investors cannot rely
on documents to prevent it. "I can't say we would never get caught in one,
but we do everything we can to avoid it. We look at their service providers,
agreements, and do background checks." He suggests that investors scruti-
nize audit firms in particular, because a common characteristic of a number
of prominent frauds was a small, unrecognized, or phony audit firm.

Liquidity Matters "The single biggest lesson" the Fauchier team learned in 2008 is that "the liquidity of the underlying portfolio matters more than the liquidity terms. If the manager gives you great terms, but he can't get out of his positions to let you out of the fund, then it's an illusion." Fauchier Partners has always had a large allocation to long/short equity, where the underlying securities have been highly liquid, but nonetheless now they are "monitoring underlying liquidity in all strategies more carefully than in the past."

Currency Matters Fawcett and his colleagues have learned that currency hedging can have an important influence on hedge fund investing. The impact of currency hedging "is underappreciated in the U.S. as a reason for redemptions."

He gives an example of how the scenario unfolds. Hedge funds tend to be denominated in U.S. dollars, but U.K investors allocate capital denominated in pounds sterling, so a fund of hedge funds manager must hedge the currency risk. If the dollar rises 25 percent in two months, the manager has to find 25 percent liquidity to meet banking requirements, so he will redeem 25 percent of the portfolio. Fawcett explains that the fund of funds manager has to remain aware of potential moves in the currency and that means, "It's more complicated to run a hedge portfolio against foreign currency. Most U.S.-based funds of funds probably did not have much of a problem."

Some U.S. investors had blamed European funds of hedge funds as the major perpetrator of redemptions, but seemed unaware of the currency hedging issue. Fawcett concurs, saying, "It's a big unknown number. We redeemed far more because of currency hedging reasons in 2008 than because of client redemptions."

Fawcett "mentioned this to hedge fund managers for many years, but the dollar went through a long, long weakening." He would explain that investments were being made with depreciating dollars and told one manager that "subscriptions are partly coming from gains on currency hedging," but got no more reaction than, "Oh, that's interesting." The dollar depreciation took five years, but it "reversed and went at once" in a matter of weeks in 2008.

Co-Investors Matter The investment team focuses more on co-investors now, not just because they may run for the exit door quickly, but also because they have more vehicles to give them an entry in the first place. The team reached this conclusion when they learned the amount of structured and leveraged hedge fund products, "whiz-bang stuff structured by investment banks," available in the market. With the industry growing in so many different directions, "co-investor risk, getting to who the co-investor is, who you're in bed with," is more important.

In the future, the profile of the ideal co-investor may shift. The conventional wisdom had been that pension managers were more likely to redeem than endowments and foundations, but the opposite proved true in 2008. Fawcett says, "Most family offices were fairly stable, because they have their own views. Private bankers felt very concerned about their clients. There was a lot of redeeming by private bankers." Therefore, the Madoff fraud, which mostly victimized high net worth investors, "came at the worst possible time."

Portfolio Matters   The Fauchier Partners investment team reevaluated and changed the portfolio composition after the crisis. Taking "a slightly different approach," they reduced their exposure to global macro managers, thinking it would not "necessarily be as big. The big move in interest rates was likely to have happened and we weren't going to go to zero." Instead, they planned to allocate more to "security selectors," continuing with long/short equity and "adding credit incrementally."

Distressed debt appeals to them, but not "a legacy portfolio." Fawcett explains, "The distressed cycle will be more difficult and more protracted than people thought. It will be more difficult because of much more intervention." Banks will not be the only interveners, especially in labor-intense industries. As banks go in and out of deals, new questions will arise. "What point will the government come in? What level of the capital structure?"

While they remain open to adding arbitrage strategies to the portfolio, Fawcett has some reservations. "Arbitrage strategies tend to be good at once or bad at once." He recommends investors "pick the strategy, then the managers," and make fewer allocations to those strategies.

Lessons from Colleagues

Asked to cite important mentors and lessons learned along the way, Fawcett replies, "This may sound quite extraordinary, but I have learned most about investing in hedge funds from some of the people we've recruited here." His colleagues might not be mentors in the traditional sense, that is his "own perception," but he believes, "the biggest single contributing external factor is my colleagues. Their different backgrounds, and experiences I didn't have, help me understand better what hedge funds do and don't do."

Saying, "I'm not doing advertising," he pays tribute to his founding partner. "Patrick Fauchier is good at getting a feeling for the personality and character of the manager. I learned a lot about that from him." Fawcett particularly admires Fauchier's judgment even when asking the most basic investment question, "Do I trust this person with my money?"

Having partners and colleagues with complementary skills and experiences may have made him a better hedge fund investor, but it raises another question. Can a single person working alone be an effective hedge fund investor today?

"One of the things about having more transparency," Fawcett says, is that "being a hedge fund analyst is a much more interesting job now because there's more to work on, more funds, and more information." Thinking further, he concludes, "More strategies, more complexity, more information, and more to work on, no one individual could do that."

LESSONS FROM A LEADER

Fawcett stepped down as chair of the AIMA in December 2008. In a press release announcing the transition to new leadership, published on the organization's web site December 10, 2008, Fawcett makes an impassioned case for the hedge fund industry.

"The hedge fund industry has found itself the scapegoat for many aspects of the market crisis. These opinions are often not fully informed. By making this commitment to secure and direct these most senior resources to engage with governments, regulators, investors, the media and the public, AIMA and its members are stating clearly their assertion that hedge funds are significant and responsible market participants within the financial system, that their benefits are numerous, positive and meaningful, and that they stand ready to participate in the revision and improvement of the world's market regulation in a material and sophisticated manner."

Several months later, he offers a more personal perspective. "I'm an optimist on the industry. I was never as pessimistic as the market in the fall of 2008. I stuck my neck out with journalists and said there would be inflows in 2009. I thought I needed to see a shrink; it sounded outlandish. By first quarter, it sounded plausible, it happened in the second quarter."

Fawcett concludes, "The industry healed even faster than even I, as an optimist, expected. It proved how resilient it is, because of the quality of the people in it."

His belief in the quality of the people in the hedge fund industry says something intriguing and important about Fawcett. In almost any industry, the people who try to set standards can be perceived as unrealistic perfectionists, self-serving bombasts, or old-fashioned scolds. Yet in his case, his commitment to setting standards clearly stems from his admiration for the people in the industry, his acceptance of their strengths and weaknesses, and his desire for them to reach their highest potential.

Fawcett modestly credits his colleagues—even those younger and less experienced—with mentoring him, but he deserves credit for mentoring the industry. Executive director Florence Lombard, quoted in the AIMA announcement, gives Fawcett proper praise.

"AIMA and its members express their most sincere gratitude to Christopher for the invaluable work he has done on the industry's behalf during his six-year tenure. He has demonstrated great leadership and commitment to our members and has proven to be a great ambassador for the industry."

No other statement could so deftly honor Fawcett for his hedge fund investment expertise and industry leadership. However, by describing his experience and sharing his advice, Christopher Fawcett makes another beneficial contribution to the industry and honors hedge fund investors.

CHAPTER 10

A Risk Management Mastermind

Deepak Gurnani, Head of Hedge Funds, Investcorp

D eepak Gurnani is the head of a $4 billion hedge fund investment business for Investcorp, a New York, London, and Bahrain banking corporation with $12 billion of alternative investment assets under management. Joining Investcorp in 1993 to establish the risk management function, Gurnani played an instrumental role in leading Investcorp into hedge fund investing and developed its hedge fund investment process. By applying his expertise and intellect to researching and solving complex investment problems, he has mastered risk management to build a unique and highly sophisticated hedge fund investment process.

Prior to Investcorp, Gurnani spent six years with Citicorp in various management and information technology consultancy assignments with Citicorp/Citibank offices in Europe. He holds a BTech from the Indian Institute of Technology in Delhi and an MBA (specializing in banking, finance, and systems) from the Indian Institute of Management in Ahmadabad.

BACKGROUND

Gurnani developed his risk management skills and mind-set while working with trading and asset management groups at Citigroup. He joined Investcorp in 1993 to establish the risk management function for its small proprietary trading operation.

Starting in 1995, Investcorp faced the "good problem" of having excessive liquid cash resulting from successfully exiting private equity investments, including Gucci and Prime Services. Gurnani embarked on a research project to determine the solution to the problem.

"How do we deploy our liquidity to get more recurring income for the balance sheet, as distinct from getting transactional income from private equity and real estate businesses?"

Research "led us quickly to hedge funds," he says. Working with the treasurer, together they started researching hedge funds in 1995 and made their first investment in October 1996. Gurnani became the head of risk for the hedge fund portfolio while continuing as the head of risk for all of Investcorp. He served in the dual roles until 2004, when he relinquished the Investcorp risk management responsibilities to focus full time on the hedge fund business.

Investcorp Investment Principles

Gurnani believes four principles distinguish the Investcorp hedge fund investing approach from others.

- **Principal Investor:** "In everything, we are a co-investor, always the principal investor. When we started investing in hedge funds, Investcorp was the only investor." Even today, when the firm introduces new products, Investcorp commits first, followed by partner investors.
- **Risk Focus from Day One:** Gurnani offers three reasons for their risk orientation.
  - *Proprietary investing:* It means they are "always focused on risk."
  - *Expertise:* As the originator and leader of the hedge fund investing program, Gurnani's experience and mind-set naturally led to a risk management approach.
  - *Necessity:* As they were researching and launching the program, they "quickly realized hedge funds attracted the best investment management talent, but not the best risk talent." Although many more investors today are focused on risk, he says, "I think it's true today as well, it's still inadequate."
- **Best in Every Class:** Gurnani says the firm "believes our job is to be the best provider of hedge fund products across the spectrum." Rather than offering a single type of hedge fund investment vehicle, Investcorp serves a range of investors with a variety of products, including funds of hedge funds, a seeding platform, single-strategy managers, and customized portfolios.
- **Lead by Changing:** Investcorp management believes the firm must continually change in order to stay ahead in the hedge fund business. Gurnani offers examples from their experience.

"Post the 1998 crisis the focus on risk was very different. It was required to stay ahead of the game." Five years later, they chose to embark on a project to do trade-based research—quantitative research based on actual hedge fund trades—to analyze sources of return.

Such actions stem from a "commitment to constantly subjecting yourself to change and thinking of ways and means to add alpha, in sync with the fact that investing is changing all the time."

RISK MANAGEMENT PHILOSOPHY

From the start, Gurnani embedded a risk management focus into the Investcorp hedge fund investment process, relying on his experience and expertise up to that point. In the 15 years since, his views of risk have evolved as his research has advanced. By putting risk management at the forefront of his investment process, Gurnani has put Investcorp at the forefront of the industry for risk management. His authoritative and definitive methodologies for analyzing and measuring risk deserve attention and implementation.

To define risk in the "traditional sense," he takes "uncertainty in future expected return, measured in volatility" as a starting point. "Any investment portfolio has uncertain outcomes. How do you quantify the outcomes?"

Gurnani thinks most investors are too focused on preventing drawdowns or losses in the portfolio. He focuses on the uncertainty and volatility, too. In particular, he tends to focus on risk as it relates to volatility. "It's very important to stay in the game. You don't want to be stopped out of trades or positions you have in your portfolio when mean reversion occurs."

Too many times, Gurnani explains, managers have "a good portfolio, good trades, but don't have staying power, or they get stopped out because of excess volatility." All the work to structure the positions becomes "no use at all," so he focuses significantly on fat tail risks. "The combination of volatility and fat tail risks is how I define and quantify risk."

Mastering Risk Management

Gurnani became a risk professional as a natural result of trading experience early in his career, but his intellectual curiosity, coupled with Investcorp resources, made him a risk master.

"Like most risk professionals, I started on the trading and liquid securities side." Citigroup focused on understanding and controlling not just investment risk, but credit, operational, liquidity, and other risks. While he gained "a tremendous amount of experience" over the course of several years, his experience prior to Investcorp "was not too distinct from how most market risk professionals got started."

After joining Investcorp, he evolved as a risk professional partly because of his involvement with its proprietary trading operations, an experience that "has been invaluable for hedge fund investing." His real growth as a risk professional came when he devised a method to identify the risks few people thought existed in certain investments.

Investcorp only invested in alternatives, mostly in illiquid vehicles like private equity and real estate. There was "no culture of quantifying risk in those asset classes in those days." When he told an internal private equity manager that his portfolio had market risks embedded in it, "he looked at me like he didn't know what I was talking about."

Responsible for managing risk for the entire investment enterprise, he endeavored to prove his case and identify the risks in their private equity portfolio. Collaborating with Barra, a company that specialized in equity market risk, Gurnani "worked from 1996 to 1998 and actually built a risk model for private equity. Barra models are based on fundamental data factors, so they lent themselves to illiquid securities, unlike price-based models."

They built "one of the best private equity risk models. You don't see private equity firms with those models today." They then created a real estate model.

"These were complex risk problems. The more complex they were, the more excited we were to focus on the ideas." Gurnani worked with a small group to accomplish this feat.

"We had the view that you don't need to be in a big bank, with hundreds of risk professionals ... to do fundamental work in risk. You can do it in a smaller setup."

Since hedge funds are based on liquid securities, Gurnani acknowledges that his success modeling risk in "tough to crack" illiquid asset classes like private equity and real estate might seem irrelevant to most hedge fund investors. The experience proved relevant, because it forms the foundation of his sophisticated, multilayered approach to analyzing hedge fund risks.

From his proprietary trading experience, Gurnani learned the two distinct areas of hedge fund risks, investment risk and operational risk. His subsequent research into the nature of hedge fund investment risk has given him strong knowledge and insights and resulted in an impressively thorough risk management process.

Hedge Fund Investment Risk

As Gurnani began researching hedge fund risk, he quickly uncovered a key difference between hedge funds and long-only investment risk.

"Unlike long-only, where positions are run through Barra equity models, the same with fixed income, there were well-established standards for quantifying risk. In hedge funds, the challenge was that you could not analyze risk at the position level. You had to have *a trade construct*, both on the long and short sides of the trade."

Convertible arbitrage provides a good example. "It is not enough to look at the convertible bond on its own; you must look at the underlying delta equity hedge, currency, and credit. You must look at the risk of the particular trade. It's a fundamental difference I learned from the proprietary desk where they had been doing hedge funds internally (without calling them that) for years."

From that insight, Gurnani concluded, "Naïve approaches to risk underestimated the risk in hedge fund strategies very easily, and that is the case today."

He offers another example, a long/short equity market-neutral portfolio. "Market neutral is a misnomer. Running positions through a basic risk model, it shows zero risk—dollar neutral, beta neutral—yet our experience shows that they're anything but market neutral."

Even in fixed-income relative value, processing trades through the "naïve model" shows limited risk, but the actual positions have interest rate, liquidity, and volatility risks. Hedge fund managers and their investors can learn from his early insights.

"You need to understand the trade for every strategy, and every strategy needs a different approach to risk. You need to run different risk models for different strategies. It means you cannot just get one risk professional and hire them to do everything. You can't just hire an equity risk professional; you need to hire specialists."

Gurnani has incorporated this knowledge into the investment process with the help of in-house research and systems support. He says it gives him an advantage, because the approach is not easily replicated.

"No risk system vendors can really help you construct the trades because they are asset class–driven, while hedge funds are not driven by asset class. Hedge funds mix and match asset classes into one trade."

To implement his approach, he recommends getting the best commercial models available for each asset class. Because those "models are not useful for hedge funds on a stand-alone basis," investors then need to integrate and adapt the models to their own process.

Risk Management Tools and Guidelines On the operational risk side, Gurnani gained other critical, early insights about valuation long since embedded in the process. "Hedge funds have difficult-to-value securities. Anyone can do equities, but with convertible bonds, derivatives, you need to build valuation tools and processes. We [Investcorp] have invested heavily in internal operational risk tools."

For Gurnani, the investment risk systems and operational risk tools go hand in hand. Combining good valuation tools with strong risk analysis enhances the investment process and puts Investcorp "in a unique position" when managing its portfolios. "Every time we look at a strategy—convertible bonds, fixed income—we have our own risk guidelines for what makes the strategy successful."

More important, the guidelines and risk infrastructure provides "an invaluable source of alpha. During difficult times having these guidelines protected our capital and that of our partners."

Gurnani gives the example of fixed-income relative value guidelines he instituted after the 1998 market crisis. Analyzing the impact on the portfolio, he observed that losing trades, if not subject to liquidity risk, tend to be short gamma trades. If his risk guidelines only applied to leverage, in a crisis the portfolio could still be hurt by losses in short gamma trades. Investcorp now has risk guidelines that not only limit leverage in stressed markets, but also prohibit certain trades.

"The guideline stops a guy from taking short gamma." Their fixed-income relative value manager had positive performance in 2008. Gurnani says that was due to the manager's expertise, but also, importantly, "our guidelines prohibit taking positions that can do badly in those conditions."

Managed Accounts   Managed accounts comprise a large part and play a crucial role in their ability to manage risk of the portfolio. Gurnani claims Investcorp was one of the first firms to actively push for them starting in 1998 and has set up 80 managed accounts since then across various hedge fund strategies. He has seen other investors pursue managed accounts, but says many drop the effort because they require a substantial investment in systems and administration. The managed account policy extends naturally from the risk philosophy.

"Most of the problems that come to bite you in bad times take place during the good times. During 2008 everyone was trying to do the right thing. The problem was, what you did when you constructed portfolios in 2006 and 2007 is what caused you to blow up or do well in 2008."

According to Gurnani, it was managed accounts that helped prevent the majority of the issues in 2008. "Our convertible arbitrage manager actually outperformed with a lower level of risk. We were not a forced seller, met redemption requests, and put up no gates." The Investcorp investment team believes the transparency of managed accounts can improve the investment process and serve as a source of alpha. Historically they insisted on managed accounts mostly on fixed-income relative value and arbitrage strategies, "anything that used financing and leverage," because it allowed them to control risk better. After the events of 2008, Gurnani says, "Now we want to use managed accounts across all strategies, period."

Opportunistic Alpha Transparency enables managers to add value to the portfolio by making tactical or opportunistic investment decisions based on their view of the entire portfolio.

In the summer of 2006, for example, Gurnani grew concerned about credit exposure in the overall portfolio. Even though he had few managed accounts with fixed-income managers and "a lower than strategic allocation to credit," he still had credit exposure.

Looking for a way to hedge the credit exposure, he considered implementing "naïve" standard swap and macro hedges, but did not find the trade-off between the risks and the returns compelling. He continued his quest.

"Then I came across the short subprime trade. We were a day-one investor with the most well-known hedge fund manager in that strategy. We did it originally as an overlay to the existing credit portfolio, but the alpha potential was strong. At the same time, it was a good beta hedge. If you were wrong you would lose a limited amount of money, but the rest of the book would do well."

Similarly, in 2007, Gurnani developed concerns about the portfolio's exposure to the equity markets and started "dramatically reducing equity beta" by redeeming from some equity fund managers. Investcorp had full transparency and it was known that one manager needed more time to refund their money. So while waiting, Gurnani implemented equity hedges using futures on specific positions in the portfolio.

During the Lehman Brothers bankruptcy crisis in 2008, he "realized that it was a liquidity seizure environment. It reminded me of 1998, except this was a lot more severe." Gurnani remembered an important lesson from 1998. That is, "Hedge funds do lose money in a liquidity crisis. There are very few ways to prevent it."

Despite the challenge, he sought a way to prevent portfolio losses. His analysis of the 1998 crisis determined that "only one thing worked." As a liquidity crisis unfolds, central banks try to add liquidity back by reducing interest rates on the short end of the curve. He could hedge the portfolio by buying the front end of the yield curve.

Gurnani immediately began working to implement the hedge with an Investcorp fixed-income manager. The manager brought insight from his experience that added even more value. "He helped us understand the forward curve. In a panic, the forward curve had higher risk return trade-offs."

Investcorp put on sizeable hedges in October 2008 and kept them on until April 2009. "As predicted we did lose money on fixed-income relative value and arbitrage, but the hedges offset the losses."

Gurnani studied overlay strategies and managed the hedge fund portfolio for 10 years before employing them. Such hedging tactics seem like a logical step in the risk management–oriented philosophy. "We always believe that using transparency, managed accounts, and risk tools are a very critical source of alpha that investors are not focusing on very much," says Gurnani.

The Alpha Project

Gurnani has applied Investcorp's intense, systematic research capabilities and deep understanding of hedge fund risks to a modeling project designed to give them more insights for selecting individual hedge fund managers.

Gurnani will typically evaluate a new manager by analyzing the historical holdings and return information in general and also for important times in market history for the strategy type.

"We ask managers for portfolio data at particular periods of time, picking both crisis and good times. For a fixed-income manager, we look at September 2001; for convertible arbitrage managers we study 2002 and 2005."

He analyzes more than just the total returns. "The key to the return series is to dissect it. What is the hedge fund beta as compared to index? What is the alpha, and what is the volatility of the alpha?" To find a method to identify hedge fund beta, Gurnani launched another ambitious research effort he calls the Alpha Project.

Coming out of an equity bear market in 2003 and seeing "a flood of institutional money" into hedge funds, being "risk and academic focused," he spent time researching publicly available information about the risk and return drivers of hedge fund strategies.

"Amazingly, I found there was very little quality research on what causes hedge funds to exist, what is the structure, and what are the inefficiencies."

Finding the indexes inadequate, he started the Alpha Project. "We took five quants and tech people and embarked on this data research project, literally locked them up. I told them not to worry about day-to-day business, because they needed to help me research the risk and return drivers of the underlying strategy."

Strategy Beta   The group studied the primary hedge fund strategies and determined the generic trade that defines each strategy. Having portfolio transparency enabled them to verify the trades. They then spent almost a year constructing a database of historical prices for securities in that strategy. For instance, the researchers compiled a database of convertible bond trade prices going back to 1990. Gurnani says it covers about 80–90 percent of the universe.

They then applied the same process to the generic trade for each strategy. "We took all the strategies—fixed-income relative value, merger arbitrage, distressed, market neutral—and used the generic trade and proprietary database to come up with our own measure of hedge fund beta."

The Alpha Project gives Investcorp the ability to calculate a proprietary index of generic hedge fund returns for each strategy. Some strategies, like convertible arbitrage, can be executed in a variety of ways, so Investcorp has a custom index for each style. A commercial convertible arbitrage index will usually have a mix of those styles.

"We have our own indices for hedge fund beta. We can look at what drives risk and return for each series. More importantly, it enables us to determine the attractiveness of the strategy. Trade by trade, we can determine what is attractive today."

Manager Alpha The Alpha Project can help determine managers who are adding alpha and gives Investcorp more flexibility when constructing investment portfolios. If they can determine whether a manager is adding value, they can then determine whether to invest more with the manager or to find a more cost-effective way, like using replication, to get the same return.

He uses the example of one year in the Japanese convertible market. A fund with a return of 25 percent would appear to have delivered outstanding performance. Yet investors could have achieved the same return by purchasing all the bonds in the market. However, if the manager in question returns 40 percent when the market delivers 25 percent, he obviously adds value.

Having transparency allows them to apply the analysis in more subtle ways, such as analyzing whether a manager adds alpha when trading in and out of a strategy.

The analysis cannot necessarily predict a manager's ability to deliver alpha in the future, but it gives a better base of information to evaluate a manager and deploy staff more effectively. Gurnani believes this method gives him a competitive advantage. "We do the analysis when evaluating a manager and look at returns, beta, alpha, and consistency. We look at the portfolio and run it through our models."

Analysts experienced in the specific strategy can focus instead on qualitative analysis and conduct more in-depth research into a manager's background, investment process, and strategy.

"We believe we have an edge, because we believe we can separate alpha and beta in the manager's return better than other people. Because of the tools, we have a better starting point. That's where the quality of the team comes in."

Alpha Strategy versus Beta Strategy   Such superior analysis capabilities seem as if they could help determine if strategies deliver alpha or not and whether they should be implemented actively or passively.

Gurnani says it depends on the strategy and describes two extreme examples. "Convertible arbitrage, it's safe to say, is easiest to replicate. It doesn't mean there aren't people adding alpha, but there are fewer people adding value." On the other hand, macro discretionary is difficult to execute passively. "The strategy is so skill-based. I haven't even started the Alpha Project on it. It is totally skill, there is no natural return."

He finds that "people have the ability to gravitate toward beta." He says that when money first comes into a strategy, it may get good returns. However, if too much capital is chasing a strategy, the investment is more likely to yield market return or "become beta over time."

In the aftermath of the 2008 financial crisis, Gurnani sees tremendous opportunities to add alpha, because "people are doing different things. They're not all trying to do the same trade."

Investcorp expects to bring investments based on the Alpha Project to market. The vehicle would charge lower fees, replicate hedge fund beta returns, and help identify alpha-producing managers to complete the portfolio.

Summarizing his comments, Gurnani says, "The right way to approach hedge fund beta is strategy by strategy. At times beta is good. At times when alpha is available, do it at a strategy level. If you want exposure to converts, get good beta exposure and look for good alpha managers. With macro, I wouldn't even look for beta; instead, look for managers who have the skill.... Don't look at hedge funds as one homogenous asset class, it isn't that at all."

INVESTMENT PROCESS

Though anchored in risk management principles and quantitative analysis, the investment process, particularly manager selection, incorporates qualitative research and evaluation techniques.

Manager Selection

Just as he builds strategy-specific models to analyze risk, Gurnani hires strategy-specific experienced analysts to handle research in their specialty.

The proliferation of hedge funds makes finding and meeting good managers challenging, so they strive to get good information flow from standard industry sources like databases and prime brokers. Gurnani and his team are "quite informally plugged in with hedge funds" thanks to their many years of experience in the industry.

Combining information from their network and their own analysis, the specialists generate a universe of good managers in their strategy and analyze the manager information for consistency and appropriate risk-taking. Calling it "basic filtering to bring the list to a manageable number," Gurnani says that at any point, "I believe there are 200 to 300 managers that would merit serious due diligence and monitoring."

He splits the due diligence research and analysis into categories, evaluating the manager's investment philosophy and ascertaining whether the manager has "a repeatable process, with inherent alpha (an advantage) and how it will continue."

The due diligence process changes depending on the specific strategy. "Quant, systematic, market neutral, or fundamental, the process is different, so there is a different focus during due diligence."

The overall manager selection process includes a number of qualitative due diligence and decision-making steps.

Qualitative Manager Selection Steps

1. **People:** Investcorp analysts study the backgrounds and quality of the people and conduct formal and informal background checks.
2. **Investment Process:** Investcorp analyzes the sustainability of the investment process and identifies the edge brought by the manager. Gurnani says it is important to determine whether past performance was due to luck or skill.
3. **Risk:** The specialists analyze risks in a fund's portfolio, and as a group they have "long discussions of the risk management philosophy and approach."
4. **Operational Due Diligence:** Gurnani says it is important to have a separate group to evaluate hedge fund operations. They meet with the CFO and COO, review the service providers, and assess operations processes, systems, and arrangements.
5. **Report:** The operations and investment due diligence reports, including qualitative and quantitative analysis and results from external sources such as background checks, are compiled into one package. The full report, averaging 100 pages, is then presented to the investment committee.
6. **Investment Committee:** Gurnani chairs the investment committee with the deputy chief investment officer. Other members include the heads of

risk, asset allocation, and quantitative research, and the leaders of the individual strategy groups.

7. **Committee Evaluation:** By the time the committee convenes to decide on a fund, Gurnani and the deputy CIO will have met with the manager and his team several times. They will have reviewed historical performance and assigned weightings to different components of the strategies to create a composite score.

8. **Manager Approval:** For a manager to be approved, the head of the strategy group must first recommend the investment. Both Gurnani and the deputy CIO must agree to add the manager for the fund to enter the portfolio. If either person says no, the manager will be rejected or kept on watch.

Winning Approval   Gurnani has some advice for the hedge fund marketing and investor relations teams as well as the individual investors responsible for getting Investcorp to make an investment. For starters, smooth sales presentations do not impress Gurnani. Before he meets a manager, he analyzes the fund and derives questions from the results. He advises investors to do the same.

"Managers tend to have a thought-out and well-presented story, telling investors what they want to hear." Doing quantitative portfolio analysis "opens up questions and gives you a lot of insight." Gurnani says it is this insight that gives the interviewer "an opportunity to talk about very different things than what most would focus on, because you're not hearing the standard party line."

Since he spends so much valuable time preparing beforehand, Gurnani wants to meet with a marketing person who can make good use of his time. He says he wants to talk to "somebody who can articulate the investment strategy, articulate the performance and the portfolio positioning."

Gurnani offers additional important advice. "The good marketing professional spends time trying to understand what we are looking for, what is our philosophy. He or she does homework and spends time knowing our needs for our portfolio."

Seeding New Managers   Investcorp does provide seed capital to new hedge fund managers, but Gurnani has narrowed the potential pool over the course of the last five years.

"Some people tend to be a real start-up coming out of investment banks. Others are coming out of hedge funds. They're not the original founders and are motivated by entrepreneurialism and economics. We tend to prefer that category. People we seed on our platform have experience, but they're not the original founder. I think that's the real opportunity."

Gurnani believes their selection parameters and partnership requirements help create the opportunity with the manager. A manager with experience at a large hedge fund, he says, "managing small amounts of capital, with good institutional infrastructure and oversight, adds alpha over big managers."

Investcorp provides initial seed capital and requires the manager to participate in their managed account platform as a subadviser. Managers accept Investcorp-mandated risk and operational oversight and service providers.

Their "institutional-quality managers on an institutional-quality platform," performed well relative to larger managers in the crisis of 2008. "Bigger managers were forced into the same kind of trades." It was not just manager skill that led them to perform better, "but oversight, and managing controlled amounts of capital. They have more flexibility and can adjust."

Terminating Managers   There are reasons Gurnani might terminate a manager, and they include the following:

- *Excessive Risk:* Too much risk on both the downside and the upside concerns him. "After a hugely positive month, we are calling them and trying to determine if there is excessive risk in the portfolio." If dissatisfied with the response, they tend to redeem.
- *Style Drift:* The manager diverts from the style and mandate of the fund. Transparency helps them avoid style drift or take action quickly when it occurs.
- *Inexplicable Performance:* If a manager has "consistent unexplained performance compared to peers," he will redeem. Examples include "a manager cannot explain consistent degradation of alpha" or "the manager is underperforming and not able to get a handle on it."
- *Organizational Issues:* They can include turnover, or a manager becoming more involved in gathering assets than managing money.

Portfolio Construction and Management

Gurnani employs a three-step allocation process to construct hedge fund portfolios.

1. **Strategic Allocation:** A medium-term time horizon—generally three to five years hence—is allocated to different strategies. After analyzing historical risk/return data, calculating correlations, and adjusting for survivorship bias, they use their own optimization model to determine a strategic allocation based on risk-efficient frontiers. As the risk level goes down, the model balances the allocation more toward relative

value, and as it goes up, the balance skews toward more macro and equity strategies. The allocation is usually reviewed and revised every two years.

2. **Tactical Allocation:** Alpha Project factors help to determine the relative attractiveness of strategies to overweight. Then they input their views and conviction level into a Black Litterman model. Controlled risk budgets constrain the portfolio to keep it from being driven by tactical views.

3. **Portfolio Construction:** Using a dual optimization, they "dissect the beta and the alpha" of the specific strategy for each manager. Using the tactical allocation guidelines as a constraint, they create a mix that is "adhering to the tactical allocation but maximizing the alpha of the portfolio."

Gurnani says many optimization methods focus on the manager's total return, resulting in "inadvertent beta creep." Other methods tend to optimize alpha using beta optimization first. Because beta and alpha drivers vary greatly, this method gives them sturdier portfolios. "Go with managers that exhibit alpha. Where hedge fund beta is dominant in a manager and tactical allocation desires beta, get that beta exposure."

Additional constraints on the portfolio include a maximum dollar amount to individual managers and strategies, a maximum risk contribution, and any investor-specific preferences, such as transparency or liquidity preferences.

Terms   Regarding lock-ups and liquidity, Gurnani concerns himself more with liquidity and the asset liability mismatch. "A distressed credit manager with quarterly liquidity, that's a problem. I would rather have a credit manager that has a 1–2 year lock-up than one that can't be honored."

Managed accounts make it less of an issue for him, but he does monitor the asset liability mismatch to determine "what is the real liquidity, and how does it match with the terms?"

The other investors in a particular fund are an important determinant of the balance between assets and liabilities, so he prefers to co-invest with other institutional investors. "We want to be in the same pool with other strategic investors." Avoiding the vagaries of other investors in an LP is another reason he demands managed accounts.

HEDGE FUND INDUSTRY OUTLOOK

Discussing the business side of individual hedge funds leads Gurnani to comment on broader hedge fund industry issues, including the impact of the financial crisis and the outlook for the future.

Fees

Gurnani has a more sanguine attitude about hedge fund fees than most. "I don't know where fees will turn out to be finally. Our view is that we don't mind paying for alpha, but do not like having to pay for beta as well. I believe investors should focus on determining who is adding alpha and who is giving you beta. To the extent they're adding alpha, we are willing to pay for it."

He thinks investors should be and will be "a lot less tolerant of people that are selling you beta, charging 2 and 20 for beta."

Regarding certain investor-organized efforts to reduce fees, he says, "I don't like indiscriminately trying to get fees reduced across the board. I think it leads to negative selection bias." In other words, managers willing to give a deal on fees are more likely to be weaker hedge fund beta providers. "When we talk privately with other institutions, they don't want a negative selection bias."

Some influential investors have advocated a fee structure wherein the performance fee is paid over a target or hurdle rate. Gurnani says, "Conceptually that is the way to go. However, I don't think the industry is geared up for that today, even managers providing alpha. I think the hedge fund industry has done a disservice by not coming up with a way to quantify beta." Without having defined hedge fund betas, he believes, it will be difficult to establish hurdles, because the industry "should have hurdles that are reflective of beta for that strategy."

His work formulating Investcorp's own trade-based approach to hedge fund beta could be adapted and taken to managers for use as a hurdle. Investors could say, "Here's a true measure of beta. It would then force people to negotiate fees; it's too early for that."

Lessons of the 2008 Market Crisis

"A lot more than people realized" could be the refrain for the lessons Gurnani learned in 2008. He says, "Hedge funds were taking excessive risk beyond what investors realized. There was a lot more concentration in portfolios than people realized, a lot more illiquidity, and a lot more style drift than investors realized."

He attributes those conditions to "the sheer amount of leverage" and the large size of balance sheets. Previously, volatility had dropped and managers could take more risk. "People had to stretch to take concentrated positions," leading to many more illiquid positions and style drift. Each one by itself was not a new lesson learned. The combination of all of them "caused a lot of damage to portfolios."

Transparency

Hedge funds have historically resisted offering any transparency of the positions in their portfolio. More have acquiesced in recent years due to the demands of institutional investors and the availability of neutral third-party risk systems. Yet Gurnani has focused on and gotten transparency through managed accounts almost from the beginning of his hedge fund investing experience. He has good reason to mandate transparency for every hedge fund in the portfolio.

"Portfolios that had more transparency outperformed by as much as ten percentage points. [Transparency] is very important to incorporate into the process going forward."

Building a managed account platform costs a lot of money for both the investor and the manager, "so if everyone wanted managed accounts, it would not work at all." Rather, Gurnani recommends that "like-minded investors should get together and seed managed account platforms, and use that to control risks."

Besides having relatively better performance in 2008, Investcorp's managers were not forced sellers. Although they "had to suffer mark to market" valuations, they could hold their positions and "bounce back in performance" when markets improved, as they did in 2009.

Don't Blame the Messenger

Although regulators have not implemented any new policies, he expects more regulation of hedge funds in the future. "Change that hurt was the temporary ban on short selling. They're quickly going to realize it is ineffective." He does not plan to institute any changes based on speculation or predictions of certain regulations, but "will react when the change comes."

Hedge funds received most of the blame as the crisis unfolded, but in retrospect the majority of it belonged to overly leveraged broker/dealers and poorly regulated CDS. Gurnani agrees, saying, "Irony is that we hedge funds were a signal for the problems. We were short the financials. We weren't the cause, we were the solution."

If you look past notable frauds and the idiosyncrasies of certain hedge fund debacles, he says, "by and large hedge funds managed risks in aggregate. Part of the reason is the investment banks were not partnerships. Hedge fund proprietors with capital on the line with their co-investors did a better job."

MIND OF A RISK MASTER

Reflecting on the current state of the industry and its direction, Gurnani says, "Notwithstanding the events of 2008, I think hedge funds actually held up well and make perfect sense to have in an institutional portfolio."

The risks associated with hedge fund investing continue to concern him. "The single most important in my view is structural weakness in hedge funds. There's an inadequate focus on risk. Investors should focus on plugging that weakness. Have more of a focus on risk through transparency, with managed accounts a prerequisite." He fears it "could be a mistake not to focus on this." Investors cannot afford to get complacent in good environments or to let managers have full control. "A lot of focus on risk is needed."

Summarizing his views on the future of hedge funds, he says, "The industry is a great industry. It continues to attract talent and will continue to do so." Risk mastermind that he is, Gurnani quickly follows up with a qualifying statement: "But you need to be mindful of risk."

CHAPTER 11

A Driver of Returns

Kathryn A. Hall, Chairman, Chief Executive Officer, and Chief Investment Officer, Hall Capital Partners

A s chief executive officer and chief investment officer of Hall Capital Partners LLC, a privately owned registered investment advisory firm, Kathryn A. Hall, known as Katie, has become one of the most prominent and well-regarded hedge fund investors. Serving primarily wealthy families, Hall and her team manage approximately $18 billion in multiasset-class global investment portfolios.

Previously, she was a general partner of Laurel Arbitrage Partners, a risk arbitrage investment partnership that she founded in 1989. Prior to that, she was a general partner of HFS Management Partners, HFS Partners I, and Hellman & Friedman. Hall began her career at Morgan Stanley, where she worked in both the risk arbitrage and mergers and acquisitions departments.

Hall chairs the board of directors of the Princeton University Investment Company (PRINCO), is a member of the board of trustees of Princeton University, and has served on a number of boards and investment committees in the San Francisco Bay Area. A director of American Century Mountain View Funds from 2002 to 2007, she serves on the advisory boards of several private investment partnerships. Hall graduated cum laude from Princeton University with a BA in economics and earned an MBA from Stanford Graduate School of Business.

While her record of accomplishment as an investor and money manager stands alone, Hall also stands out as one of the leading women in a segment of the investment business even more dominated by men than the rest of the industry. In mid-2009, the industry trade organization 100 Women in Hedge Funds announced she would receive its Industry Leadership Award for 2009.

BACKGROUND

Katie Hall says of the circumstances that led to her investment career, "All of us would probably say this about our careers. I just ended up in the midst of a lot of interesting investment issues that formed my investment interest in hedge funds."

As a senior majoring in economics with a math focus at Princeton University, Hall had to write a thesis. "I laugh at myself when I think about how absurd it was. I wrote a thesis on 'quote, unquote' the explanatory model of Treasury bill futures. How funny is that?" The serious point is "not to say I developed a great model, but how my background and interest in math and finance all fits together."

Hall joined Morgan Stanley, working in merger and acquisitions from 1980 to 1982. "Those were rocking and rolling times. Interesting work was being done responding to hostile takeovers. It was when you had different proration dates, different tender dates." Learning the "theories around how you wound your way though all those transactions was really fun."

She left Morgan Stanley to attend Stanford Business School in Palo Alto, California. After getting her MBA in 1984, Hall returned to Morgan Stanley in the risk arbitrage department. "It was the public markets phase of M&A," an extremely active time in that market. She remained there for two years before moving back to Northern California to join "a brand-new start-up."

The firm, HFS Partners, took its name from the founders Hellman, Friedman, and Steyer. Under the leadership of Hall's friend, former Morgan Stanley colleague, and Stanford Business School classmate Thomas F. Steyer, the firm eventually became the highly regarded hedge fund firm Farallon Capital Management. When she joined, it was "less than a year old."

Risk Arbitrage Training

Risk arbitrage, Hall says, "is the absolute best training for thinking about investments broadly. You need to understand the different strands, then how they weave together to make a specific decision." She elaborates, "It's a very disciplined framework: identifying a critical path, understanding financials, understanding other aspects that could interrupt that critical path, integrating legal and financial vocabulary." Observing the way people made decisions and whether they trusted each other also helped her learn. She adds, "It was a great field."

The lessons of her risk arbitrage experience "all boiled down to how you assessed your upside and your downside with whatever complexities were attached." The basic framework she learned in risk arbitrage, "risk taken for returns desired in the time frame expected," Hall says, is "the absolute backbone of my style and perspective today."

At around the same time she and Steyer got their risk arbitrage education, the disciples of hedge fund legend Julian Robertson, known as the "Tiger Cubs," got more of an equity value investing experience. Since all have had successful hedge fund management and investing careers, how do the two styles reconcile?

"Cut through the good ones," Hall says, and the risk arbitrage stars like Steyer and the highly regarded value investors like Tiger Cub Steve Mandel "share more in common." Each approach essentially employs a framework for analyzing portfolios and investments rooted in fundamental analysis, just "expressed in a different way." She concludes, " At its heart, it's a very deep fundamental analysis and understanding of the positions, the risks associated, and how the expected downside and upside will occur."

Hall spent three years with the HFS organization, becoming a partner in 1986. By 1989, although she and Steyer remained good friends, HFS Partners was "his baby" and she "really had an enormous bee in my bonnet to have my own show." Montgomery Securities provided capital and fund-raising resources, and together they launched "classic risk arbitrage hedge fund" Laurel Arbitrage partners. The timing was so inopportune, she is "literally not sure whether to laugh or cry."

Risk Arbitrage Reality

The fund began trading October 1, 1989, "the month of the earthquake in San Francisco and of the world earthquake in risk arb. The United buyout failed." Hall likens the period leading up to the launch of her fund to the financial crisis of 2008. "It was the era when buyouts were happening at a tremendous pace; there was ever higher and higher leverage. Northwest Airlines had no business 'LBO-ing,' but did. Then United Airlines came up and pushed it even farther, to the max. They pushed too far and the banks balked at providing funding at the very last minute. In my opinion, the banks were squeezed too hard."

The immediate lesson, "Financing doesn't go away in a continuous curve, it goes away on a dime," had lasting repercussions for her nascent fund. "It just ended. Buyouts ended overnight."

Hall kept a "very risk-controlled book" and despite having fewer opportunities, she continued to run the partnership for the five years. The experience taught her a personal development lesson.

"I had chosen to focus my investing efforts on classic risk arbitrage. Partly by organization limits, and in retrospect through my own decision-making failing, I decided not to aggressively broaden and go into distressed debt. It ultimately proved more lucrative in the early '90s. Part of it was a function circumstance, but part was not being willing to adapt to the environment at the time."

During that period she got involved in helping a large, wealthy family "think about the whole universe of their investments." At the time, the problem she was asked to help solve—structuring a large charitable investment trust to invest in hedge funds—was uncommon. Having found the experience interesting, Hall realized her "training and framework, of identifying the problem, the solution, and the probability," suited the task. The hedge funds and a legal team worked with her "to design a solution to meet the need. It was an accomplishment."

Hall finished the project in early 1994 as risk arbitrage "started to just pick up enough. I had to make a choice of what direction to go." She felt she had done good work during a boring time, but now "had an acute sense of the cyclicality of M&A opportunities." Deciding that she "wanted to look at things from a broader perspective," Hall liquidated her hedge fund, received capital from Warren Hellman and others, and started Laurel Management Company.

Although she "used different vocabulary at the time," in today's parlance, the firm was charged with "building global multiasset-class portfolios of outside managers." As the firm has grown, it has changed its name twice to reflect changes in its ownership structure, but the approach has remained consistent. Through it all, Hall says, "We have had a relatively meaningful allocation to hedge funds and other alternatives. That's not surprising because of my background."

When she started the company, Hall stopped managing money directly and allocates only to external managers across all asset classes. The policy serves as "a good cornerstone" of the firm to avoid conflicts and remains "an important tenet."

Although Hall built the business with a broader investment mandate, it has benefited from her market knowledge. "It's an advantage to have real-life scars and experience in the investment landscape. It makes you a better gatherer and consumer of information."

Risk Arbitrage Returns

Specifically, her experience managing money in active markets makes Hall "more critical, from the analytical perspective, of return patterns. I think I have a real understanding—it's a cliché, but—good returns can be as big a problem as bad returns, sometimes more so." This perspective enables her "to have a nuanced capability to assess the believability of returns" when hearing a manager describe the risks taken to achieve those returns.

Her perspective serves as a "point of differentiation" for the organization and makes her investment team "push further" with managers to determine concentration and leverage and assess their sources of information. "It helps us go farther in trying to understand whether returns were generated by rising tides, a home run that went the right way, uncomfortable risk, or an appropriate path."

Their in-depth analysis of return patterns does not just serve as an inquisition tool. "Conversely, it can give you staying power during periods of trouble." Hall describes a "clear case in point. We lived through it in the fall of 2008, in and around credit. Anybody buying senior secured debt that thought they had the steal of all time at 80 had to live with it at 60 in December. You had to understand what the market was doing; who the buyers and sellers were; who the distressed and leveraged sellers were, and why." Emphatically, Hall says, "It was ug-LY!"

Meanwhile, her team was monitoring credit managers who were analyzing larger amount of credits at a much faster pace. "We had a very high degree of visibility into what was happening." Her read on the situation helped her react better to "unlevered returns down 20 to 25 percent." Hall explains, "Sure I'm not happy, but it was not like I had to say, 'Oh my, the world has ended!' It gave us, in an uncomfortable time, the ability to stay with it. Focusing on the returns gave them "greater staying power and the ability to add capital where we could."

INVESTMENT PROCESS

The framework for analyzing companies and securities Hall acquired in risk arbitrage infuse her investment philosophy and investment process. The way she summarizes the lessons of that experience could also describe her investment philosophy and approach to manager selection.

"In the end, it is not that anyone or anything has a unique ingredient. It is synthesizing and judgment; how you pull together and weight information and then make an assessment."

Manager Selection

Even though Hall is "really not a label person, and resists them in any way, shape, or form," to describe the managers she prefers, "If you had to slap a label on, it's 'Concentrated High Conviction Investors.' I would probably add a value modifier onto it as well." The broad description serves as a "bit of a road map for thinking of managers generally."

The concept ultimately represents the common set of attributes they seek in every manager across every asset class. Being value-oriented rather than price-oriented means they prefer processes and investment styles that are "fundamental in nature." Managers who analyze cash flows, whether from a security, company, or property, and who understand "the actual drivers of value in the asset class" fit this profile. The managers dominating their portfolio are "driven by fundamentals, or by specific catalysts, or by knowing something before the rest of the world knows it." These traits, Hall reiterates, are "common across everything."

They also like managers with a strong risk return framework and the ability to pinpoint and explain why and how they can continue to generate return.

Specific Strategy Criteria   When they begin considering a specific strategy, they need "good reasons why the investment has a high probability of being successful." Hall says, "We're agnostic," about the strategy type and execution; it can be "complicated, simple, global, domestic; we're broadminded about that." But in questioning the manager and evaluating the strategy they "will come back to the succinct driver of return. Why will it persist? Why is the market giving you the opportunity?"

On the surface, her "only absolute other rule" sounds like a test of the manager's client service policies. Some shortsighted hedge fund managers may see it as such, but it becomes clear that it has more to do with assessing the manager's mind-set and attitude toward co-investors and limited partners.

"We have to be able to speak to the investment decision makers. It doesn't mean we will do it all the time or abuse the relationship, but it will permit us, when needed, to actually get to the person that is making the investment decisions. We won't make the investment if we don't believe we can get that call through." The policy "keeps us out of certain investments, good and bad," she says, but she has a "fundamental reason" for adamantly abiding by it.

"You do hit brutal air pockets. Having a direct pipeline in gives you an understanding of the manager's conviction and insight into the calm of the organization and the objectivity and stability of the decision maker." She stresses, "It is one really important rule."

They seek managers who have explainable and sustainable attractive, risk-adjusted returns. Hall says, "The best nominal returns are not always the best returns." They rigorously use analytics, so if nominal returns are lower, they are then comfortable that "true risk-adjusted returns are higher and more attractive."

She thinks her experiences running a business have made her more sensitive to a manager's business skills. "I have a great respect for the difficulty and challenges of running the business. If you don't invest in your own infrastructure, or don't have enough respect for the roles of the companies or the people that provide it, you probably won't have good returns and a good business." She and her team carefully observe how the business is managed in order to assess its likely stability.

Personal Characteristics Hall cares less about liking a manager personally, since deciding whether the person is a "good guy" is such a "subjective assessment," and she focuses more on finding him or her trustworthy. "If we think a manager cuts it close from a legal and ethical standpoint, no matter how good the returns are, we don't care. We just won't invest with him. People do draw different lines; we draw a brighter, hard line."

Similarly, recognizing the difficulty of making a subjective assessment of a manager's ethics, they work to find a systematic way to make that determination. They review and evaluate the incentive program to make sure it "rewards the manager to do the right things, as opposed to stretch." The team will analyze the program and cross-reference it against other information and observations, looking for signs the incentive program could foster questionable ethical or risk-taking behavior. Some organizations "give big rewards and disproportionate payouts" that may lead to behaviors like "stretching."

Unfortunately some "people are always willing to be too cute by half." Besides incentive compensation practices, the manager's negotiating style provides an insight into his ethics. They avoid those with a "take no prisoners, stomp on the other guy" approach. She says, "Investors can get at that by doing as much reference checking as you can on business management and business behaviors."

When considering a manager's personal characteristics, "Another kind of totally squishy armchair psych area investors must think about is, why is the person getting up in the morning? When will they meet their personal goals? Is it just to make money, so will they lose focus?" Some managers find motivation in personal competition and achieving or besting personal goals. Investors should consider whether such managers "will go into other fields like politics or bicycle racing." Investing can be another form of personal competition. "Some people eat, live, and breathe investing and use money as a count." Investors need to think about the manager's psyche, because "it helps you think about his caliber and the kind of person he is."

Due Diligence   Hall prefaces her thoughts on due diligence practices by reminding investors that effective hedge fund investing requires more than knowing some tactics. "This business is an apprenticeship business, a cumulative knowledge and experience business." Although her firm has as "thorough an approach as possible, in the end, the ability to make judgments, good or bad, is the sum of those experiences."

When they evaluate a manager, the due diligence analysis encompasses the entire firm. "Having multiple points of view and insights within the organization deepens your understanding. If you have conversations with junior analysts, the CFO, a mid-level person, you learn a lot." The approach helps them determine the fund's decision-making process, the people doing the work, the pace and objectives of the work, the ways and topics they're communicating, and "obviously the set of references."

They cross-reference the information in multiple ways "in as authentic a way as possible." Investors need to do "classic reference checking to not miss anything obvious" and to have the "broadest network possible as a source of confidential references." Although the latter tactic "may be controversial," Hall finds it necessary. "People might be cautious about answering questions. They are wary of making negative comments."

Strategies to Avoid   Asked to describe hedge fund strategies she avoids and why, Hall laughingly responds, "At the risk of sounding arrogant, we think we can analyze almost anything." Seriously, she says, they generally avoid strategies they consider "too narrow" and names merger arb as an example. "It's too cyclical, too hard to get in and out."

They "keep looking," but have never invested in a macro fund, "largely because of the investment framework that I and the company live by." Hall adds, "We have yet to really find a macro investor who can articulate clearly not just how they made money in their strategy, but why there's a reason to believe those attributes, beyond trend trading, will persist in the future."

Even though managers profit from trading trends, "I don't think it has an inherent economic sustainability. They keep being right until they're not." She "wants to be convinced" and planned to invest with a well-known manager until he refused to give them direct access to him, so the team keeps looking.

Otherwise, they "look and invest across the spectrum, including highly quantitative strategies." Because of the analytical process in place, Hall says her team is "quite comfortable" with evaluating a variety of different and complicated strategies.

Portfolio and Risk Management

Hall identifies "permanent capital loss" as the real measure of risk. "That is the single most important risk we focus on." She believes investors "can't avoid the risks associated with human behavior and other external consequences" and says those risks are "typically encapsulated in some discussion of volatility." In other words, while some investors consider volatility a risk, she says, "Volatility per se is not a risk in my book. It is only a risk in that it magnifies human behavior or changes external relationships to other investors and funding sources."

The Hall Capital Partners team focuses on identifying potential sources of volatility and causes of permanent capital loss. Losses are usually caused by investment decisions, but Hall says, "They're also a function of staying power, meaning organizational stability. You may be fine if you hold the investments, but if you don't have the organization to hold your investments, you book the loss."

Liquidity Risk During the 2008 financial crisis, illiquid investments caused problems for long-term investors like endowments and put liquidity risk in the spotlight. Liquidity risk is not a young ingénue making her debut, but an old pro making a comeback.

"I would not identify liquidity or illiquidity as a new risk, although I think some people are acting like it's a new risk. Having a really good understanding of the liquidity of the underlying investments, the appropriateness of the terms being provided, and their consistency or inconsistency, is very important, but that's not a new insight." People seem "shocked, shocked" that managers investing in illiquid securities "put up gates when they had high withdrawals." Hall seems more shocked others were shocked and asks, "What's surprising about that?"

She offers an explanation. "Most people were not being harsh enough. They were complicit in kind of a deal. 'I will invest in a bunch of stuff and get returns, as long as I get quarterly liquidity when I want it.' They were almost demanding an asset liability mismatch, and then were unhappy when it happened."

Lock-Ups Discussing liquidity brings on the subject of lock-ups. A fund with a diversified equities portfolio "would have a pretty hard case" justifying a lock-up. "Not as often as claimed," Hall says. "The need to constrain capacity to generate returns in a particular investment segment might merit a bigger commitment of time." The lock-up can be justified in those situations not only to match assets and liabilities, but also to maintain a stable investor base. When considering whether a lock-up is justified for any manager, investors need to consider both objectives.

As the hedge fund industry has evolved and different types of investments have come to market in hedge fund vehicles, one-size-fits-all terms and conditions will not work for all investors. Hall points out that it may be the investment, not the structure that can be the problem in some cases.

"All this gets to a bigger issue: These structures are horrible for high-volatility investments. To be in something that goes up 200 percent is insane. It's the wrong structure."

She tends to avoid "that type of home run hitting manager," recalling one year when "global macro went all the way up 80 to 90 percent." The managers rode it back down the next year, shut their funds, and "took the huge carry [performance fee] with them." Even in funds where they expect to see a good amount of volatility, she still thinks it sets up a "heads I win, tails you lose" structure.

Hall expects the discussion of the appropriate length of lock-ups and related fee structures to continue. She supports the concept of removing a portion of capital if a manager with a longer-term lock-up reaches a certain performance target before the lock-up period expires. Investors may have more difficulty getting managers to agree to let them pay the performance fee at the end of the lock-up, because "there are some funky tax issues" for managers with that solution. The conversation seems headed in the right direction. "Hurdles, structures with some version of a claw-back—there are ways to get at the problem that will ultimately be better for investors."

Transparency and Managed Accounts   Similarly, Hall says, "The market is coming our way on transparency." Post the 2008 financial crisis, "even those that clung to the old way [no transparency] have to appreciate the reshaped environment."

Transparency relates to being able "to talk to the decision maker and understand the actual portfolio." The consistency and continuity of the report matters more than the amount of information. "I don't need a position sheet from a prime broker every night. I think that's fake transparency. I know what they look like. Very few people can even read them, much less process all the information, especially on a complicated strategy." A high-level, consistently produced report of the risk exposures, leverage, and strategy-specific data is fundamental for all investors.

Managed accounts feature transparency, so interest in them has also increased since the crisis. The wishful thinking regarding liquidity provisions appears to have shifted to managed accounts.

"I personally think it sets up a false dichotomy. People were extrapolating terms that you could have in equity managed accounts to a separate account across any other class. In my experience, that's not necessarily true."

Hall says investors may get enhanced transparency in managed accounts, but fears an "implicit belief that if you have more transparency, you would have more influence." That idea is not likely to be true either, but if investors could extract such terms from good managers, it would mean the managers would have too many separate deals and would spend too much time handling the accounts. If she found either behavior in a manager, it would "be fatal." The situation would be rife with conflicts, allocation problems, and back office issues.

"Managed accounts require a different apparatus than most of these organizations have. Investors think it's like equity, 'I can get in and out.' It's just not practical." When investors and managers are too willing to arrange such deals, it creates too many conflicts and managerial problems.

INVESTMENT PERSPECTIVES

No matter how their investments performed as a result of the 2008 financial crisis, many leading investors took the opportunity to review and reconfigure their organizations, asset allocations, and hedge fund portfolios. Hall describes how her organization and portfolios are positioned and offers advice to investors and her thoughts on the future.

Return Drivers

The firm manages approximately $18 billion, mostly large capital pools from wealthy families, although they do work with small and mid-size foundations and endowments. They make allocations across multiple asset classes and organize the investment team around "drivers of return." Thus "spread-based" investments like credit and absolute return are grouped together, while "distressed for control" debt resides in the private equity group along with more typical venture capital and buyout funds. Equity strategies, both long-only and long/short, belong in one group. Finally, they have a capital markets function that "drives collaboration and coordination among four groups, identifying central themes to pursue more aggressively, such as inflation across asset classes."

Multiple Asset Advantage When asked if investing in multiple asset classes enhances their hedge fund investment process, Hall responds, "You're talking my own book!" Elaborating, she says it is "incredibly valuable to be talking to people across multiple asset classes," because it keeps investment team members from getting mired in an asset class mind-set. For example, "I'm a private equity guy so that's what I'm investing in," or "I have to invest in it, because that is how I get paid."

Hall mentions an "emerging concern" for asset class purists. Because of her firm's multiple asset class approach it is "less likely to get hung up on structures. We were early and happy investors in hybrids and are not concerned about private or public structure. It releases us from getting unduly wound up about, say, a credit guy that needs to have call-down structure and a three-year payout."

Many investors will not make such investments because they cannot figure out how to classify them. To the extent good investments come in uncommon vehicles, her firm can benefit from their multiple asset class perspective. "We have the capacity to look at the returns and return patterns, and then worry about the structure."

Hall believes the firm's openness to multiple asset classes and structures gives it a "distinct advantage." It is one of the main reasons the investment team is organized by return drivers and works mostly in an open-plan environment.

Additionally, investment firms that remain entrenched in an asset class mind-set tend to have difficulty differentiating in the marketplace and spend too much time and energy protecting a structure rather than making investments. Such behavior provides Hall and her firm the advantage, because "We don't have to be hung up on it. We think about it purely from an investment standpoint and then worry about boxes."

Portfolio Themes

A significant theme stems from the "viewpoint that the market is permitting us to be simpler. We have less need to be in complicated strategies and don't need to use leverage at the manager or investor level. Simpler, blunter strategies are providing as good or better returns."

Managers and investors that own assets outright, without leverage, will generate good returns and protect their portfolios from "other people's problems" such as failing counterparties and panicky co-investors.

When discussing her background, Hall referred to the work she and her team had done to capitalize on opportunities in credit resulting from the financial crisis. As a result, they are "beefing up credit and distressed exposure through hedge funds and private formats and reducing specialized and niche strategies." She elaborates more on their thinking and approach to this important theme in the sidebar titled Credit Runway.

CREDIT RUNWAY

In the aftermath of the financial crisis, it felt as though new "credit opportunity" funds had materialized overnight. This development seemed surprising at first; then it just seemed like a replay of every other postcrisis scenario. Hall explains how she and her team assessed the environment and positioned their portfolio to capitalize on the opportunities in credit.

"Yes, this happens every time," Hall says. "I don't feel it came out of nowhere. If you go back to 2005 until early 2007, there was a lot of discussion of spreads tightening, issuance picking up, and distressed funds being launched.

"There was a much longer buildup to this, even once we got past the first wave, the statistical arbitrage losses at the start of the summer of 2007. There were renewed discussions of the usage of leverage; the markets seized up. I feel there was a longer runway than it seemed to build up relationships with potential partners.

"We felt we were working on this that whole time, digging deeper into our big universe of managers with exposure and expertise. We were in increasingly constant dialogues with managers. It was all really building, going into the summer of 2007, but even well before that when pricing got crazy.

"We looked at managers we had close relationships with, those who chose to access the classic, credit-distressed markets, because spreads had gotten so uninteresting. Those who were sitting back and preparing and then who were able to raise pools in late 2007 and early 2008, could begin to deploy it in an increasingly chaotic market.

"These were seasoned people with experience in the last cycle, back to 1994 to 2002. Those are the people that I think point to point will be very successful. They are a good example of people that go in with a different sort of duration-matching sensibility on their investments than I think the broad hedge fund industry was attuned to. Even with prices dropping and liquidity disappearing, they could be out there buying into it, because they had set up to have capital deployed more slowly. They did not take in all the capital at once and had withdrawal provisions in line with the more episodic nature of the opportunities.

"I think these managers will fare well, but in the short term, no. It's too early. We see a lot of totally new managers and we approach them

(Continued)

CREDIT RUNWAY (*Continued*)

with a high degree of skepticism. They take 'what was good yesterday' and are building a fund around it. Dedicated senior secured loans, dedicated DIP funds. Hello? Again, they might be good marketing pitches, but they are way too narrowly specified. They don't take into account the rate markets are changing and the way opportunity sets are evolving."

Although they worked diligently to implement the increased allocations to credit, Hall says, "It's a tactical shift for two to three years, not a permanent shift." The investment team has also reduced exposure to long/short equity strategies in favor of long-only equity and distressed debt strategies. "We still think there is money to be made, with the balance shifting more toward long."

The investment team has prepared for interest rate shocks and inflation risk, moves less relevant to their hedge fund portfolio, but important in their global equity portfolio with its hard asset exposure. She says they do not adhere to one overall macro view. "We have scenarios, never just one scenario," assign probabilities to various scenarios, and allocate according to those probabilities.

Even if they had a negative view on a market, they would not allocate to short-only strategies. "We have used short-only in the past. The problem is they never change or reduce exposure to adapt to conditions. They are heroes, then give it all back." The problem is compounded from "the investor behavioral perspective. It drives people nuts." She has observed that when short-only strategies drop in value, investors' pain is too disproportionate to the happiness they feel on the upswing. It works better to have a short view embedded in long/short hedge fund strategies.

Allocations to Alternatives

The firm still has a significant allocation to hedge funds, largely because "in a time of great uncertainty, I think the managers are more comfortable making decisions with a more visible shorter term payoff, particularly in the credit area. You can have a high probability of an expected two- to three-year return, as compared to equities with a high probability of a five- to seven-year return, with no opinion of whether you are actually going to get that."

They have allocated significantly more to both hedge funds and long-only public market funds than they have to private structures. "The cost of the illiquidity in private structures is high. In the areas I think will be the most interesting, you have yet to see enough price adjustment." Hall names oil and gas and real estate private partnerships as targets for allocations when prices adjust.

Many endowments reportedly suffered their liquidity problems due to excessive private equity commitments, leading to some secondary sales and rumors of more to come. Hall says, "So much discussion about it and so little trades. The private equity placement firms are talking about $100 billion of overhang. My instincts are that the number is significantly inflated, that there are substantially fewer distressed sellers than people thought. At the right pricing, I think people would adjust their portfolios, but they're not distressed enough to give it away."

They have looked at secondary hedge fund sales in the past, but "when we want to transact, we haven't been able to."

Hedge Fund Industry

Commenting on the state of the hedge fund industry Hall says, "I think we have seen a significant washout of what I would call naïve investors in hedge funds." She describes a group "clinging to a circa 1980s perspective of 1 percent of month and quarterly liquidity, as both a reasonable expectation and a God-given right. They're gone. But that hadn't been available or true for a decade."

Looking toward the future, she thinks managers and investors now have a better understanding of the opportunity set and the asset liability match, as well as an understanding of "the biggest advantage hedge funds had, if they had answered those questions correctly." That advantage, "being able to provide liquidity when other people are panicking as opposed to being the panickers, that's attracting people."

Hall says that is why assets have grown in strategies like distressed and why institutions have remained invested. "Even with the disappointment hedge funds did fulfill their promise." Being down 18 percent in hedge funds is not great, but it is better than being down the 38 percent equity long-only portfolios were in 2008. She thinks investors will look at the trade-offs between hedge funds—higher fees, less liquidity—and equities and increase their commitment to hedge funds. She also thinks the opportunity set is more robust in hedge funds. Nonetheless, "It has been a huge and appropriate wake-up call."

Lessons of the Financial Crisis   The overarching investment lessons from the financial crisis are not new lessons, says Hall. "We just get to learn them again. How many times do we have to learn that leverage cuts both ways? Leverage absolutely imports other people's problems into your portfolio."

Another lesson is, "You can absolutely be too clever by half. Strategies that are finely tuned—in terms of their investor relationships and investment strategies—and that don't leave cushions for the completely unexplained and inexplicable tend to be more brittle than expected, especially at times of great stress."

Hall says we relearned "the importance of having 'robust businesses of the businesses'" to be able to get through challenging times. "The incentives, maturation, sophistication, experience, and calm of the guys at the helm" became glaringly important during the crisis. "Those that had the most difficulty compounded the hard environment by freaking out themselves."

Her awareness of such situations reinforces her lesson. "Investing with people that have the temperament, experience, support, and discipline to keep their composure through good times and bad is really important."

Lesson from the Madoff Fraud   A client told Hall about a "great investor, we should invest." She said, "Great, let's learn about it, send us some information." The great investor, Bernard Madoff, replied "No." For Hall, it was "dead on arrival, on the 'won't talk to us' list." Another client had an indirect investment through a different advisor. When the client asked Hall her opinion of it anyway, she told him, "A. It's dead on arrival due to the behavior. B. The numbers aren't believable." She explains, "Numbers don't work that way. It goes back to experience. Nothing has the kind of consistency that he was purporting to return. Thankfully, the client reduced the position."

Hall saw the biggest red flag almost immediately. "If any organization is not willing to engage in a very professional conversation with an adviser about the sources of returns, because 'it's so exclusive,' people should never invest, period, regardless of what the returns are."

This opinion "hasn't made me the most popular person. It's not that we think we know better, it's just that you can't actually count on the person whose coattails you are riding to have done the work." Investors cannot assume the marquee investor is doing the same rigorous work they would do before making an investment.

In the Madoff situation, the other investors were not doing the work, and "it began a daisy chain. Before you know it, the promoter is marketing the marquee investor's credibility as the de facto due diligence." Investors cannot and should not make investments based on the reputations of the other investors. "You have to have your own viewpoint."

Career Advice

Her investment advice to "have your own viewpoint" could count as career advice too. Another "overarching theme" of her own career, Hall says, is, "You have to be willing to do the hard work and be true to yourself. If it means go out on your own, do it. Accept the consequences and the time it takes. Don't look for quick fixes."

Hall advises, "Be flexible, things change." Looking back on her own career, she remembers "times when I showed a great willingness to be flexible, and times I'd wish I'd had more flexibility." People face trade-offs "between what they know and what other areas they can learn," and they need to assess those trade-offs throughout their careers.

GLOBAL, DIVERSIFIED INVESTOR

The question Hall says she was not asked, "Why are there fewer women running hedge funds and private equity funds?" is one she answers anyway. "There's absolutely no good reason," she says, "except that it's an apprenticeship business and requires a degree of immersion."

Hall explains the implications. "In apprenticeship businesses the leaders tend to hire people in their image. Over time this will prove to be a limiting factor." Opportunity sets have grown, but to capitalize on them, "you need a wide array of perspectives, need to be more global and have broader experience."

She hopes it will change, not as "a political statement," but for more practical reasons. Having a "diverse set of views makes for better investors." As world economies and opportunities evolve, "How are you going to make money?" Hall says managers and investors need to develop "flexibility" or risk they "will miss something big." She urges more managers and investors to approach all they do "with as clear a view as possible."

Organizations like 100 Women in Hedge Funds exist because people like Hall lead the industry forward and because not enough men or women follow her advice to diversify their organizations. The organization's statement announcing Hall's award said, "She has bona fides as both an investor and hedge fund manager." The conclusion reads, "Katie has a well-established reputation for communication with investors; her leadership in this area makes her a role model for so many women in the industry."

The 100 Women in Hedge Funds announcement needs a slight, but important, revision. As a former hedge fund manager and leading hedge fund investor, Katie Hall is a role model for all the investors in the industry.

CHAPTER 12

A Better Way

Ted Seides, Co-Founder, Protégé Partners

I n many ways Ted Seides represents both the past and the future of hedge fund investors. Having learned to invest under the tutelage of David Swensen, the legendary Yale University chief investment officer and author, Seides went on to co-found Protégé Partners and serves as senior managing director of investments. He has also contributed to the industry as an educator, writer, and bettor. Although he is relatively young—age 39 at publication time—his track record of expertise and accomplishment rival those of more senior investors.

He did not start out that way.

"I was fortunate to fall into something right out of college that suits me very well," he says. Until entering Yale University, his limited exposure to investments consisted of having a real—not proverbial—uncle in the business and watching the scrolling ticker on the Financial News Network (the precursor to cable channel CNBC) with his father. Taking Swensen's portfolio management course in his junior year at Yale eventually led Seides to begin his career at the Yale University Investments Office in 1992.

Prior to co-founding and launching Protégé (a multibillion-dollar alternative investment firm that invests in and seeds small and specialized hedge funds) in 2002, Seides gained experience in a variety of investment disciplines. From 2000 to 2001, he was a senior associate at J.H. Whitney & Company, working on hedge fund seed investing and conducting equity research for the firm's long/short hedge fund. Prior to J.H. Whitney, he was an associate at private equity firm Stonebridge Partners and interned in equity research at Brahman Capital, a 20-year-old long-short U.S. equity hedge fund.

Seides holds a BA from Yale University, cum laude, with distinction in the economics and political science major, and an MBA with honors from the Harvard University Graduate School of Business. An active participant in industry trade associations and charitable organizations, he chairs the programming committee of a professional educational forum, the Greenwich Roundtable, serves on the investment committees of the Bruce Museum Endowment and the Wenner-Gren Foundation, and sits on the advisory board for Citizen Schools New York.

Additionally, Seides has written articles and columns for various trade publications, including the late Peter L. Bernstein's *Economics and Portfolio Strategy* newsletter, the *CFA Conference Proceedings Quarterly*, and the NMS Exchange. He wrote "A Matter of Trust: The Issue of Risk Transparency," a chapter in the book *Hedge Fund Strategies: A Global Outlook* by Brian R. Bruce,[1] and the Harvard Business School case study "Woodland Partners: Field of Dreams?"[2] Seides was also a protagonist of the Harvard Business School case study "Protégé Partners: The Capacity Challenge."[3]

BACKGROUND

Seides does seem to have stumbled into his investment career. His parents were not business people—his mother a teacher, his father a psychiatrist—and his father discouraged him from becoming a doctor, saying, "There are better ways to make as good of a living." Even though his father's profession, psychology, fascinated him, Seides trusted his father's advice and thought he had to earn a living another way. As it turns out, his knowledge of psychology factors into his success investing in hedge funds, while one of his mother's often-repeated aphorisms, "Patience is a virtue," similarly influences his investment philosophy.

His uncle in the business lived on the West Coast, so Seides saw him infrequently and felt his influence only on the periphery. Watching the Financial News Network with his father, he became intrigued by stocks. Although he was not one of those teenagers who made a fortune investing bar mitzvah gifts, the more he learned about markets and people, the more he thought investing suited him well.

Seides essentially backed into getting an economics degree at Yale. "I referred to my educational major as Random Studies. I took a broad spectrum of introductory courses I found interesting, and by sophomore year I had almost completed a major, so I finished its requirements and continued my pursuit of Random Studies."

Turning Point

The portfolio management course Seides took with Swensen in his junior year set him on the path to becoming a professional hedge fund investor.

Swensen hired one graduating student a year as an analyst in the Investments Office. When Seides graduated from Yale in the summer of 1992, "the economy had hit a bottom and the job market was tight." He had worked through final-round interviews for the Goldman Sachs training program, but "it sounded brutal, my older friends in the program were miserable, and nobody said it was a great experience until years later; I figured there had to be a better way."

Swensen, with his bias against Wall Street firms now well documented, confirmed Seides's fears. As a result, Seides understates, "I was lucky enough to get the Yale Investments Office job."

Yale Investments Office

Seides learned investing at the Yale Investments Office. The training had "academic underpinnings" similar to the disciplined approach of the Chartered Financial Analyst (CFA) program, with an investment philosophy he describes as "value investing, executed through managers." Although he had taken investment courses, including Swensen's, "I didn't really understand what a stock was until the day I walked into the Yale Investments Office. I learned about hedge funds the same day I learned about stocks."

When Seides joined the Yale Investments Office in 1992, institutional investors had not yet begun to invest in hedge funds extensively. Yale is credited as being among the first to do so, but in the early days Seides spent the bulk of his time analyzing long-only managers. He believes it was important to have learned to invest in that structure first.

"I don't understand how someone can learn to invest in hedge fund managers unless they can see through the managers, into their portfolios, and understand what they are actually doing. There is no way to confirm what someone tells you they're doing unless you can look at it on a position level and track it over time. I was able to learn about investing and the investment process—finding managers, analyzing managers, and monitoring managers—in a very transparent way, because my work involved long-only managers with assets held in custody accounts."

He found Yale's "very disciplined approach" an extremely valuable experience, saying it was "incredibly important for me to learn good habits before I developed bad ones on my own."

The benefit of the Yale training and experience, Seides says, is "working with people like David Swensen and Dean Takahashi [Swensen's long-time deputy] who think every day with a perpetual time horizon and are phenomenal selectors of talent. I got to spend the lion's share of my time being around the people David and Dean believed were the very best at what they do. After experiencing that every day for five years, I found it much easier to recognize when other managers were not on the same tier as the ones Yale employed."

Seides believes it is hard to learn the investment business "when the epitome of what you're trying to achieve in a portfolio is something you have never seen done before. So much involves pattern recognition, and having witnessed mentors who made great decision after great decision makes a huge difference in seeing the right patterns down the road."

At the same time, he realizes that he had a rare professional privilege. He believes he was the only junior analyst at an endowment or foundation in the country during the time he worked in the Yale Investments Office, mainly because "there were no more than a handful of fully staffed investment offices in the late '80s and early '90s."

When Seides joined the Yale Investments Office, Swensen had been its leader for seven years. The timing turned out to be fortuitous. "It takes that long to craft an endowment portfolio into a new leader's image." Seides joined "at the end of a restructuring and at the beginning of a long execution period. I hit the sweet spot."

Several prominent nonprofit chief investment officers overlapped with Seides under Swensen in the Yale Investments Office. "They were imminently qualified to move into senior leadership positions in part because they had similar training, and there *is* a training, a set of rules, that generally holds true." Although Swensen documented those lessons in his book, *Pioneering Portfolio Management* (Free Press, 2000), Seides says, "The day-to-day reality is different from simply reading a book." That training gave him the fundamental underpinning for much of what he knows and does as an investor.

As much as he liked his job at Yale, he found his life in New Haven outside of work isolating. Single, in his late 20s, and interested in starting a family, he made plans to move on. "Had I been married, I [might] have spent my entire career at Yale. It was an absolutely wonderful place to work. David preached balance, and I thought I stood a better chance experiencing a full life outside of work living elsewhere. At the end of the day, I care a lot more about my family than about making money."

Transition from Yale

Seides was admitted to Harvard Business School and decided to go. He says, "I had long aspired—somewhat irrationally—to go to HBS," in part because his uncle had attended HBS and his mother had been a Harvard graduate student. However, he considered the move quite rationally. He observed that many investment managers had Harvard MBA degrees and strong connections through that network, and he concluded that its interactive teaching style and the quality of student body made it the best business school for him.

The majority of the people he knew in the industry were investment managers selected by Swensen. Lacking peers in the industry or at other institutions, Seides felt a void. "One thing I missed while at Yale was the ability to build my own network. I wanted to be around a group of peers that could constitute that group, the next generation of investment managers."

Swensen discouraged Seides from going to business school, so "even though in my heart I knew I wanted to go," he researched the decision among the members of the Yale Investment Committee. Many had gone to graduate business schools, and all the Harvard graduates "to a one" said, "If you get in, just go. Don't think about it, don't ask why, you'll figure out what I mean when you get there." When he spoke to investment managers with Stanford MBAs, "They gave more rational and thoughtful responses about the strengths and weaknesses of modern business education. I thought there must be something special about HBS when such luminaries, in good faith, consistently said 'just go, you'll figure it out later.'"

Although HBS did not disappoint and he "definitely understands what they meant," his experience of graduating from college and going directly into working in an investment organization "at the top of the food chain" caused him to struggle somewhat in his career moves after business school. "The only jobs I knew how to do well were managing a couple of billion dollars and taking out the trash." So he "dabbled around" to see if his interest in what he did at Yale would apply to roles with more direct involvement in the markets.

He had aspired to be a portfolio manager, so he worked at an investment firm in the summer of 1998. Seides says, "It wasn't the most pleasant experience being in a value-oriented shop that was short Internet stocks at the beginning of the bubble." After business school, he joined a small private equity firm. "I thought I wanted to dive in and learn how to analyze companies, but the time-intensive nature of deals took me away from being around the markets."

Seides joined J.H. Whitney to conduct research for its hedge fund, but to his surprise, he was not happy doing it. "I couldn't figure out why. I always thought I wanted to pick stocks. But for reasons I couldn't explain at the time, I didn't like business analysis as much as I enjoyed the statistical and interpersonal analysis involved in investing through managers."

Seides took a step back to analyze his predicament. "I knew that I loved public investment markets, being around and analyzing people, and sports," but that didn't tell him enough. Upon further analysis he realized, "I played a lot of sports growing up, but I was never a guy who thrived on external competition. A lot of top, top people in the industry were competitive athletes—the guy you want on the free-throw line, down one point, with the clock expired. I was never that guy—I was the clubhouse guy. The guy you wanted to have in the locker room to bring the team together."

Seides realized he loved being on a team. As a high school wrestler he would compile stats on the entire league and prep his teammates about their opponents. He had followed the Yankees religiously since childhood, yet tended to follow box scores as much as the games. "I discovered that what I did out of college was a perfect fit for me, for what I love doing, and I already had the best training in the world." He decided to look for an opportunity to invest in markets through other people, in a role that would allow him to choose investment managers, similar to the experience he had had at Yale.

A Focus on Small and Early-Stage Hedge Funds

Choosing to specialize in hedge funds, as opposed to other asset classes, boiled down to a simple analysis. "Hedge funds are a structure—no more, no less. Hedge fund managers have the flexibility to think broadly across asset classes, investment markets, and risk versus reward in a relatively unconstrained way, similar to the way we at Yale thought across asset classes. Yale ate the free lunch of diversification by looking around the world for the best opportunities, which is one of the things I loved about my time there." His post-MBA hedge fund experience gave him an additional advantage, because "I'd learned more about what goes on inside the sausage factory—and it's usually messy, even when the ultimate product is good."

In the midst of his self-assessment, the portfolio manager of the J.H. Whitney hedge fund decided to start his own hedge fund and asked Seides to join him. Facing a longer commute—and its potential for social isolation—he declined, but offered to help his colleague set up the new firm. After watching the project evolve, he realized that he "really enjoyed the process of creating the business and having the knowledge to be helpful."

Seides looked at how his passions and skills combined to determine what he wanted from his next role.

- **Portfolio involvement:** He wanted to be involved in decision-making at the portfolio level and have access to underlying manager portfolios at the position level.
- **Advisor:** He wanted a role that allowed him to be helpful to people and to offer them sound, unbiased advice.
- **Greater than limited partnership:** He wanted a closer relationship with managers than just being another outside investor.

As a result, he decided to pursue seeding new hedge funds and investing in smaller managers, an approach "that bore a striking resemblance to Yale's investment style."

Between 1997, when Seides left Yale, and 2001, when he began an active search for career opportunities involving seeding managers, his mentor David Swensen had published his book *Pioneering Portfolio Management.* Seemingly overnight, Seides's once obscure professional past became popular conversation. Everyone, especially potential employers, wanted to talk about David Swensen. While Seides admits lacking an entrepreneurial instinct, he saw an opportunity to capitalize and thought, "If others wanted to monetize my resume, I figured I might as well try to do it myself."

Swensen introduced Seides to David Salem, the founder of the Investment Fund for Foundations (TIFF). Salem had an interest in expanding TIFF's hedge fund team, but after their meeting Seides told him, "I'm interested and would love to continue nonprofit investment work, just not for another 15 years or so." Salem then connected Seides with Jeffrey Tarrant from the TIFF board who was working on a similar idea. That introduction led Seides and Tarrant to form a partnership and launch Protégé.

The entrepreneurial Tarrant brought business acumen and experience Seides lacked, having founded Altvest, the first Internet-enabled hedge fund database (now a division of Morningstar), and having seeded and invested in hedge funds for a family office. Tarrant already had plans to start a fund as a division of Reservoir Capital, a firm led by Dan Stern.

"Dan Stern is a great investor. He understands patient investing at its core and is one of the best, if not the best, relationship seeder in the business." Seides knew of Stern from his Yale days, but Tarrant and Stern were longtime personal friends and were ultimately hesitant to launch a business together for fear it could interfere with their friendship. After separating from Reservoir, Tarrant and Seides forged ahead independently, launching Protégé Partners in July 2002.

The two shared similar business philosophies. Starting with the notion that "the world doesn't need another asset-gathering fund of hedge funds," they had a clean slate to design an optimal, investment-driven model. "We come into the office every day trying to help people—help our investors generate returns, help managers navigate their careers. If a person across the desk from me can receive my honest feedback about the best thing for them, in the long run that will be best for us and our clients as well."

Their interests and skills complemented each other. Seides says, "I'm an investment guy and an interpersonal guy. I've learned about the business side, but it doesn't get me as excited as being a full-time investor and a part-time psychologist for hedge fund managers." He adds, "I'm a great number two in an entrepreneurial environment."

A New Model Hedge Fund Investment Firm

Lessons from dabbling earlier in his career coalesced at Protégé. Seides and Tarrant shared a common belief with Yale that "size is the enemy of performance." Surveying the industry in 2002, they expected hedge funds would be adopted in more and more portfolios and lead to bifurcation. Most investors would focus on larger managers and "there would be real differentiation between larger funds and smaller ones. So we decided to specialize in the universe of smaller managers."

Regarding portfolio construction, the partners knew that many smaller managers would have trouble competing with larger managers. As Seides puts it, "A three-person shop can't compete with Och-Ziff across the breadth of their activities." They decided they would build a portfolio of smaller managers, akin to a multistrategy fund, by finding the most talented managers in a variety of single-strategy niches and diversifying the portfolio qualitatively. An example would be combining a Korean long/short equity fund in a portfolio with a dedicated U.S. equity short seller.

Seeding new funds was a natural extension of the strategy. Yale had invested in new managers, essentially putting them in business, but did not take stakes in those businesses. Protégé planned to fund new managers as a part of its strategy, but intended for its clients to have a share of the business. Seides had been involved in emerging manager analysis at Yale and Tarrant had extensive experience seeding new managers prior to starting Protégé, so for Seides, "having the ability to be one level closer to managers and understanding the analysis of new managers made it a natural fit."

The numbers worked too. "If you can do a good job picking managers, you get the upside for free." That presents an attractive opportunity "in a world where diversified portfolios used to make 12 percent to 15 percent, but now looked like they would make 8 percent to 10 percent, because assets were flooding into hedge funds and diluting elusive alpha. We could turn the negative industry dynamic on its head and benefit from the growth of the industry."

"Focusing on smaller managers, executing in thoughtful ways," is how Seides summarizes the Protégé model.

Alignment of Interests

David Swensen had engrained in Seides the importance of proper alignment of interests between investor and manager, but it must be handled delicately in seeding. Taking ownership stakes in funds can create situations that might cause conflicts of interest.

Seides and Tarrant asked themselves, "How do we create a structure so that our clients know that we have their interests at heart?" They concluded, "You have to have everything in the same pool of assets." Seides says, "In the seeding business, you have to serve all of your masters at once. Starting de novo, we could create a great structure."

They created a hybrid model, one they believed few others could replicate. As they analyzed it in 2002, many large hedge funds were closed to new investment, so a new fund of funds needed to have existing relationships with managers in order to access top talent. Yet newly launched organizations often did not have that access. Those with experience and access usually were already managing significant pools of capital and thus couldn't combine their best hedge fund ideas with seeding opportunities without cannibalizing their base business. In forming Protégé, they aspired to combine investments in the best existing small managers with seeding emerging managers in new funds. They thought, "Two guys with great relationships, deep experience, and a fresh pool of capital could invest very creatively for their clients."

Seides stresses that Protégé is not a seeding-only fund and says they have refused to create one despite being asked. "For what we know and understand about seed investing, we would never put our own money into a seed-only fund. We'd never go out and ask someone to put their own money in something we wouldn't invest in ourselves."

INVESTMENT PROCESS

Regarding his hedge fund investment process, Seides states that while he has some personal biases, he thinks that overall his approach is not demonstrably different from that of other sophisticated investors. But just as investors seek hedge fund managers who can add value with unique skills and insights, the personal biases and ideas a hedge fund investor brings to the table in selecting hedge funds can make a big difference in performance.

Manager Assessment

Protégé documented its investment process in a policy statement, listing "a sense of humor" among the prerequisites for choosing a manager. Although that statement may seem flippant on the surface, Seides and Tarrant have found it to be true. "Investing is a humbling business, and managers who cannot release the tension tend to have short half-lives."

Seides offers a summary of other characteristics they look for in a hedge fund manager.

"At the core, managers need to have a philosophy about what they're trying to do—not just what works, but why it works—and have an execution strategy that makes sense. They must have an identifiable competitive advantage, meaning they either gather or process information better than their competitors. Underpinning the fund should be a sector, strategy, or assets that—independent of the manager—provide an attractive opportunity set."

Regarding the personal qualities of individuals, he used to "always want to hire a hedge fund manager I would never want to work for." Back when he worked at Yale, Seides saw that to be great in the business, a manager needed high degrees of intensity, obsession, and competitiveness, and he had thought the manager's "drive to succeed almost should, by its nature, be difficult for another person to keep up with." Seides now thinks that may not always be the case.

"That changed somewhat, because over the years I found that I became more and more like one of those types of people."

Organization Assessment

Seides believes partnerships can be better than sole proprietorships. "However, successful partnerships require self-awareness by the principals and take a lot of work, like marriage. Most partnerships in a male-dominated industry don't work well. A sole proprietorship or at least a lead decision maker is preferable to a poorly functioning partnership."

His approach veers "way on the qualitative side." Seides explains why.

"One, I have yet to meet a hedge fund manager that could promise they would deliver the returns in the future that they had delivered in the past. Two, hedge funds change much more frequently than traditional long-only strategies, so prior performance not only isn't indicative of future performance, but also often doesn't look anything like it."

While he is biased toward qualitative assessment, he believes "it's important to measure everything you can." His team uses numerous metrics to assess manager skill and ability to generate alpha, such as calculating the return on the long and short sides of the portfolio, looking at spreads and leverage, and comparing that information to the market to determine market exposure and timing.

But, he says, "At the end of day it doesn't matter. The data set is much shorter than the likely life of the relationship. You have to be very careful that your analysis is not garbage in, garbage out."

An element of pattern recognition imbues his qualitative approach. The most striking comparison "is the similarity between analyzing a company and investing in hedge funds. Equity analysts assess management teams and their ability to execute against a set of metrics." Seides lists a few questions an equity analyst would likely ask to evaluate a company:

- What are the management team's incentives?
- Are management incentives aligned with yours?
- What is their motivation?
- How do they motivate their team?
- What distractions do they have?

The same questions can be used when looking at a fund.

The comparison to equity research conventions applies to the smaller funds in the portfolio. Seides says, "We invest in a lot of small-cap companies that all have a single product." In comparison, he thinks most hedge fund investors "invest in GE. If you're a research analyst looking at GE, you have to go meet every manager at every subdivision to conduct a comprehensive analysis. It's a lot of work, and you don't really have the access to do it." Investing in small hedge funds is akin to investing in small-cap stocks, because "there is a lot of work to do, but you can do it, because you can go and meet each manager."

According to Seides, even Yale, with its capability and resources, had few investments in large hedge funds during his tenure, so he cannot fathom how other organizations can analyze them effectively. "I wouldn't know how to do it; how to get their time and attention to grant you access when you're just another of their 300 clients."

He thinks excessive manager monitoring can become counterproductive and aims to spend an appropriate amount of time with a manager to have the information needed to make decisions. For instance, some hedge fund investors require their managers to participate in monthly calls. Seides calls them "tremendously helpful for the fund of funds, but equally detrimental for managers. If everyone required it, the managers wouldn't have enough time to manage money."

Yet he says industry metrics indicate that most hedge fund investors—whether fund of hedge funds or institutions—have 85 to 90 percent of their assets invested with the same 170 to 200 large hedge funds.

In rare instances, Protégé will make a conscious exception and invest in a specialized product sponsored by a large firm. "There have been niche opportunities we wanted to pursue that were best executed by a larger manager in a segregated product. We don't invest in the flagship fund."

Isolating a strategy in a larger organization has allowed them to pursue opportunities in attractive sectors or asset types and to structure the investment in ways that benefited them, such as limiting fund size or reducing fees.

Incentive Fees

One of the single most important questions Seides asks when evaluating a new fund is, "Where is the manager's money?"

He says, "Sometimes it's not appropriate for the manager to have all of their money in the strategy. It may be too risky for all of their eggs and create a misalignment between the manager and the other investors. The amount of money has to be appropriately meaningful for the manager."

The hedge fund incentive fee is supposed to align the interests of managers and investors, but the 2008 financial crisis caused investors to question that construct. New types of fee structures should match lock-up periods more closely to the liquidity of the underlying assets and investor liquidity. Some are seeking claw-backs, a private equity convention requiring managers to pay or earn back incentive fees paid on unrealized gains, if those gains are then actually unrealized.

Seides calls himself an "internal perfectionist," meaning he's a perfectionist "in a flawed way. I want to have the best performance in the industry all the time and tend to dwell on our mistakes when we've fallen short." When it comes to fee structures, he says, "In a world of imperfection, you can't have absolute rules about hedge funds—you need to make compromises." He feels he can only do so much to influence proper structures, saying that the laws of supply and demand, and the decisions of other investors, ultimately determine the deal between general and limited partners.

"We would love to see structures properly align the GP and the LP. In an ideal world, what I refer to as a David Swensen world, the manager couldn't take incentive fees until you [the investor] took money out of the partnership."

However, he adds, "Pricing—incentive fees included—is a consequence of supply and demand. With some smaller managers, important clients are in a better position to create fair rules. There are so few truly great hedge fund managers, though there are many more today than 10 or 15 years ago, that sometimes you're a price taker, sometimes you're a price maker."

In addition to fee structure, Seides pays attention to fund size. "We view size as a qualitative, not a quantitative, dimension. How big is a fund that's too big for us? It depends."

When assessing a manager's size, he asks, "Has the manager grown in such a way that we think their prospective returns for the strategy are as good or better than anyone we can find that is smaller? An appropriate size may be different for different people and strategies, and may change over time."

Seides shies away from absolute rules about many investment criteria. "Someone may say, 'I'll never invest in a manager who lost 85 percent of my money.' In general, that makes a lot of sense, but with any rule, there could be exceptions. What if the market fell 90 percent as it did from 1929 to 1932?"

Investors need to have a set of rules they generally follow and believe to be true, be "very thoughtful and conscious when making an exception," and be certain the reward is worth it.

"If rules are too tight, you can create your own adverse selection. I'm not a big believer in artificially limiting the opportunity set." Seides says investors already have enough limits. "If we agree that Jim Simons of Renaissance cracked the code on the market, and that his Medallion fund will be the best-performing hedge fund in the years to come, then by definition everyone, except for his employees, has adverse selection."

Due Diligence

Although his due diligence process may not differ broadly from that of other investors, Seides has developed interesting tactics to elicit the insight and information needed to evaluate a manager.

Like other investors, he asks a basic set of questions and advocates spending a lot of time with managers over time. Investors need to "get inside the portfolio and get past the pitch."

In order to get to know managers, investors should spend time with them "in a variety of settings other than sitting across the business table, talking about their portfolio." David Swensen applied this tactic "brilliantly" at Yale. "Maybe it's easier in New Haven, but go out to lunch, play golf," or, he jokes, "Go see a movie."

He learned a great questioning tactic at HBS while working on a case about the Toyota Production System; it's a philosophy called "The Five Whys." Seides gives an example from the case to describe the tactic.

> *If the assembly line experienced a breakdown, the foreman would ask the worker, "Why isn't it working?" and kept asking why until he resolved the problem.*
> *The piece fell down. Why?*
> *The belt tilted over. Why?*
> *There was a screw missing. Why?*
> *Quality control didn't check.*

The point of the exercise is, "If you ask the question 'Why?' five times, you will get to the heart of the issue." Now he teaches his team, "When you're questioning a manager, all you have to do to get in depth is ask them

'Why?' five times. It's a simple application, but works incredibly well at getting to the core of what managers do."

Aspect Expertise One tactic Seides uses to gain deeper insight into a manager's portfolio and investment skill has the added benefit of enhancing the Protégé team's understanding of investments. They gather a detailed amount of information and develop strong knowledge about one aspect of the manager's area of expertise.

"If managers spend all day doing something, they'll know more than you. So know something in detail in their sphere of influence in order to ask better questions." For this reason, Protégé has developed the capability to make direct investments. "The more you're in the game, the better able you are to ask questions and have relationships that inform."

Verify, Then Trust One of the most basic steps in conducting manager due diligence, checking references, can also be among the most difficult to accomplish in a "litigious society." When contacting people on a manager's list of references, Seides has found "they never say anything bad; they tell the story the person wants to hear. I know—I've been on a lot of reference lists." His knowledge of psychology and interest in people helps him work around some of the weaknesses of the reference process.

"Any time managers come in, they come with a life history. Their success or lack thereof is known to someone—what they do well, not well, what they need to work on—it's just not known to you. Our goal in reference checking is to learn the truth."

When he talks to a reference he does not already know about a manager, Seides tries to determine the person's biases, objectives, and psychology. Despite the obstacles, he finds it helpful to call references. "If you don't find people that say good things, that's telling. Any worthwhile manager can find at least five or six people to say good things about them."

He offers a particularly valuable piece of advice for extracting good information from references. "Keep asking the manager for someone else to talk to. The way we get to the truth is by finding someone that knows the manager intimately, that has worked with him, but *that we just happen to know better than the manager knows him.*"

Being able to do that requires having a lot of relationships and an expansive memory bank of people in the business. He and Tarrant have networks akin to a "binomial tree of the many portfolio managers and analysts we have held relationships with over the years."

Seides lists reference tactics many investors probably do not know about, but he says are easy for anyone to do.

Easy and Helpful Reference Tricks

- **Early Life:** Seides always talks to someone the manager knew growing up or attending school. "People change, but not that much; you can learn what makes someone tick."
- **Admin:** Seides recommends talking to the person's former administrative assistant. He knows this from his own life. "My assistant knows everything about me." Furthermore, "the best person to do that reference check is your own administrative assistant."
- **Google Alerts:** This service allows the user to input the name of a manager or fund and receive an e-mail when the Google search engine detects news or information about the entity.
- **Ghin.com:** Check the golf handicap registration site. Seides recalls a story of a manager whose clients discovered that he had played 50 rounds of golf one summer during a particularly tough year. "After the fact, they weren't too happy." Now he makes checking this site a routine part of due diligence.

Creative Insights A junior analyst on the Protégé team known affectionately as "Doogie Howser" (the seminal role of television star Neil Patrick Harris) has a natural gift for playing Twenty Questions. The analyst learned a lot about investing in school, and, Seides says, "He constantly asks questions; some are right down the middle, some are out in left field and seemingly way off base, but also might be brilliant." Seides has "Doogie" review material and compile a list of questions he would ask the manager.

While unique to Protégé, the idea demonstrates the need to think creatively and resourcefully when conducting due diligence on a manager.

Seides uses Ghin.com and similar services not because he believes managers should have no other interests, but in order to discern whether the manager has any distractions that could affect management of the portfolio.

"Distractions can be both negative and positive parts of a manager's life cycle and are always a consideration. At any point things can change meaningfully, especially since managers can make so much money in such a short period of time."

Monitoring the person and where he is in life helps him get a sense of a manager's personal qualities, approach to work and life, and how he spends time and money.

Manager Characteristics

Accurately identifying and assessing a manager's characteristics is crucial for deciding whether the manager warrants an investment. Some investors employ a "Beer Test," making one of their investment criteria whether they want to have a beer with the person. Seides finds fault with that approach.

"One great thing about this business and investing through managers is [that] you can pick people you think are the best at what they do, and by virtue of that relationship and respect, you may become friends with them."

More important than a personal connection or "a behavioral bias grounded in commonality" is the manager's degree of integrity. Seides looks for a person who displays intellectual honesty and self-awareness and who "believes, at times to their own detriment, their mission is to serve their clients."

According to Seides, "Yale had a tremendous focus on getting the people right." He quotes Glen Greenberg of Chieftain Capital, a Yale graduate and money manager. When asked the three most important criteria in selecting a stock, he said, "It's the management team, the management team, and the management team." Because Seides heard that message for years, he believed it from a mostly academic perspective, until he "experienced things people did that I never thought they would."

He now cares much more about the character of the people he invests with. "Not sure I'd always want to have a beer with all of our managers, but if I know that person has such passion about what they do, and to a fault, passion about doing it for the clients, that's the kind of person I want to invest with."

Portfolio Management

Protégé allocates its money at the margin to attractive investment opportunities it identifies through research, analysis, and brainstorming. It develops a medium-term view of the world's direction and invests 20 percent to 30 percent of the portfolio tactically, based on an investment thesis with a finite life.

Asked if they pursue style selection over manager selection, Seides responds, "We're on the cusp of a shift in the thinking. At Yale, we would go out and find the best jockey. Now people have realized you also have to be riding the right horse. You could have the best jockey, but the horse could be galloping into the Hudson River."

Protégé considers a blend of its time horizon and liquidity when making decisions. Seides compares it to navigating a battleship. Although making tactical moves is important, he says, "You can't make tactical moves over two to three months in our structure, it's more like two to three years. You need time, often don't have liquidity, and markets move too quickly." More importantly, he believes "if there is one common flaw I see across all of investing, it is chasing performance. Hedge fund investors generally aren't patient enough with their managers. I follow a lesser known cliché—don't just do something, sit there."

The team can invest in mutual funds or long-only investments in addition to outside hedge fund managers. "The problem for most funds of funds is that they have to invest only in hedge funds, narrowing the opportunity set. There are times when the investment opportunity is in tactical beta or a co-investment with a manager. Being one step closer to the markets also helps us get an edge when interviewing managers."

For example, at the end of 2008 investment-grade bonds offered "equity-like returns with bond-like risks" (a classic description of hedge fund return objectives), making them an attractive investment for a period of time, but Protégé does not have a policy allocation to always invest in high-quality bonds.

If they had attempted to execute using a hedge fund manager, Seides says, they would have paid fees of 1.5 and 20 for bonds yielding 9 percent, and "there goes the equity-like return." Instead, they conducted further research and invested in a mutual fund with daily liquidity. "That was the most efficient way to pursue the opportunity." The investment demonstrates that "we are able to be more tactical and nimble when appropriate."

Style Biases Surrounded by a group of value-oriented investors when learning to invest at Yale, Seides absorbed their message. Seemingly influenced by Ayn Rand, these investors "firmly believe there's only one way to invest: Buy things with a margin of safety and nothing else matters. That's absolutely the Yale mantra and the way I learned to invest."

A value mantra makes sense to him at an intellectual level and it makes an "incredible amount of sense from an allocator's perspective. When something is going wrong, you know what to do."

For instance, "with a long-only value manager, you know what to do in a situation. If he's down and your thesis is still intact, give him money; up, take away some money; buy low, sell high."

It took him years before he could stop saying, "If it's not a value fund, I'm not interested."

His perspective started to change when he began working with Tarrant. Seides says they share strong skills and experience in assessing value-oriented investments, but partners Tarrant and Soros alum Scott Bessent also "have much more experience, judgment, and pattern recognition ability in nontraditional value areas such as global macro."

Seeing Yale miss "some extraordinary hedge fund" investment opportunities after his tenure there and realizing that "the long term" means different things to different investors also helped him get past his value bias.

"The proverbial long time horizon is much shorter than anyone wants to admit. In hedge funds, it is two to three years. If a value style is out of favor for long enough, the market will stay irrational longer than you can stay solvent."

While no longer militantly biased toward value managers, he remains largely in favor of equity and credit hedge fund strategies. He has gained comfort with global macro investing by agreeing with Tarrant and Bessent to focus solely on fundamentally driven macro managers. Seides tends to avoid systematic and quantitative strategies, but not because he doesn't understand them.

"Statistical arbitrage—I'm not a believer, not on the investment side, but the business side. It's a classic principal-agent dilemma. You give them money, but no model works forever. The problem is, if a manager isn't doing well, they know from their research that the model no longer works, but they have no incentive to tell you and lose their revenue stream. So they will tell you, 'We're working on new things.' It's impossible for the investor to know whether the model is working or not, and therefore, whether your capital has migrated from buying a functioning product to buying R&D, because the manager has the incentive not to tell you that the model is broken."

Seides dislikes strategies that require leverage and those he calls "high-octane trading," especially in volatile markets, because of the trading costs.

Protégé does not invest in CTA (commodity trading advisor) funds, because his team's evaluation capabilities are stronger in other areas. "My strong bias is to invest in something I can understand. Occasionally, we will meet with a manager that seems really smart. But when they leave, I realize I don't have a clue what they just said. In those cases, I've learned that the problem is with them, not me."

It takes discipline to avoid strategies that may be interesting or in favor, but as Seides points out, "Theoretically there are 7,000 funds to overturn. We can't meet them all, so let's focus on funds we can get right."

Positioning for the Market Environment   Looking toward the future, Seides expects the financial crisis of 2008 to have ongoing repercussions. "History shows that financial and banking crises take a long, long time to work through, much longer than most can envision."

He takes pride in the fact that he and his team had been bearish on credit, the asset class hit hardest during the crisis. "The real carnage—or call it impairment—happened in the two manager buckets of credit and big multistrategy funds that invested in credit. The drift into private equity was also a disaster for hedge funds."

For one thing, he is focusing on hedge funds that do what they are actually supposed to do—hedge—with long and short positions, "because we are not going to have the tailwinds that we became accustomed to."

Managing Risk   Managing risk in the Protégé portfolio begins with the steps they take to mitigate the risks of the underlying funds when they make the initial investment. "In a world of trust but verify, we think we know what they're doing. We have full, position-level transparency on over 75 percent of our portfolio, but we are still big believers in the 'you never know' risk." To protect against what they "don't know," they take an operational risk management approach and do not invest more than 5 percent of the portfolio with any one manager.

When seeding, Protégé always gets 100 percent transparency of the positions in the manager's portfolio and over time, has been able to increase the amount of transparency it gets from other managers. Managed accounts offer investors more control of portfolio assets, liquidity, and full transparency, so Protégé has moved toward using them more. "Transparency is a wonderful thing," Seides says, but investors need to know "what to do with information once you get it."

Because Protégé has individual position information, they approach risk management in their overall portfolio more like the managers of multistrategy hedge funds. "Who the managers are and how many are in the portfolio doesn't matter as much for assessing position-level risk," Seides says. The questions that concern them include:

- What do we own?
- What exposures do they create for us?
- What do we think about those exposures?

To answer those questions, they aggregate the portfolio at the individual position level to the best of their ability. Having full transparency with many managers allows them to do so, but when lacking full transparency, they rely on 13F filings, manager correspondence, and audited financial statements to fill the gaps. They use the data to create their own model of each individual manager's portfolio and link these to the Bloomberg system so they can monitor the portfolio on their own. If their model tracks the actual performance reasonably well, they conclude there is sufficient transparency. If their model does not function well enough, they work with the manager to refine it.

The approach allows them to ask better questions. "If a manager says they're down 2 percent, we know they're down 2 percent. But if the market is up 6 percent, we don't have to ask what happened. We can ask, 'What happened with that stock?' Or better yet, I can see that this or that happened, how did you react?"

Knowing portfolio positions and performance not only allows them to ask better, deeper questions, it also allows them to act quickly if necessary.

Seides acknowledges the approach cannot handle every eventuality, or what he calls the "known unknowns or unknown unknowns."

"Even if you have a quant model, how is the manager going to behave? You really only learn how a manager will behave after experiencing the extremes, periods of great success or periods of great failure. Most people don't have enough of those data points to make a determination about what will happen the next time."

Nonetheless, they continue to seek ways to prevent the unknown risks of their underlying managers from impacting their portfolio. Chris Endgall, a former prime brokerage lending executive with 20 years' experience working with hedge funds, recently joined Protégé in a senior risk management role, adding a new dimension to their analysis.

"He takes individual managers and analyzes them from the credit perspective, while we use metrics more akin to equity analysis. Chris looks at things in a completely different way, because he's concerned about return *of* capital. We may have one metric for liquidity, he has five."

Every quarter, the team reviews the overall portfolio from a big-picture perspective. After aggregating all the position-level details, they look for cap biases, sector biases, and style biases, and evaluate the performance of the long and short positions across equities, credit, currency, and commodities. They then focus on investment management, assessing the current state of the portfolio, evaluating their market exposures, and determining their goals for the portfolio based on their themes and expectations.

Ultimately their two most important considerations for managing risk are knowing what securities and positions comprise their portfolio and understanding and mitigating the risks of the individual managers.

Seides makes an important point about the difference between risk management and risk measurement. "There is a tremendous difference between risk measurement and risk management. While it is important to measure everything you can—market exposures, VaR, factors, stress scenarios—that has nothing to do with managing risk. Risk measurement is backward looking. Risk management is forward looking. It has more to do with experience than it does metrics.

"Part of our role as an investment manager is to be a risk manager."

INDUSTRY ISSUES AND CHALLENGES

Considering the issues and challenges he expects the hedge fund industry and investors to face for the foreseeable future, Seides worries most about the industry's poor and misunderstood image among the general public and with some investors.

Bad Public Relations

"For many years the hedge fund industry has suffered from really bad, misguided PR. It's understandable. Investigative journalists have the same skill set as stock analysts, but they don't make as much money. Their incentives are to report what's news, what's sensational, what's hot, big ups and big downs. It is ironic, because the outlier stories they report are the antithesis of what hedge fund investing is all about."

The industry's poor image with investors stems from oversimplified and overblown marketing messages. The problem is, Seides says, "The output of the hedge fund became the input used to sell them. Fifteen years ago, managers who ran widely diversified portfolios of merger arbitrage transactions provided liquidity to the markets, captured spreads, and delivered smooth annual return streams of 12 to 15 percent because deals closed at different times." Over time, managers added distressed investing to have a portfolio of two counter-cyclical strategies, providing return opportunities through the cycle.

In the last 10 years, Seides says, "People who were selling hedge funds said, 'Look at this, you can make 1 percent a month!' Make money in up times and down times."

Hedge fund managers and investors seemed to forget the true meaning of certain investment concepts. "Absolute return means you aren't tied to a benchmark. It's absolute versus relative. You are trying to make equity-like expected returns with less correlation to the markets. That's an entirely different proposition from absolute value—the mathematical expression of an always positive number.

"Equities are also supposed to make equity-like expected returns, but no one assumes equities must go up all the time!"

In other words, like equities, hedge funds can go down in value, but in theory hedge funds should drop less. Seides adds, "Hedge funds have done well when markets fell, like in 2000 to 2001 or even from January to September of 2008. But they don't do well when markets fail."

The fallout from the collapse of the capital markets in 2008 and from the misunderstood perception of hedge funds is one of his "unknowable" risks. "I'm not sure what it means for the industry, but it has to factor into how you participate in investing." Therefore, Seides advises investors, "Invest your capital in a way that if you need it, you have access to it."

Fraud Protection

Seides relays a story about the renowned long-only equity investor, Michael Price of Mutual Shares, a victim of the Sunbeam-Oster fraud perpetrated in the mid-1990s. When Seides asked what he had learned, Price said, "Absolutely nothing!" making the point that "fraud is fraud; the best way to protect against it is diversification."

He agrees with Price and explains why. "We spend 98 percent of our time trying to assess the investment opportunity. Maybe we spend 2 percent of our time asking whether what we just saw actually exists. For every minute you spend trying to determine if what you saw is real, that charlatan is spending a month making sure they stay a few steps ahead of you.

"If someone really wants to defraud you, if they're that clever and motivated, they will."

That said, from an investment perspective, Seides believes the Bernard Madoff fraudulent fund that came to light in December 2008 was relatively easy for investors who understand and conduct due diligence to avoid.

From the psychological perspective, he says, "Madoff is a sociopath. There was a scary elegance to everything he did, playing on people's emotions and desire to be in the club. He lulled some smart people to sleep with steady, but not spectacular returns."

Although he believes diversification is the best way to protect the portfolio from fraud, there's a trade-off with being too diversified.

"One manager that is 5 percent of the portfolio can lose all their money and we might survive as a business. If a manager is 20 percent of the portfolio and loses all the money, then there's no chance we survive." The trade-off at the extremes is between concentrating best ideas in 10 to 15 managers or thinking "you know nothing" and having as many as 100 managers in the portfolio. Protégé falls somewhere in between. From a risk perspective, Seides thinks it matters little if an investor has 15 managers or 100 managers if they all own the exact same positions, so he believes investors need to look at the positions in their underlying portfolio.

IDEALS, OBSERVATIONS, AND ADVICE

Just as Seides seeks managers with a passion for investing and for serving clients, he strives to live up to those same ideals. He continues to be motivated by his desire to help investors. "The value we try to add is not just the return on the funds, but helping our clients be better investors and earn higher returns on their capital. For example, if we figure out the right horse and tell them about it, they might be able to pile on outside of their investment in Protégé."

Seides urges investors not to delegate decision making. "You can't delegate the experience and judgment that come from being in the meetings. I'm not a believer in pyramid organizations with armies of analysts. There is often information Jeff or I can suss out in a meeting that a junior analyst can't; tangential connections we happen to know from having been around. Our team is essential to make sure we have all of the necessary information at our disposal to make good decisions, but at the end of the day our investors are buying into the senior partners' experience in the business."

While he believes having "raw horsepower" and a certain IQ can help younger, junior people succeed in the investment business, he also believes it is no replacement for the skills and insights gained from years of experience.

Investors need to seek out the good investments. "Most great investments are bought, not sold. Very few hedge fund managers are also good marketers. I've almost never found an investment from a salesman calling me and saying, 'Hey, you want to look at this.' When investing in funds, you have to seek out and find talent through your relationships."

Career Advice

For those considering a career in hedge funds, or any career for that matter, Seides firmly believes you need to have passion for your work.

"I never heard the phrase 'Do what you love' until I went to Harvard Business School." His father's advice resonated with him probably a little too much. "I thought work was about making a living and making money, instead of finding what you love and letting the rest take care of itself."

Partnership

Seides believes a strong partnership can be better than a sole proprietorship, because he has experienced it working with Jeffrey Tarrant. In his opinion, that is not only because they have committed to making it work, but also because working together has helped both become better investors.

"We have very different personalities, interviewing styles, investment biases, and varied strengths and weaknesses both as business managers and investors, but our mutual respect and recognition that bringing our skills together makes a better whole is incredibly important to Protégé's success. In many ways, it reminds me of the partnership that David Swensen and Dean Takahashi have at Yale; David's success is greatly enhanced by working alongside Dean. The same is true for Jeff and me."

Seides considers Tarrant a mentor, along with David Swensen of Yale.

Betting against Buffett

With one prominent, much-admired investor, one most investors can only dream of having as a mentor, Seides has a somewhat adversarial relationship.

In 2007, Seides decided to bet against legendary investor Warren Buffett. The high-stakes public challenge will not be decided until December 31, 2017.

In the short version of the story, at the Berkshire Hathaway annual meeting in May 2006, Buffett apparently offered to bet anyone $1 million that in 10 years time, and accounting for fees and expenses, an S&P 500 index fund would beat a portfolio of 10 hedge funds.

Seides entered the picture on a slow July day. "I had heard about his claim that a year had passed and no one had taken him up on it, so he must be right." Knowing that Buffett's legend extends to his clever responses to written correspondence, Seides wrote to him, saying he would take the other side of the bet. "It's not often you can catch someone as smart as Buffett making a mistake. He picked the wrong benchmark at the wrong time."

A healthy negotiation ensued. "What I experienced in bringing the bet to fruition was a lot different from the image of Buffett buying huge companies on a napkin. The only way I could make heads or tails of it was a realization that he might be the patsy at the poker table, but he had the most chips."

After some negotiation about the format and size of the bet—Seides agreed to pick five funds of hedge funds rather than 10 individual hedge funds, and Protégé, not Seides, bet the $1 million—it was announced in June of 2008 in *Fortune* magazine.

The bet "is what hedge funds are about—seeking to generate equity-like expected returns." At the end of the 10 years, "equities are going to be higher or lower than their historical average would dictate. If they are meaningfully higher, hedge funds should lose. If lower, hedge funds should win." Based on his analysis of the market valuation at the end of 2007, he concluded, "any way you look at it, markets were poised to do badly.

"We're going to win."

It's a good-natured bet for a good cause—each side has chosen a charity that will receive the winner's proceeds—but Seides hopes it helps improve the image of hedge funds. "It's not the reason I made the bet, but if it ends up evolving as I suspect it will, the results could show hedge funds doing what they are supposed to do and not doing what the press so eloquently describes."

NO BETTER WAY TO MAKE MONEY

Although hedge funds have been "massive money-making machines" for a number of years, in the aftermath of the financial crisis of 2008 and with the likelihood of challenging markets and business conditions for a long while, Seides says, "The people that were truly in it for the money are going to leave the industry, because they would have made their money or won't be able to make as much."

Seeking a better way to make money, Seides found it by stumbling into an investment career. But making money is not the only thing driving him. A "clubhouse guy" with a passion for helping hedge fund managers, investors, and the industry to succeed, Seides represents his own ideal investment manager.

Whether or not Seides wins his bet with Buffett on December 31, 2017, if he is right about those who will leave the industry, then it is a sure bet that Seides will be in the industry and investing in hedge funds for many years to come.

CHAPTER 13

The Quality of the People

A Review and Preview

H edge funds began to rebound during the same period that we interviewed the talented hedge fund investors profiled in Part Two. As the year progressed, hedge fund performance indexes approached record-breaking heights and assets flowed back. Some predictions the subjects made had come true or were coming true. Even so, industry participants continued to experience and struggle with the consequences of the financial crisis.

If it is true that you are never a superstar until you make a comeback, then hedge funds made a perverse comeback in late 2009 when Raj Rajaratnam, the founder of the $3 billion Galleon Group hedge fund, was indicted for insider trading. When a different scandal has captured your attention, then you truly have moved on. Or the government has decided to divert your attention from its previous colossal missteps. Future top hedge fund investors will consider those issues.

This chapter reports on the postcrisis period when we profiled these top hedge fund investors and uses their insights, ideas, and advice to comment on developments and highlight important lessons.

HEDGE FUND RECOVERY

Christopher Fawcett from Fauchier Partners said, "I'm an optimist on the industry. I was never as pessimistic as the market in the fall of 2008. I stuck my neck out with journalists and said there would be inflows in 2009. I thought I needed to see a shrink; it sounded outlandish. By first quarter, it sounded plausible; it happened in the second quarter."

In the year following the financial crisis, hedge funds on average delivered outstanding performance. Two separate publishers showed substantial gains in their primary hedge fund indexes.

Sol Waksman, founder and president of BarclayHedge, when reporting November 2009 results said, "The Barclay Hedge Fund Index is now up 21.60 percent in 2009, and hedge funds appear to be on the way to their best performance since 1999, when the index gained 36.96 percent." The Barclay Fund of Funds Index was up 9.41 percent for the year.[1]

In the same period, the HFRI Fund Weighted Composite Index gained 18.8 percent, a result indicating hedge funds could end 2009 with the best performance in a calendar year since gaining 19.55 percent in 2003. Meanwhile, the HFRI fund-of-funds index was up 10.69 percent.[2]

Assets under Management

Good performance news coincided with good asset growth news. Hedge fund assets reached the $2 trillion mark again, less than a year after the losses and redemptions in the last quarter of 2008. The monthly net positive inflows of capital that began in May 2009 continued through November. Much of the asset growth came from positive performance. The net inflow of investor capital in November 2009 amounted to $26.3 billion, while another $40.5 billion came from positive returns. Hedge fund assets remained $900 billion away from their peak in the second quarter of 2008.[3]

However, the assets managed by funds of hedge funds continued to fall in 2009. Another industry tracking service and data provider, Eurekahedge, reported the worst year on record for funds of hedge funds, with $164 billion in net redemptions through November. Total assets stood at $440 billion, almost half the $823 billion at the peak in May 2008.[4]

Given the return of assets to hedge funds, this seemed a surprising development, since the growth in hedge funds has largely been fueled by institutional capital flowing into funds of hedge funds. To the extent investors chase performance, with the substantial difference in performance between the respective Barclay and HFR hedge fund and fund of hedge fund indexes, this is a completely logical development.

Funds of Hedge Funds as Investor   Similar to HFR, the Eurekahedge fund of funds index was up 9.17 percent while its hedge fund index was up 18.24 percent, a differential significantly worse than in previous years. According to HFR, historically hedge funds outperformed funds of hedge funds by just a few percentage points, with the difference attributed to fees.[5]

Some industry observers found the difference in the results puzzling and dismaying, while others sought an explanation. Robert Howie, a principal at investment consultant Mercer, was reported as saying, "The typical fund of hedge funds performance is much more representative of what investors are actually getting than the overall hedge fund index. In many cases, investors are still trying to get their money back from funds that imposed gates."[6]

In other words, on the strength of the numbers reported to databases, hedge fund returns are high, but that does not necessarily mean investors are profiting. If one considers that before the crisis, funds of hedge funds represented at least two thirds of the capital invested in hedge funds, then they may now serve as a proxy for all hedge fund investors.

Bryan Goh, the head of hedge fund research and manager selection at First Avenue Partners LLP in London, writing on the blog Hedged.biz, makes an interesting observation about the disparity between the performance of the hedge fund and fund of hedge fund indexes.

> *Notice the difference in performance between HFRI and HFRI FOF.... There appears to be a vast underperformance by funds of funds that cannot be simply explained by the additional layer of fees. Applying 1 and 10 fees on top of the HFRI still gets you to 14 percent YTD. The volatility of the funds of funds index, however, is 13 percent lower than that of the hedge funds index. If that is explained by cash, then the funds of funds index should still return around 12 percent. If we assume a much higher level of cash, say 24 percent, then we get to a ballpark of 10 percent YTD for funds of funds.*
>
> *This appears to be what has happened. In the wake of the 2008 crisis, funds of funds raised more cash than they needed. They could not know how much cash they would need to meet investor redemptions and had to be conservative.[7]*

A Predictable Pattern   Whether assets flow into hedge funds directly or through an intermediary, the activity supports the conclusion in the Casey Quirk white paper, *The Hedge Fund of Tomorrow: Building an Enduring Firm* (2009), that the hedge fund industry will continue to grow after a transitional period. Permal's Hodge referenced the paper when he said, "Institutions are in to stay. The industry will grow again."

Hodge also expected the industry to be "a smaller but much more profitable business" for one to three years after the crisis with so many players exiting the business.

Early signs indicate the period may end closer to one year than three years. HFR released another set of data in the third quarter of 2009 that indicated further "Signs of Revival in the Hedge Fund Industry." For the first time since the crisis, more hedge funds launched than liquidated. Although liquidations continued, they slowed, and a net positive 34 new funds brought the total tracked by HFR to 6,775, the highest number of funds since the

6,845 recorded in 2008. The 858 fund closures in 2009 were the second highest on record after the 1,471 shut in 2008.[8]

The number of new funds in 2009 was nowhere near the average of 1,400 a year opened in the years from 2002 to 2007. It is still too early, but it looks likely that Hodge's next prediction—"Then, of course, greed will overpower fear and the money will pour back in"—will come true.

INVESTMENT ISSUES

The following section references articles and white papers that analyzed different aspects of the industry's response to the crisis. It reviews key issues and highlights the thoughts and opinions of the top hedge fund investors profiled in this book.

Operational Due Diligence

Morten Spenner, the CEO, and Andrew Gibson, the head of asset allocation with International Asset Management (IAM), expect hedge funds and funds of hedge funds to continue to invest in operations, including hiring people, improving processes, and adding infrastructure.[9] That is an understatement in "the post-Madoff world" of due diligence described by Corgentum Consulting founder Jason Scharfman.

> *The hedge fund operational due diligence process from the investor perspective is likely to be altered in the following major ways:*
>
> *Institutions which invest in hedge funds and in particular money managers like fund of hedge funds will dedicate more resources to due diligence with a particular focus on operational due diligence.*
>
> *Hedge fund investors will take greater ownership and involvement in the operational due diligence process and no longer completely outsource operational due diligence to professional hedge fund allocators such as fund of hedge funds and consultants.*
>
> *There will be a marked increase in both investment committee voting authority and veto power extended to operational due diligence analysts at more hedge fund allocation organizations.*
>
> *Investors will increase both the scope and depth of operational issues covered during a due diligence review, with a particular focus being placed on operational risk.*

> *Investors will place a premium on those hedge funds that allow*
> *them both:*
> ■ *Access to operational information; and*
> ■ *Proactively provide this information on a frequent basis.*
> *Hedge fund investors will increase the frequency with which they*
> *perform operational due diligence reviews.*[10]

When Ted Seides from Protégé Partners described his overall approach to due diligence, he thought it did not differ broadly from that of other top investors. His extensive set of creative due diligence tactics offers more than a few good ideas. Suggestions to talk to a manager's childhood friends and monitor his golf handicap may sound simple, but they are clever ways for an investor to gain insight into the manager's character and psyche.

Investors can also learn from Seides that while they may need to rely on more due diligence experts, they also need to be wary of getting too dependent on outside and syndicated information. Nor should they become dependent on name and reputation. Investors should do their own due diligence and implement unique techniques for eliciting qualitative information during the process.

Risk Management

The IAM executives expect that more systematic risk management will be important.[11] All the top investors had a definition of risk and a methodology for evaluating and managing it. Fawcett and Katie Hall of Hall Capital Partners defined it as capital preservation, while Richard Elden, the founder of Grosvenor Capital Management, uses a simple and effective "tire-kicking" approach honed in his 40 years of experience.

Louis Moelchert, Jr. of Private Advisors dismisses value at risk (VaR) analysis as "a cruel joke played on the financial community," saying it did not work during the crisis. Seides adds to Moelchert's comment by explaining the difference between risk measurement—calculating stats like VaR—and risk management. "Risk management is forward looking. Part of our role as an investment manager is to be a risk manager."

The majority sought transparency from their underlying managers to help them evaluate and manage risks, but in varying degrees. Deepak Gurnani of Investcorp, a consummate risk manager, expresses ongoing concerns about managing hedge fund risk. "The single most important, in my view, is structural weakness. There's an inadequate focus on risk." Investors should focus on plugging that weakness by focusing on transparency and requiring managed accounts. Investors cannot afford to become complacent in good environments or to let managers have full control. "A lot of focus on risk is needed."

Managed accounts for transparency and liquidity control purposes remains a prominent industry topic, but movement toward using them seems limited. Gurnani and Seides advocate managed accounts, Hodge has increased his use of them, but the others mostly express ambivalence.

Fee Structure

Many industry observers perceive investors as having gained the upper hand in the business relationship with hedge funds and expect changes in the hedge fund fee structure. Top investors largely agree.

Mark Anson of Oak Hill Investment Management summarized the hedge fund fee issues and represented the opinions of the majority of top investors when he described his work on the "Asymmetry of Incentives." As investors gain more understanding of hedge fund fee structures and find lower-priced "alpha extension" funds like 130/30, he believes they will be less willing to accept the classic 2 and 20 fee structure.

Top hedge fund investors discussed "claw-back" provisions that would allow investors a refund on performance fees for unrealized gains. Most agreed with Anson that if hedge fund managers institute the same contractual terms as private equity structures, then those contracts should include similar investor-friendly fee provisions.

Commenting on the traditional 2 and 20 fee structure, Howard Marks of Oaktree Capital Management told Reuters, "Getting money with incentive fees should be special. The fact that everybody could do it means something was wrong."[12]

The 2 and 20 fee structure may have more to do with a manager's marketing practices. As some managers told Anson, "If we don't charge 2 and 20, no one will take it seriously." He says that now managers have to prove why they deserve 2 and 20. "It's no longer a right of hedge fund existence."

Neither Anson nor other top investors expect high fees to disappear completely. "Some managers have legitimate skill and can add a lot of value." If they do, then investors will have to pay a premium.

Lock-Ups   Olympia Capital Management found that few hedge funds had changed their liquidity terms after the crisis. Those that did reduced investor rights to withdraw capital. It appeared that hedge funds had aligned the liquidity promised to investors with the liquidity of the underlying instruments. Olympia supported such a move, in agreement with the majority of the top investors.[13]

An appropriate lock-up, according to Fawcett, factors in the strategy type, the liquidity of underlying securities, and the likely liquidity needs of the co-investors. Moelchert thinks longer lock-ups would encourage a long-term investment horizon and benefit the entire industry. Hall points out that the lock-up serves to match assets with liabilities and to maintain a stable investor base. Investors need to consider both objectives when evaluating lock-up provisions.

Business Management

Poor business management practices, including inappropriate liquidity provisions, factored into many of the problems faced by hedge funds during the financial crisis. No surprise to Frank Meyer, the founder of Glenwood Capital Investments. He adamantly stated that a hedge fund manager's business management skills are an incredibly important selection factor.

"Looking at a manager that you're going to give money as a passive investor, I don't care what the strategy is, the manager has to succeed in carrying out two key tasks: He has to run the money, and he has to run the business."

The crisis reinforced for Hall "the importance of having 'robust businesses of the businesses'" to be able to get through challenging times. "Those that had the most difficulty compounded the hard environment by freaking out themselves."

INDUSTRY ISSUES

Business management tactics will become increasingly important as institutional investors continue to prefer more established, stable, and service-oriented firms. Leon Cooperman, the head of Omega Advisors, said, "Hedge funds will become larger, more professional; fewer one-man and two-man shops. There's a certain scale needed. Investors will put their money with a firm that's been around. It's all about process and controls and reputation."[14]

The top investors tend to agree that big hedge funds will get bigger. A recent Goldman Sachs report gives evidence of that fact, according to an analysis by Christopher Holt, founder of AllAboutAlpha.com:

> To be sure, the sampling only looks at equity assets under management, and it only looks at U.S.-based funds. But the results paint a very interesting picture: The days of multitudes of multi-billion-dollar long/short hedge funds are over—at least for now.

Indeed, what Goldman's "Appendix D" ranking illustrates quite nicely is the top 10 hedge fund firms in terms of equity assets under management are light years ahead of any of their competitors, while those in the $1 billion to $2 billion category are equally well ahead of their multiple-million brethren.

In other words, the big are getting bigger, the small are staying smaller and those in the middle are shrinking. It will be interesting to see if this is still the case a year from now. Even more interesting, and a topic we've touched on before, is whether the divergence between big and small will do anything to help returns.[15]

The divergence between small and large managers is also referred to as "bifurcation." Hodge thought it would take the form of categorizing funds by liquidity, while Seides thought smaller funds would more likely engage in idiosyncratic asset classes with limited capacity. Both are probably true since liquidity is not normally associated with idiosyncratic asset classes.

The biggest hedge funds have the potential to become even bigger businesses, a huge shift from when Elden founded Grosvenor Partners in 1971. Legendary hedge fund manager Michael Steinhardt commented on it recently.

The hedge fund business today is a business. It wasn't always a business. Years ago it was a profession. It certainly wasn't an enterprise that required a great deal of organizational skill.[16]

Yet the leaders of Fortress Investment Group, a publicly held alternative investment company, hired a professional manager in 2009 so they could focus on investing.[17] Elden would agree with the move, since he advises hedge funds to emulate the most successful macro managers and hire strong internal business management partners.

Elden has been an influential participant in the industry's evolution for more than 40 years, and his advice relates to a recent phenomenon, the "exit strategy." In Steinhardt's heyday, hedge fund management companies did not have natural buyers, so they did not focus on creating a saleable enterprise. He produced compound annual returns of 24 percent over 28 years[18] and then closed the business. Today, hedge funds have more potential buyers for their enterprise, but Elden believes that possibility has made hedge fund managers more risk-averse. For that reason, today a Steinhardt might not achieve such a track record.

Regulation

The threat of regulation hovered over the industry in the first year after the crisis. In March 2009, Treasury Secretary Timothy Geithner described likely hedge fund regulatory reforms such as mandatory SEC registration. Another Obama administration proposal would make the largest hedge fund advisers subject to additional supervision by the Federal Reserve.[19] U.K. hedge funds adhere to similar FSA regulations. Fawcett says the system has worked well.

HEDGE FUND INVESTING OUTLOOK

Each of the top hedge fund investors spoke eloquently and at length about the hedge fund investment philosophy and process. This section highlights common threads and thoughts for the future.

The Big Picture

Writing in early 2009, Alexander Ineichen named "three overriding themes" he thought would affect long-term investors over a period of decades. The three themes were:

- Changes in demographics ("peak labor")
- Global power rebalancing ("reverse pax americana")
- Green and Clean (or "peak energy") movement, i.e., economies and business becoming greener and cleaner[20]

Historically, a hedge fund investor would discuss similar macro investment themes with a manager, but would not necessarily build portfolios along thematic lines. Most of the top investors that we interviewed build the portfolio from the bottom up, although both Moelchert and Elden believe strategy selection is important. Hall and Moelchert both invest in other assets besides hedge funds and find the knowledge and perspective they gain benefits their hedge funds portfolios. Gurnani developed his deep understanding of risk partly by creating a risk model for private equity securities.

Where Investors Will Be Rachel S.L. Minard, a highly respected veteran hedge fund marketing executive, says that even before the financial crisis in 2008, she began to believe that hedge fund investors were missing the big picture. Having built two global funds of hedge funds, Cadogan Management and Corbin Capital Partners (a firm she renamed from Dubin and Sweica Capital Management), while responsible for their branding, marketing, and client service, and having raised assets for more than 18 years, Minard offers great insight into the minds of investors and the direction of the industry.

"Investors increasingly showed a heightened interest in fund of hedge funds managers that could not only identify qualitative long-term themes, but also had the experience and acumen to choose the right instruments to capture those opportunities." Elaborating, Minard says, "Investors wanted to understand the undercurrent of the sectors and strategies in which they were investing and would no longer choose a fund of hedge funds strictly for its ability to secure capacity and access to strong managers."

Essentially, investors increasingly expect their fund of hedge funds managers to have a specific investment opinion, yet, she says, few do. Rather than relying predominantly on analyzing historical information, Minard predicts that many hedge funds of funds will have to adapt their current processes to incorporate "forward-looking outside macroeconomic, thematic factors." Hedge funds of funds will provide value by their ability to choose the best alternative investment "to capture the nuances no historical analysis can clearly define."

Minard likens this emerging thematic approach to her favorite Wayne Gretzky quote: "Skating to where the puck is going to be." Given her successful track record on the marketing side of the industry, it seems Minard is pointing hedge fund of funds managers to where investors will be.

People

Elden remembers the good advice of a fellow investor. "The number one criterion for selecting managers is character, character, character." The investor may have been David Swensen, Ted Seides's mentor at the Yale Investments Office, where he learned to focus on "getting the people right." The top investors all value a manager's integrity, some after learning the hard way that they had not valued it enough in the first place. Related to the character of the individual is the culture of a hedge fund organization. Both Fawcett and Elden focus on a firm's culture when selecting managers.

PORTFOLIO OF TOP INVESTORS

In an increasingly complex, global, competitive investment environment, advised Katie Hall, it will be increasingly important for investors and hedge fund managers to incorporate diverse viewpoints and new ideas and to keep open minds.

Starting with Richard Elden, the founder of the first U.S.-based fund of hedge funds, and ending with Ted Seides, the co-founder of Protégé Partners and willing bettor for hedge funds against Warren Buffett, this book tells the stories of a diverse group of experienced, accomplished, and influential investors. The group includes industry pioneers, specialized practitioners, and next-generation innovators. The strategies and advice of these asymmetrically talented individuals, when combined and read together, provide a guide to investing in hedge funds and succeeding in the investment industry no textbook could surpass.

Richard Elden said that investors would find in certain hedge fund managers "some of the best and the brightest people. They have had great records, are on top of all kinds of things, and have lots of interests." He could be describing himself and the other top investors profiled in this book.

When Christopher Fawcett discussed his views of the hedge fund industry in the aftermath of the financial crisis, he inadvertently wrote the conclusion to the stories of the top hedge fund investors.

"The industry healed even faster than even I, as an optimist, expected. It proved how resilient it is, because of the quality of the people in it."

Notes

CHAPTER 1   The Truth about Hedge Funds

1. Ineichen, A., 2003, *Absolute Returns: The Risk and Opportunities of Hedge Fund Investing*, Hoboken, NJ, John Wiley & Sons, 34
2. Ineichen, A., Silberstein, K., 2008, *AIMA's Roadmap to Hedge Funds*, The Alternative Investment Management Association, Limited, Investor Steering Committee, 37
3. Kochard, L.E., Rittereiser, C.M., 2008, *Foundation and Endowment Investing: Philosophies and Strategies of Top Investors and Institutions*, Hoboken, NJ, John Wiley & Sons, 49–50
4. Ineichen, Silberstein, 4
5. Kochard, Rittereiser, 50
6. SEI Knowledge Partnership, Greenwich Associates, 2009, *Hedge Funds Under the Microscope: Examining Institutional Commitment in Challenging Times*, 6
7. Kochard, Rittereiser, 50
8. Ineichen, Silberstein, 37
9. Ineichen, 35
10. Ineichen, Silberstein, 93
11. Ineichen, 31–34
12. Ineichen, 29
13. Investors' Committee to the President's Working Group on Financial Markets (PWG), 2009, *Principles and Best Practices for Hedge Fund Investors, Report of the Investors' Committee to the President's Working Group on Financial Markets*, www.amaicmte.org, 9
14. PWG, 10
15. PWG, 10
16. Ineichen, 35
17. Ineichen, 35
18. Kochard, Rittereiser, 267
19. Ineichen, 19
20. Ineichen, Silberstein, 131–135
21. Kochard, Rittereiser, 51
22. Ineichen, 5

CHAPTER 2   The Investment Process

1. Investors' Committee to the President's Working Group on Financial Markets, 2009, *Principles and Best Practices for Hedge Fund Investors, Report of the Investors' Committee to the President's Working Group on Financial Markets*, www.amaicmte.org, 16
2. Ineichen, A., Silberstein, K., 2008, *AIMA's Roadmap to Hedge Funds*, The Alternative Investment Management Association, Limited, Investor Steering Committee, 53
3. *AIMA's Roadmap*, 6
4. *Principles and Best Practices*, 18
5. Ibid.
6. *AIMA's Roadmap*, 42
7. *Principles and Best Practices*, 18
8. *Principles and Best Practices*, 19–20
9. *AIMA's Roadmap*, 43
10. Ibid.
11. *AIMA's Roadmap*, 65
12. *AIMA's Roadmap*, 47
13. *Principles and Best Practices*, 18
14. *Principles and Best Practices*, 62
15. *AIMA's Roadmap*, 42
16. Ibid.

CHAPTER 3   The Hedge Fund Investment Landscape

1. Herbst, M., Wessling, G., 2nd Quarter 2009, "Trends and Developments in the Hedge Fund Industry," *swissHEDGE*, Harcourt AG, 12
2. Herbst, Wessling, 13
3. Ibid.
4. Strauss, L.C., January 5, 2009, "Hedge Funds Meet Their Match," *Barron's*, http://online.barrons.com/article/SB123094644823550755.html
5. Ineichen, A., February 2009, *A&Q Industry Research Hedge Fund Industry Update*, UBS O'Connor Limited/UBS Alternative and Quantitative Investments Limited, 30
6. Strauss
7. Ibid.
8. Ibid.
9. Herbst, Welling, 13
10. Strauss
11. Herbst, Welling, 13
12. Strauss
13. Herbst, Welling, 13
14. Strauss
15. Herbst, Welling, 13

16. Ineichen, 7
17. Strauss
18. Ineichen, 8
19. Goh, B., July 2009, "Hedge Funds and Investors"; June 2009, "Hedge Fund Law Blog," www.hedgefundlawblog.com/hedge-funds-and-investors-june-2009.html

CHAPTER 7   An Asymmetrical Talent

1. Anson, M., May 4, 2009, "Hedge Funds Are Hurting But They Still Have an Edge," *Pensions and Investments*, www.pionline.com
2. Ibid.
3. Ibid.

CHAPTER 12   A Better Way

1. Institutional Investor, 2002
2. Harvard Business School Publishing, 1999
3. Harvard Business School Publishing, 2005

CHAPTER 13   The Quality of the People

1. Waksman, S., December 16, 2009, BarclayHedge Press Release, www.barclayhedge.com/research/press_releases/PR_Dec_16_2009.html
2. *The Hedge Fund Journal*, December 8, 2009, www.thehedgefundjournal.com/news/2009/12/08/hfri-fund-weighted-composite-index-1-75-in-nov.php
3. Herbst-Bayliss, S., December 9, 2009, "Assets: Hedge Fund Assets Climb Back above $2 trillion," Reuters.com, www.reuters.com/article/idUSN0821505920091208
4. Hutchings, W., December 17, 2009, "Assets at Funds of Hedge Funds Drop by Nearly Half Since Peak," *Wall Street Journal* Online http://online.wsj.com/article/SB10001424052748704541004574599732732069514.html
5. Hutchings
6. Hutchings
7. Goh, Bryan, November 16, 2009, "Hedge Fund Performance 2009 09," hedged.biz
8. Sanati, C., December 9, 2009, "More Signs of Revival in Hedge Fund Industry," DealBook Blog; *New York Times*, http://dealbook.blogs.nytimes.com/2009/12/09/more-signs-of-revival-in-hedge-fund-industry/?ref=business
9. Spenner, M., Gibson, A., December 15, 2009, "Comment: Review and Outlook for 2010," HedgeWeek, www.hedgeweek.com/2009/12/15/27267/comment-hedge-funds-2009-review-and-outlook-2010
10. Scharfman, J., March 2009, *The Madoff Identity: A New Operational Due Diligence Paradigm in a Post-Madoff World*, Corgentum Consulting LLC,
11. Spenner, Gibson, 4–5

12. Giannone, J.A., December 10, 2009, "Hedge Funds Tip-Toe toward an Uncertain Future, Reuters.com, www.reuters.com/article/idUSTRE5B90NV2009 1210

13. Holt, C., September 30, 2009, "Hedge Fund Mid-Term Report Card," Seeking Alpha.com, http://seekingalpha.com/article/164080-hedge-fund-mid-term-report-card

14. Giannone

15. Holt, C., September 14, 2009, "Goldman Hedge Fund Report: More Consolidation Ahead" Seeking Alpha.com, http://seekingalpha.com/article/161326-goldman-hedge-fund-report-more-consolidation-ahead

16. Giannone

17. Ibid.

18. Ibid.

19. Ibid.

20. Ineichen, A., February 2009, "A&Q Industry Research Hedge Fund Industry Update," UBS O'Connor Limited/UBS Alternative and Quantitative Investments Limited, 14

Index

Printed in the United States
By Bookmasters